D1547148

DATE DUE

CLARENDON LIBRARY OF LOGIC AND PHILOSOPHY

General Editor: L. Jonathan Cohen

THE EMERGENCE
OF NORMS

THE EMERGENCE
OF NORMS

—

EDNA ULLMANN-MARGALIT

OXFORD
AT THE CLARENDON PRESS
1977

Oxford University Press, Walton Street, Oxford, OX2 6DP

OXFORD LONDON GLASGOW
NEW YORK TORONTO MELBOURNE WELLINGTON
CAPE TOWN IBADAN NAIROBI DAR ES SALAAM LUSAKA
KUALA LUMPUR SINGAPORE JAKARTA HONG KONG TOKYO
DELHI BOMBAY CALCUTTA MADRAS KARACHI

© *Oxford University Press 1977*

British Library Cataloguing in Publication Data

Ullmann-Margalit, E
    The emergence of norms. – (Clarendon
    library of logic and philosophy).
    1. Social psychology
    I. Title II. Series
    301.1   HM299
    ISBN 0-19-824411-8

*Printed in Great Britain
at the University Press, Oxford
by Vivian Ridler
Printer to the University*

Dedicated to

AVISHAI

and to the memory of my father

DAVID THEODOR ULLMANN, M.D.

PREFACE

THIS is an essay in speculative sociology. Its subject matter is the rise and function of social norms, and hence belongs to the domain of social theory. Its approach and conception, however, are philosophical—hence the 'speculation'.[1] The account of the emergence of norms this book is concerned to offer is not an experimental, or historical, one. At the same time it is an empirically constrained speculation: social facts are taken seriously as delimiting the outside frame of the picture hereby drawn.

Put very crudely, the main thesis of this book is that certain types of norms are possible solutions to problems posed by certain types of social interaction situations. The problems are such that inhere in the structure (in the game-theoretical sense of 'structure') of the situations concerned. Three types of paradigmatic situations are dealt with. They are referred to as (1) Prisoners' Dilemma-type situations; (2) Co-ordination situations; (3) Inequality (or Partiality) situations. Each of them, it is claimed, poses a basic difficulty, to some or all of the individuals involved in them. Three types of norms, respectively, are offered as solutions to these situational problems. It is shown how, and in what sense, the adoption of these norms of social behaviour can indeed resolve the specified problems.

The basic line of reasoning underlying the essay can now be seen. It is pointed out, first, that a large number of real-life situations are, upon analysis, revealed as falling, roughly, under one of the three categories just mentioned. Secondly, it is pointed out that norms of the types suggested as solutions do in fact exist. The demonstration of this correlation—between certain types of situational problems on the one hand, and certain types of norms which facilitate their solution on the other—is offered as an account of the emergence of these norms.

A question which naturally arises in this connection concerns

---

[1] For a persuasive appeal for the revival of a kindred discipline, speculative psychology, see J. A. Foder: *The Language of Thought*, New York: T. Y. Crowell, 1975.

the status of the three paradigmatic problem situations and their associated norms: do they exhaust the possibilities or do they just represent them? And if the latter is the case, then what can be said of the other possible types?

I am afraid I do not know the answer to this question. I am unable to provide arguments for the exhaustiveness of the three types I deal with. Indeed I am in doubt as to what *sort* of arguments are called for. On the other hand, I have not been able to find (or to manufacture) an additional class of a significantly different situational problem, i.e. one that neither falls under one of the three categories dealt with nor represents a case which is in some sense intermediary between any two of them. In default of conclusive arguments or persuasive counter-examples, my hunch is that the three types of cases taken up by this study form the *core* cases in this field of inquiry. I surmise, that is, that further cases turned up by further work are more likely to fall somewhere between two of the three paradigmatic cases than outside their range.

There are many people to whom I am happy to acknowledge my debt of gratitude. While agonizing over my Oxford D.Phil. thesis (1973), which forms the basis of this book, I was greatly aided by my Oxford teachers and advisers: the late Arthur N. Prior, Anthony Kenny, and especially Peter M. S. Hacker who painstakingly sifted and improved early versions of all chapters. I was fortunate to receive detailed and helpful comments and suggestions in writing from John L. Mackie and Carl G. Hempel. I did try to incorporate them in the final version of the text, but I dare not hope to have truly met their challenge. Sidney Morgenbesser contributed various points of insight; the late Yehoshua Bar-Hillel and Maya Bar-Hillel read the text through and corrected many mistakes. I am indebted to them all.

During my year's stay at Cambridge, Mass. (1974/5) I benefited from discussions with—and kind encouragements by—Israel Scheffler and Hilary Putnam. I wish more of their ideas could have permeated the final product. I would also like to express my gratitude to the Principal of Somerville College, Oxford, Mrs. Barbara Craig, for her unfailing support at various junctures.

Above all I want to thank Avishai Margalit, my husband, friend, and true mentor throughout. What I owe him extends far beyond the gratitude for shouldering a heavy burden all decent preface-writing authors express to their spouses. What I owe him is the near-ineffable gratitude one owes a teacher, tutor, inspirer. It was his never-failing resource, concern, and patience which miraculously turned my barren notes into ideas, deadends into thoroughfares. Perhaps the best indication of how much of *him* is in the following pages is that I hesitate to add the standard disclaimer that all the errors, gaffes, and blunders remain my own.

EDNA ULLMANN-MARGALIT

Jerusalem
March 1976

CONTENTS

I

AIM AND METHOD

1. *The Subject Matter*

IT is often impossible, and always dangerous, to compress a long, complex study into one all-embracing statement: it is almost bound to sound either banal, or else pompous. Yet I do see merit in taking this calculated risk with the present study. The characterization I venture to offer, then, is this:

This study attempts to provide a rational reconstruction of the formal features of states of social interaction in which norms are generated.

I shall now explain this statement through breaking it up into its constituents and examining each in turn.

1.1 *'Rational Reconstruction'*

By a rational reconstruction of an event, or, more precisely, of a description of an event (Carnap, 1962, pp. 576–7), is not meant a reconstruction of the specific historical circumstances in which the event occurred; this is taken to be the task of the historian, or archaeologist. Rather, it is a description of the essential features of situations in which *such* an event *could* occur: it is a story of how something could happen—and, when human actions are concerned, of what is the rationale of its happening that way —not of what did actually take place. The sense of 'could' here is, of course, narrower than that of mere logical possibility. It should be taken to mean that, given accepted common-sensical assumptions about the nature of the world and of human beings, the story of the emergence of the phenomenon under discussion is plausible. Thus, the role played by rational reconstruction is in the first place explicatory, and only in the second place explanatory; hence it is a philosophical rather than an empirical task. In our present case a rational reconstruction would refer to a description of the essential features of social states in which norms could emerge, or, in fact, in which norms are likely to emerge.

As exemplifying the practice of providing rational reconstructions in the realm of social philosophy I would regard the account given of the origin of the state in Plato's politics (compare Caws, 1965, p. 9), the theories of social contract such as those of Hobbes, Locke, and Rousseau, and Rawls's reconstruction of the just, or fair, society. Nozick's more recent account of the emergence of the 'minimal state' can also be added to this list.[1]

A rational reconstruction does not necessarily involve a commitment to confine one's discussion to rational creatures only. Indeed, in spite of the use I make in this study of game-theoretical methods, I am not presupposing that the participants in the game-like situations analysed are fully rational—at any rate not in the strict game-theoretical sense of rationality (see Luce and Raiffa, 1957, pp. 5, 49–50). In fact, the Carnapian expression 'rational reconstruction' could be given up in favour of 'ideal reconstruction'. However, the term 'ideal' is apt to involve one in its own host of troubles: witness the fate of this term in the expression 'an ideal speaker' in the linguistic theory of Chomsky.

But if I do not take a rational reconstruction to be normative, that is, to specify those patterns of behaviour which a creature should exhibit if it is to be considered rational, then what can its empirical import be? Or, more to the point, in what after all does the difference lie between the rational reconstruction of states in which norms are generated—which I consider the job of the philosopher—and what the sociologist or the social-psychologist does when dealing with the same problem?

One difference mentioned earlier is that a rational reconstructionist is interested in what could happen rather than in what actually happened. Secondly, the empirical assumptions on which a rational reconstruction is based are, unlike those of scientific theories, received ones, whose truth is taken for granted and considered obvious. A rational reconstruction is not expected to discover, or to predict, new empirical facts; it

---

[1] In characterizing the methodology of his project Nozick does not in fact speak of rational reconstruction. Rather, he regards his account as a 'fundamental potential explanation' which is possibly 'process-defective'. This means, roughly, that it is an explanation that *would* explain the whole realm under discussion correctly *were* the processes it describes the actual ones. (See Nozick, 1974, pp. 6–9.)

I can see no essential differences between this and a rational reconstruction—although I am aware that differences of connotations of some of the key words describing these two methods might strike different notes, in various contexts.

aims, instead, at providing a better understanding of a given, received, body of beliefs, this better understanding being achieved through a systematic description in which the vague concepts of the received views are exchanged for more precise ones.

Indeed, the more obvious the empirical assumptions on which a rational reconstruction is based, the larger its explicatory force. At the same time, though, the more obvious these assumptions, the larger the danger that the product of the reconstruction will appear to be trivial. But here two senses of 'trivial' have to be distinguished, only one of which is dangerous:

(1) 'trivial' in the sense of 'obviously true';
(2) 'trivial' in the sense of 'marginal', 'uninteresting', 'devoid of theoretical implications'.

A proposition can be such that its truth is known to all, and yet it might have important theoretical implications. For instance, although the fact that children acquire their mother tongue between their second and fourth year is obvious, it is most significant for theoretical linguistics and for psycho-linguistics. In the context of appraisal, therefore, the attribute 'trivial' in sense (1) is not necessarily to be taken as disreputable. It is of course when the product of a rational reconstruction is trivial in sense (2) that it is bad, but the trouble is that it is not always that easy to be clear about the application of the two senses. Incidentally, when dealing with 'trivial' in sense (2) one should take care not to fall into a form of the fallacy of composition: a collection of propositions trivial in sense (2) might yield a result which is far from trivial, if, for instance, this collection has an interesting structure. Hyperbolically, this is what mathematics is all about.

An empirical theory, on the other hand, is expected to discover new facts such that we have no previously set intuitions regarding the truth value of the statements asserting them, or indeed facts which are interesting precisely because they run *counter* to our preconceptions and intuitions. And in any case it is central to any scientific theory that the truth of its statements be tested and verified through confronting them with the facts.

The rational reconstruction I am here concerned with is different from, though related to, the Popperian concept of the *logic of the situation* (Popper, 1966, pp. 97, 265; 1961, p. 149). Popper understands by this concept an attempt to reconstruct a concrete historical situation in terms of the interests and aims of the individuals taking part in it; that is, an attempt to understand the behaviour of people taking part in some historical event in the light of the alternatives they believed to be open to them, and on this basis to try to appraise the extent to which they actually fitted means to the ends they wanted to achieve.

Popper's approach, unlike the way I propose to deal with norm-generating situations, constitutes in fact a proposal of a methodology for historical research, its object being specific events which took place at known and well-defined periods of time. However, what Popper proposes under the title of the logic of the situation might converge upon what I—following Carnap—understand by a rational reconstruction once one shifts one's interests from specific past events to *types* of situations (or, in our present case, from specific contexts which have generated specific norms to types of situations capable of generating types of norms), as well as from concrete historical personalities to Weber-like 'ideal types'.

From a historical account of the origin of norms one expects to learn which initial conditions are claimed to be the cause, or at least a contributing cause, of the emergence of some particular norm in a given community and at a definite point of time. Thus, to the question concerning the origin of the norm, among the Ashkenazi Jewry, forbidding the opening of a letter without its author's permission, a historian might give the following answer: Commerce relations among the European Jews were often conducted through letters carried by emissaries. Secrecy and confidence were in general guaranteed by the fact that it was mainly with family members, dispersed all over Europe, that such commerce relations were maintained. However, in the eleventh century the number of cases in which the confidential contents of such letters were leaked increased. This, the explanation goes, eventually led Rabbi Gershom (960–1028) to impose a ban on unauthorized opening of letters—*any* letters, the ban being backed by a severe sanction of excommunication.

This historical explanation might be challenged by an alternative one, for instance that it was not until the twelfth century that this ban was imposed, by various communities' rabbis, and, furthermore, that its initial conditions were not leakages of commercial letters but leakages of rabbinical communications containing information on matters of personal status such as marriages and divorces.

In general, then, while drawing on all relevant facts, a historico-sociological explanation of a particular norm strives to provide sufficient chronological conditions for the emergence of that norm. Explanations of the type to which the present study belongs, on the other hand, strive to provide a scenario of conditions that, on currently accepted common-sensical assumptions, are conducive to—or, ideally, necessary for—the generation of wide-embracing types of norms.

It is my hope that the conditions cited in this work—falling short, as they do, of being necessary ones—nevertheless furnish us with a clearer picture of some norm-generating types of situations. We should then also gain thereby better understanding of the concrete contexts in which such norms do as a matter of fact emerge.

1.2 'Formal Features'

There is a huge variety of situations, or contexts, in which norms actually come into existence. This variety might—and usually does—conceal the fact that it is possible to discover formal structures common to many of these situations, and thus generalize over contexts. It is a known fact from the realm of pragmatics of natural languages that the large variety of contexts in which linguistic expressions are uttered was considered an insurmountable obstacle for the construction of a formal theory of pragmatics; that is, a theory which takes into account the concrete circumstances in which linguistic transactions are conducted. This is one reason why pragmatics was relatively neglected and only those aspects of language which readily lend themselves to systematization were dealt with —viz. those compressed under the headings of syntax and semantics.

A parallel phenomenon is discernible in the study of general norms. A considerable portion of recent philosophical discussions has concentrated on the linguistic aspects of normative statements, the main effort being directed toward analysing the meaning postulates[2] (or 'the logic') of terms like 'obligatory', 'permissible', and 'forbidden', and investigating the validity of arguments in which these terms occur in an essential way. The result has been a rapid development of the semantic study of normative statements known as normative, or deontic, logic.

It is my feeling that the pragmatic aspects pertaining to the socio-psychological contexts in which norms emerge, exist, and disappear have been relatively neglected in recent and current philosophical discussions, possibly because of the aforementioned reason—that the great variety of contexts concerned precludes adequate systematization. At the same time it is my belief that the theory of games, as a branch of mathematics, has contributed a good deal to the development of a conceptual web which makes it possible to discover the traits common to situations which appear to be very different from each other. I tend, therefore, to accept the recommendation of thinkers like Braithwaite, Harsanyi, Rapoport, and Schelling to introduce to philosophers this conceptual network, as well as the tools it involves. To wit: somewhat as the tool of one who deals with the logic of norms in the accepted narrow sense is formal deductive logic, the tool of one who deals with norm contexts would be the game-theoretical pay-off matrices.

The term 'formal' in the expression 'formal features' should be taken with a grain of salt. I do not intend to propose a formal theory in the sense of an uninterpreted calculus in which theorems are deduced from axioms by means of rules of inference. Moreover, it will be shown that the framework of the theory of games as a formal discipline is too narrow, and hence inadequate, for an account of the generation of norms. Rather, my present use of 'formal' should be understood as a partial intersection of 'abstract' and 'structural'. That is to say, it refers to situations as stripped of their idiosyncratic elements on the one hand, and to their synchronic—rather than diachronic—traits on the other.

As an example of a treatment of norms which *cannot* be regarded as formal in the above sense, though it does in a way classify them according to the contexts in which they have emerged, one might consider Montesquieu's concept of the

---

[2] For the introduction of the concept of meaning postulates see Carnap, 1956, pp. 222–9.

general spirit of a nation. Very roughly, according to Montesquieu it is the specific conditions of geography and history which produce the way of living, behaving, thinking, and feeling of a people, which in turn determines causally its laws, customs, and manners. Hence, in Montesquieu's account it is precisely the idiosyncratic and diachronic features which are of paramount importance, not the formal ones.

1.3 'Social Interaction'

The theory of games can be viewed as an extension of the theory of decision. The theory of decision is concerned with an isolated decision-maker who has to make decisions under conditions of risk or uncertainty; the theory of games deals with problems of deliberation in situations of social interaction. These situations of social interaction are further characterized as being ones of *strategic* interaction among rational agents, either individuals or groups. The modifier 'strategic' points to the fact that these are situations of interdependent expectation, decision, and action: each participant's best choice of action depends on the actions of the others and hence on the actions one *expects* the others to take, which he knows depend, in turn, on the other's expectations of his own.

Thus, these situations cannot be viewed as simple generalizations of ones in which decisions are taken by an isolated individual. They involve a *number* of persons who cannot behave as if the actions of the others were given and hence still make their decisions in isolation; rather, these persons are interacting in an essential way, such that no choice of action can be made wisely without taking into account the dependence of the outcome on the participants' mutual expectations. It is in this sense, of the interdependence of expectation, decision, and action, that the expression 'states of social interaction' is to be understood here.

1.4 'Generation of Norms'

There is a suggestion[3] according to which one ought to give up the question of how norms come about and ask instead what

---

[3] Raz, 1970, pp. 67–8. The suggestion is brought up in the context of a proposed distinction between norms which belong to normative systems and norms—'isolated norms'—which do not. It is the latter to which Raz's suggestion refers.

are their conditions of existence. The rationale of this suggestion is simple and pointed. Norms do not as a rule come into existence at a definite point in time, nor are they the result of a manageable number of identifiable acts. They are, rather, the resultant of complex patterns of behaviour of a large number of people over a protracted period of time.

I take this approach to be valid and important in curbing historical discussions concerning the emergence of some particular norm, discussions which are, I believe, likely to be as futile as those concerning the origin of language, or of a folk-joke. And indeed, just as there was a shift, in the study of language, from genetic explanations to structural ones, there ought to be a similar shift in the study of norms. However, I am not here concerned with specific norms, and hence not with specific initial conditions for their emergence either. Instead, it is in *types* of norms, in a sense yet to be explained, that I am interested. I therefore consider it safe enough to speak of their generation, where the notion of generation is employed in a structural, not a historical, sense.

As to the problem of the norms coming into existence as a result of complex patterns of behaviour on the part of a large number of people, I contend that it is possible to provide an abstract and relatively simple description of some such patterns which would make the task of accounting for the generation of some types of norms feasible. I admit, at the same time, that these patterns of behaviour become extremely complicated when the explanation of the origin of specific norms in some given historical situation is at issue. It is my hope that this contention is sufficiently clarified and defended in the main body of this work.

A study of the conditions of existence of norms can be taken to deal with two comparatively independent questions:

(a) Under what conditions would we say that a norm x exists?

(b) Why does norm x exist?

The philosophy of law is chiefly concerned with question (a), whereas I am primarily interested in a certain version of question (b), namely:

(b′) Why do norms of type X exist?

I believe that theories in the field of social psychology which, relying mainly on theories of learning, have attempted to answer (b), or even (b') (e.g. Suppes & Richardson, 1960, p. 256), have in general failed since they did not relate to the conditions of the *emergence* of the norms x (or of norms of type X). To the question, Why do we behave in accordance with x?, they replied, roughly, that this is what we were taught to do by our parents, teachers, the party, the police, etc., through (negative) sanctions or (positive) rewards. But then one has got to answer the further question, Why did our parents, teachers, etc. teach us to behave in accordance with x and not with some alternative to it, say y? Now a common answer to this last question is that they did so because of the culture to which they belong. But since an account of culture can hardly avoid being given, at least in part, in terms of prevailing social norms, the circularity in this approach becomes apparent.

In order to prune this regression it is necessary, I contend, to cite conditions of generation: where x is a specific norm—specific historical conditions, and where X is a type of norms—general structural conditions.

Since this study is concerned with types of norms and not with specific norms, the concept of generation, as I have said, cannot be taken in its genetic, historical sense. So what, after all, do I refer to when speaking of the generation of norms? My basic argument is that certain types of norms are solutions to problems posed by certain interaction situations. These problems inhere in the structure—in the game-theoretical sense of structure—of the situations concerned, pertaining to some or all of the interacting participants. Very generally, three types of paradigmatic interaction situations are dealt with in this study. They are referred to as (1) Prisoners' Dilemma-type situations, (2) Co-ordination situations, and (3) Inequality situations. Each of them, it is claimed, poses a certain problem:

(1) In Prisoners' Dilemma-type situations the state which is mutually desired by the participants is such that there is a strong temptation for each to deviate from it unilaterally. The state which results when they all deviate, however, is bad for all, jointly as well as severally. The problem, therefore, is to devise a method which will protect the 'good' state and annihilate the temptation to deviate.

(2) In Co-ordination situations there are several mutually beneficial states, none of which is strictly preferred to the others; there is perfect (or almost perfect) coincidence of interests. There is, however, no possibility of coming to an explicit agreement among the participants as to which of these states is to be aimed at by their actions. Their problem, then, is to find some device which will enable them to co-ordinate their choices of actions so as to 'meet' each other at one of the 'good' states.

(3) In Inequality situations the state of inequality is not completely stable; owing to its structure it is potentially threatened. The problem here is for the participant(s) favoured by the inequality to determine how to fortify the state against upset, or, put otherwise, how to maintain their favoured position.

From this point the line of argument continues as follows: It is shown how, and in what sense, norms of specified types might solve each of these problems. It is then noted, on the one hand, that a large number of real-life situations reveal themselves on analysis as falling roughly under one of the three categories just mentioned and, on the other, that norms of the types suggested as solutions do in fact exist. The demonstration of this correlation between certain types of situational problems and certain types of norms which facilitate their solution is considered an account of the generation of these norms.

This is, then, an account of norms in terms of the *role* they play, and might therefore be viewed as a functional explanation of their generation. The term 'functional', though, should not mislead owing to the connotations associated with it from the sociological doctrines called functionalism: it is by no means presupposed here that the solution achieved through norms is one that satisfies all the parties to the interaction situation, or, for that matter, the 'needs' of society as a whole. It might be a solution for only some of them, who are able to impose it on the others (as in the case of the Inequality situations), or it might indeed benefit all those involved (as in the case of the Co-ordination situations and—with some qualifications—in the case of the Prisoners' Dilemma-type situations). This question of the relation between so-called functionalism and the present study is, in any case, entered into in the main body of the work.

Another way of looking at the account of norms given here[4] is as exemplifying the so-called invisible-hand type explanations. Such explanations attribute the generation and maintenance of a social institution (norms, in our case) to people's 'stumbling upon establishments which are indeed the result of human action but not the execution of any human design'. (Adam Ferguson, *An Essay on the History of Civil Society*, Edinburgh, 1767, p. 187.) Based on the classical Adam Smith account of the market mechanism, invisible-hand type explanations do not as a rule postulate anything beyond the motives, goals, and actions of individuals. And yet, if successful, they account for an over-all social pattern which emerges as the unco-ordinated product of the scattered, self-interested actions of numerous individuals.

Yet another angle from which it may be illuminating to view the account of norms offered here is that of evolutionary explanations. The abuses incurred by the biological theory of evolution when transported into the social sciences[5]—mainly in the form of so-called Social Darwinism—are notorious; the eugenic and class-structure purposes to which terms like 'struggle for existence' and 'survival of the fittest' were put hardly need to be dwelt upon. It is with caution, therefore, that I propose to regard the argument underlying this book as, in a borrowed and somewhat metaphorical sense, a natural selection theory of the development of norms. It is metaphorical because, of course, it has nothing to do with physical and inheritable properties of individuals. Rather, it deals with the selection of norms as successful social institutions. The types of norms discussed here are selected for because even their faint beginnings—through design, stumbling, or whatever—contribute to the survival of something. This 'something' has to do with the concept of solution developed in this work, and it varies with the various types of norms under consideration.

---

[4] The remarks which follow pertain mostly to co-ordination norms, to some extent to PD norms, and not at all—as far as I can see—to norms of partiality.

[5] It is of interest to note that all the indications are that in fact Darwin and his contemporaries derived the suggestion for their biological theory from the rather well entrenched theories—predominantly of the Scottish school—of social and cultural evolution. The abuses of the evolutionary ideas occurred when the social sciences re-imported the biological notions into their fields, toward the end of the nineteenth century. (See F. A. Hayek, 1960, p. 59.)

To sum up: it is the specific connection, in the form of a solution, between norms and certain paradigmatic interaction situations which is offered here as an account of the generation of these norms, rather than a detailed description of some mechanism which actually brings them into existence. To be sure, there are references to such mechanisms, especially in the case of co-ordination norms, but they are of a rather general nature and should be considered of only secondary importance.

1.5 *Norms*

It is a complicated matter to account for the concept of norm, or, more particularly, for that of social norm, within the framework of a description of the subject matter of this work. Indeed, to provide an account which would be philosophically adequate is an enterprise in its own right. For the over-all purposes of this work, however, all that is needed is some general characterization of the concept of social norm, which would count as a useful working definition thereof.

The first, rough characterization to be proposed is the following: A social norm is a prescribed guide for conduct or action which is generally complied with by the members of a society.

For more specific purposes within this study this characterization would be found to be too broad. I shall therefore focus upon a subclass of social norms which is called by Hart 'rules of obligation' and which will here be referred to as *norms of obligation* in order to maintain a uniform terminology.[6] I shall, furthermore, use Hart's formulation of the characteristic features of this subclass of norms (1961, pp. 84–5). It is, essentially, this (with 'norms' substituted for 'rules' throughout):

(i) '[Norms] are conceived and spoken of as imposing obligations when the general demand for conformity is insistent and the social pressure brought to bear upon those who deviate or threaten to deviate is great.'

---

[6] The term 'norm' tends to be used mostly by authors whose educational background is Continental, whereas Anglo-Saxon ones seem to prefer the terms 'law' and 'rule' to cover more or less the same domain of discourse. (It might be true, though, that there is a difference in connotations between the terms 'norm' on the one hand and 'rule' and 'law' on the other: those of the first seem to be more on the moral side, those of the latter pair on the legal side.)

(ii) 'The [norms] supported by [a] serious pressure are thought important because they are believed to be necessary to the maintenance of social life or some highly prized feature of it.'

(iii) 'It is generally recognized that the conduct required by these [norms] may, while benefiting others, conflict with what the person who owes the duty may wish to do.'

To wit, it is proposed that the main elements in the characterization of norms of obligation be: a significant social pressure for conformity to them and against deviation—actual or potential—from them; the belief by the people concerned in their indispensability for the proper functioning of society; and the expected clashes between their dictates on the one hand and personal interests and desires on the other.

The features (i)–(iii) are not intended to provide necessary conditions for obligation norms. I believe, that is, that examples can be found of norms of obligation to which one, or more, of these features does not apply. What might, however, be rightfully claimed with regard to these features is that they are *typical* of norms of obligation. Generally speaking, a typical feature is useful for explicatory purposes if it is sufficiently common in the class characterized by it, if it applies to its paradigmatic cases, and if, moreover, it requires a certain degree of ingenuity to provide counter-examples to it. In these senses the above characterization of norms of obligation seems to me to be satisfactory.

With regard to the types of norms dealt with in this study it can be said that:

(a) the norms referred to as PD Norms in general answer to the description provided by each of the three features listed above;

(b) the norms referred to as Norms of Partiality answer to the description of features (i) and (iii) but only partially—and in some cases not at all—to that of feature (ii);

(c) the norms referred to as Co-ordination Norms do not all classify as norms of obligation. For them is needed, therefore, a somewhat broader characterization such as the one offered at the outset of this discussion.

2. *Methodological Individualism*

Methodological individualism is the view according to which statements about social collectives can be reduced to statements referring solely to individual human beings, their actions, and the relations among them. (The 'individualistic' statement, even though it cannot be said to have the same *meaning* as the 'collectivistic' statement it paraphrases, has to be equivalent to it in respect of its *truth value*.)[7]

The concept of social norm is clearly a 'collectivistic' concept. The question we are to turn to, then, is whether it is possible— and if possible, whether worth while—to explain by means of concepts pertaining to beliefs, expectations, incentives, and interrelations of individuals all that is explained through use of the concept of social norms. If it *is* possible, then the concept of norm itself receives its explanation in the process; after all, to explain a concept is, as Quine has put it, to show how it can be avoided.

John Harsanyi has put forward (1968, esp. pp. 313–14) the rather radical claim that all that is explained in terms of social norms can be explained through use of the conceptual machinery of the theory of games, which, taking as its primitives only the interests of the individual 'players', complies with the strictest requirements of methodological individualism. I agree with Harsanyi that there is merit in explaining social norms in individualistic terms, and, moreover, that the game-theoretical apparatus renders this enterprise feasible. I differ from him, however, in that I do not believe that the theory of games alone can deliver the goods.

By way of justifying my position I would at this point offer sketches of two arguments. Firstly, I believe that what are sometimes called the 'connotations' of games (compare Schelling, 1960, esp. pp. 95–6, 162–3), i.e. the non-formal, contextual features of the situations represented by the game matrices, play a decisive role in explaining the generation of social norms. These connotations, however, remain outside the game-

[7] The expression 'methodological individualism' originated with Popper, 1966, pp. 91, 323–4. For a comprehensive discussion of the issues involved (holism, reductionism, etc.) see: Brodbeck, 1968, Chapter 4 (comprising articles by E. Durkheim, E. Gellner, J. W. N. Watkins, M. Brodbeck, A. M. MacIver). See also the exchange between J. W. N. Watkins and L. Goldstein in the *British Journal for the Philosophy of Science*, Vols. ix–x (1958–9).

theoretical treatment of these situations, or, rather, they are chopped off in the process of abstraction involved in this treatment.

It is a certain type of contextual detail of a given situation, rather than its bare mathematical structure, which determines that a certain game-theoretical 'solution' stands in need of being made conspicuous, or that its stability needs to be protected or indeed that it cannot be accepted as a social solution at all, and that some alternative state of affairs has to be stabilized and defended instead. And it is precisely these factors, extraneous to the theory of games, that have to feature prominently in the explanation of the generation of norms—or at any rate they do in mine. (Incidentally, note that by granting admittance to connotative features of the game-like situations the discussion is brought somewhat closer to reality and is made to a certain extent less abstract than it would have been had it been strictly confined to the framework of game theory proper.) Any further elaboration of this point at this stage would, I feel, be pointless: the main body of the study is in fact aimed at lending substance to this contention.

Secondly, my work is largely based on the assumption that the game-like situations most significant for the analysis of the generation of norms are those which are taken by game theory to be either trivial or else paradoxical. Situations for which game theory is unable to specify a unique solution, since they have two or more possible solutions regarding which game theory can do no more than prescribe indifference (as in the case of the co-ordination and the inequality situations), on the one hand, and situations for which game theory prescribes a solution which, being mutually destructive, is socially unacceptable (as in the case of the Prisoners' Dilemma-type situations), on the other, seem to me to constitute the best potential recruiting fields for norm-generating contexts. It is precisely because the game-theoretical solutions to such situations are either indeterminate or paradoxical that the participants in them face a real problem arriving at a unique, satisfactory solution, and this is where norms are likely to emerge and come to their rescue.[8]

---

[8] It might be mentioned in this connection that von Neumann and Morgenstern contended that whenever there is more than one game-theoretical solution to

To sum up, then: although I believe, with Harsanyi, that game theory provides a rich source of insights as well as useful tools for the explanation of social norms, I also believe, in opposition to Harsanyi, that this undertaking cannot be carried out within the rather too narrow framework of game theory proper. Accordingly, notwithstanding the important role that the game-theoretical mode of representation plays in the present study, the over-all explanation of norms offered in it should not be mistaken for a game-theoretical explanation.

Once it is realized, however, that the discussion will transcend the boundaries of game theory proper, an individualistic methodology is clearly no longer guaranteed. So the question has to be asked again: is it possible to account for norms in individualistic terms exclusively? Well, 'possible' can stand for 'logically possible' or for 'practically possible', and the question just posed must be answered for each of these senses in turn.

As to the logical feasibility of achieving the objective at hand, or in general of reducing theories about collectives to theories about individuals, I shall just state that I have not been convinced that there are any good *a priori* reasons to the contrary.[9]

---

a game, the solution which is actually arrived at depends upon the norms and conventions (or, as they put it, on 'standards of behaviour') in the community to which the players belong. (See Luce and Raiffa, 1957, pp. 205, 219.)

[9] Let me consider in some detail one of the more forceful arguments which purports to demonstrate the logical infeasibility of reduction programmes.

In his article 'Societal Facts' (1955) Maurice Mandelbaum claims that there exists a (social scientific) language S, which comprises such ('collectivistic') terms as 'marriage', 'banking system', 'presidency', etc., and that this language cannot be fully reduced to any (social scientific) language P which comprises terms relating to actions and beliefs of individuals only. The reason: the problematic terms of S occur in many of the actual thoughts and speech acts of people.

It seems to me that this argument fails in that it does not distinguish between use and mention. Sentences of P, which are 'translations' from S, may certainly contain terms of S, but they will be mentioned, not used. And when this is the case, there is no ontological commitment to the existence of irreducible collectives involved—just as to mention the term 'witch' does not presuppose a commitment on the part of the speaker to the existence of witches. What Mandelbaum has to prove, therefore, is that the translated sentences of S in P necessarily *use* the problematic terms, not merely mention them; and this he fails to do.

So much for the claim that people actually speak in terms of S. As to the claim that people *think* in terms of S, here the problematic terms of S will necessarily occur within opaque contexts in their P-translations; i.e. these terms will occur only in clauses of propositional attitudes in P. Thus P might contain sentences like

And even if I have no conclusive *a priori* argument that such an undertaking *is* logically possible, I deem it worth while—for reasons which will be mentioned presently—to consider it at least as a regulative idea, even an approximation to which deserves to be attempted. With regard to the practical possibility of accounting for norms in individualistic terms, here—whatever the degree of success of attempted reduction programmes in general (say, of thermodynamics to mechanics, or of sociology to psychology)—what more can be said other than that the purport of the ensuing chapters is to offer just such an account?

It remains, finally, to be made explicit just why it is that I see merit in this reduction programme. The advantages of adopting an individualistic methodology in the context of an explanation of social norms seem to me significant, in the first place, in view of the ever-present and ever-tempting danger of reification: in fear of succumbing to views about the term 'social norm' according to which it might denote 'an entity which has causal power and which interacts with and directs people and groups' (Morgenbesser, 1967, p. 161). To be sure, I do not in this study avoid using expressions such as 'norms guide behaviour', or 'he observed the norm' etc., but it seems to me that this use is harmless so long as there are sufficient indications as to how these expressions can be paraphrased, or 'unpacked', in individualistic terms, within some general theoretical framework.

Secondly, and lastly, whenever a reduction programme of the type here under consideration is feasible, or even whenever it is merely *likely* to be feasible, it is *ipso facto*, in my opinion, worth while and valuable to carry it out. Any reduction of one theory (or type of theory) to another carries the prospect of being a clarificatory achievement—at least philosophical, if not downright scientific—again from the consideration that in a sense to clarify or explain something is to show how and under what conditions it can be done away with.

'*a* believes that mob hysteria brought De Gaulle back to power' but from this it does not follow that *P* contains sentences like

'It is (was) mob hysteria of which *a* believes that it brought De Gaulle back to power.'

That is to say, when the terms of *S* occur within opaque contexts in *P*, there is again no ontological commitment to the existence of the collectives denoted by these terms.

II

PD NORMS

1. *The Prisoners' Dilemma*

1.1 *Presentation*

THE well-known story of the prisoners' dilemma is the following:

Two guilty prisoners, against whom there is not enough incriminating evidence, are interrogated separately. Each faces two alternative ways of acting: to confess the crime, or to keep silent. They both know that if neither confesses, they will be convicted of some minor offence, concerning which there is sufficient evidence against them, and will be sentenced to a year in prison. If both confess, each will be sentenced to five years in prison. However, if only one confesses, he thereby turns king's evidence and is thus set free, whereas the other receives a heavy term of ten years.

Matrix 2.1 depicts the situation in terms of years in prison awaiting the prisoners in each of the possible combinations of their actions.

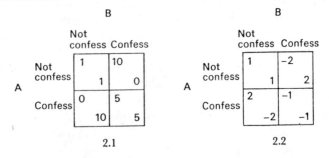

2.1

Matrix 2.2 depicts the situation in terms of the desirability of each of the possible combinations of their actions for each prisoner. That is to say, the numbers, or 'pay-offs', indicate roughly the participants' relative strength of preferences over the possible outcomes, on some ordinal scale. (In both matrices prisoner A is Row-Chooser and prisoner B is Column-Chooser, their gain-and-loss measures being indicated in the upper-left and bottom-right corners of each cell, respectively.)

Two points are to be noted about matrix 2.2. First, the action 'confess' *dominates* the action 'not confess', for both A and B. That is to say, if A confesses, his pay-off is higher than it would have been had he decided not to confess, regardless of B's choice of action. And the same goes for B. In terms of the matrix this finds its expression in the fact that, for Row-Chooser, each entry in the second row is higher than the corresponding one in the first row ($2 > 1$ and $-1 > -2$), and similarly for Column-Chooser with respect to the dominance of the second column over the first.

Secondly, the state of affairs obtained when both choose their dominant actions (i.e. the state represented by the bottom-right cell of the matrix) is an *equilibrium* in the sense that each stands to lose were he alone to deviate from it (as the pay-off for uni-lateral non-confession is -2, which is worse than -1). This implies that this state of affairs is *stable*. (It is, moreover, stable in the strong sense, since each stands actually to lose by uni-lateral deviation from it, and not just not to gain from it.)

Note, finally, that any matrix of the form shown in 2.3, where $T > R > P > S$, repre-sents a situation embodying a dilemma the same as the prisoners'. (The letters stand, almost traditionally by now, for the following: 'R' for 'reward', 'T' for 'temptation', 'S' for 'sucker', 'P' for 'punishment', 'C' for 'co-operation', and 'D' for 'defection'.)

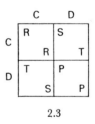

2.3

1.2 *The Dilemma*

Let us examine the prisoners' considerations as to which course of action they are to opt for. The lines of reasoning to be presented are of course well known, indeed they almost belong to folklore by now. I consider it worth while, however, to ela-borate them here since this is the basis for most of what follows.

Suppose, first, that there is no way for them to discuss their situation, and in particular no possibility of coming to an (explicit) agreement between themselves as to how they are to act. Each prisoner will realize that the worst he is to expect from choosing to confess is a term of five years, whereas from choosing not to confess it is ten years. So it is reasonable for each to regard confession as a *safer* course of action than non-confession. If, as a result, they both opt for confession, their choice is said to reflect the consideration of *maximizing security level*.[1]

There is, moreover, a stronger argument for preferring confession to non-confession. Each prisoner will realize that whatever the other does, he himself stands to gain more (or actually to lose less) by confessing than by not confessing. The consideration is based on what is known as the *dominance principle*: the choice of confession dominates (as was shown on p. 19 above) the choice of non-confession, regardless of what the other does.

(I have said that this is a stronger argument for preferring confession than was the former. The reason is that any combination of the participants' chosen actions which is an intersection of their dominant strategies is, in particular, also an intersection of their maximum security level strategies.)

The state of affairs arrived at on the basis of these forceful and convincing considerations, viz. double confession, is, however, jointly undesirable. It implies a sentence of five years to each. And it must be felt to be all the more frustrating once the prisoners realize that there is in fact an alternative outcome which is mutually desirable: they could have ended up with a relatively light term of only a year in prison had they coordinated their choices of actions appropriately.

But prisoner *A* will not decide not to confess unless he is absolutely sure that *B* will not confess, for if *B* confesses while *A* keeps silent, *B* goes off free and *A* is condemned to the heaviest sentence. The same goes for *B* with respect to *A*. But of course there is no way of being sure what the other will do if there is no possibility of communication before taking their decisions. And the risk involved in assuming, or hoping, that the other will not

---

[1] This, basically, is the idea behind the famous game-theoretical principle of mini-max, which instructs a player to examine all the (pure) courses of action available to him, find out what is the maximum loss he may expect to suffer in each, and finally choose that action which minimizes that loss.

Strictly speaking, however, the mini-max principle applies to games of *pure* conflict only (i.e. only to zero-sum games, in which one person's gain is the other's loss)—a class of which the Prisoners' Dilemma is not a member.

confess is, under the circumstances, too great for either of them to take. So once again they are locked in on the jointly destructive course of double confession.

Let us now remove, therefore, the restriction on communication, and suppose that they are allowed to discuss their situation. Would this solve their dilemma?

Clearly, they will come to a quick agreement to co-ordinate their choice of actions so as to achieve the mutually desirable outcome. That is to say, they will agree not to confess. But this is not the end of the story. Having come to this agreement and having persuaded each other that it guarantees the best they may hope for under the circumstances, each will have good reasons to walk out on it. Reasonably expecting B to keep the agreement, A will find that he stands to gain a lot—his freedom —by treacherously choosing to confess. While hesitating whether to resist this temptation he may further reflect that this consideration is likely to occur to B too, which means that perhaps B may after all *not* be expected to keep the agreement. And this, obviously, is all the more reason for A not to keep his own part of the agreement. So either way, whatever he expects B to do, A will decide to confess. The same, of course, applies to B with respect to A. So once again the available-yet-unattainable attractive outcome produced by joint non-confession eludes them. Their having come to an agreement, provided it is not enforceable, does not prevent their being stuck with the harsh consequences of having both confessed.

The dilemma of the prisoners is thus clear. The most rational choice for each leads to a state of affairs which is jointly destructive and at the same time stable. The jointly beneficial outcome, on the other hand, although available in principle, is highly unstable and hence is all but unattainable in practice.

2. The Main Proposition—PD Norms

What the prisoners need, quite clearly, is to find—or to develop —some means of stabilizing the jointly desirable state of affairs brought about by their both keeping silent. To be sure, the prisoners' problem is not in principle unsolvable; there might be instances of the dilemma where such means *are* present. For instance, the existence of trust, solidarity, or friendship between them might directly resolve their dilemma (on this issue see section 8 below). So also would an agreement between them, once it is enforceable; that is, provided that its breach is certain to be punished and, furthermore, that the threat of this punishment outweighs the temptation of breach.

However, my concern in the present chapter is not the particular problem of the two prisoners as presented thus far. Rather, I shall be interested in situations the structure of which is revealed on analysis to be similar, in its main features, to that of the Prisoners' Dilemma (henceforth to be referred to as PD) situations, but which is a generalization, in a sense yet to be explored, thereof. It can be said, therefore, that I shall be interested in situations which are generalized PD-like ones.

Regarding such situations it might already be noted by way of a preliminary conjecture that the larger the number of participants in them, the less the likelihood that there will exist trust, solidarity, or friendship among them, and also the more problematic (and possibly costly) the possibility of their coming to an explicit and enforceable agreement capable of co-ordinating their choice of actions in a mutually satisfactory way.

With the intention of providing an early guideline to the arguments in this chapter, I shall now state its main proposition. It is that generalized PD-structured situations constitute a type of contexts which are prone to generate norms. Unfolding this contention somewhat, the idea is the following: A situation of the generalized PD variety poses a problem to the participants involved. The problem is that of protecting an unstable yet jointly beneficial state of affairs from deteriorating, so to speak, into a stable yet jointly destructive one. My contention concerning such a situation is that a norm, backed by appropriate sanctions, could solve this problem. In this sense it can be said that such situations 'call for' norms. It can further be said that a norm solving the problem inherent in a situation of this type is *generated* by it.

Such norms I shall call PD norms.

3. *A Generalized PD-structured Situation*

Having said that I shall here be concerned with generalized PD-structured situations, I have yet to state more precisely first, what 'essential features' a situation has to possess in order to qualify as a PD-structured one, and, second, in what sense such a situation is considered to be a generalization of the prisoners' predicament.

3.1 *First Approximation*

Stripping the story of the Prisoners' Dilemma down to its bare skeleton, we get, as a first approximation, the following characterization:

A PD-structured situation is any situation involving at least two persons each of whom is facing a decision as to whether to do A or non-A,[2] such that

(i) If all of them do A the outcome is (and is known to them to be) mutually harmful;

(ii) If all of them do non-A the outcome is (and is known to them to be) mutually beneficial—or at any rate *better* than the outcome produced by their all doing A;

(iii) Each of the persons involved stands to gain most by singly doing A. That is to say, one's highest pay-off is obtained when one does A while all the others do non-A;

(iv) One's doing A when the others do non-A is—at least to some extent—at their expense. That is, when all-minus-one do non-A, the outcome to the non-A doers is less beneficial than it would have been had *everyone* done non-A.

Examples of familiar situations which might be seen to answer this description are, say, those involving a decision between payment of income tax *vis-à-vis* tax evasion, conscription *vis-à-vis* draft dodging, voting in the general election *vis-à-vis* picnicking on that day, and—on a smaller scale—situations involving decisions such as whether to take the longer path or to short-cut through the well-tended lawn, whether to keep a promise or to break it, and the like.

The generalization involved in passing from the story of the prisoners to the types of situations described above is conceived as being carried out along two axes. The first obviously concerns the size of the class of participants, which is allowed to be indefinite. A clarification is in order here.

---

[2] It does not matter which of the two involves doing and which refraining from doing (or, for that matter, they might both involve doing: if A is voting, non-A might be construed either just as not voting, or as some alternative B—like going to the beach for the day).

In game theory, a single participant is not necessarily envisaged as a single individual. It might be an aggregate of individuals (e.g. a firm, a political party, etc.). So that in fact a two-sided game might involve a (possibly large) number of persons as participants. However, it is not the number of persons involved in a game situation which is of significance to the game theorist; it is, rather, the number of decision-makers. Thus, when one considers a game between two firms, one might take them as two single players—even though they might each be composed of many individuals—once it is understood that each firm (regardless of how the processes of arriving at decisons are carried out *within* it) speaks with just one voice, and that in this respect its 'moves' are analogous to those of a single individual.

The generalization intended here, on the other hand, is genuine in that it refers not just to a large class of participants, but to a class of participants each of whom is a unit in terms of decision and action. Of course, a generalized situation *cannot* be represented by a 2×2 matrix of the familiar type. (See, however, section 9 below.)

The second axis, which does not find an explicit expression in the above list of features, concerns the factor of time. The original Prisoners' Dilemma is ordinarily conceived as a 'one-shot' game; i.e. as a situation involving a dilemma which is presented to the (two) participants just once, and simultaneously. A generalized PD-structured situation, on the other hand, is one in which the dilemma faced by the (multiple) participants is recurrent, or even continuous.

As a result, in addition to yielding a situation involving a large number of people among whom the dilemma is recurrent, the generalization should also yield situations in which the class of participants is not only large, but also indeterminate. That is, situations of particular interest to us here will be such that involve a community which is neither fixed nor closed, but which admits initiation of the young, of newcomers, etc. In such a situation, therefore, where people come and go, the recurrent dilemma is not in general faced, in each of its occurrences in the community concerned, by exactly the same people, but rather by a community with somewhat fuzzy borderlines.

Moreover, the participants involved in such a situation *know* this to be the case, and have to take the indeterminacy of the class, as well as the anonymity of its members, into account in their considerations as to what they might expect the others to do, and ultimately as to how they themselves are to act. Consequently, a solution to such a generalized dilemma would have to be one that is capable of being extended to cover the many instances of the problem, possibly among the anonymous members of an indeterminate class, and not one that solves, *ad hoc*, just a particular occurrence thereof, among specific participants.

Each of these generalization axes is of crucial importance to the central contention of this chapter. It might be said, somewhat schematically, that the smaller and the more determinate the class of participants in a generalized PD-structured situation, and the more isolated the occurrence of the dilemma among them, the more likely it is that there might be solutions other than (PD) norms to the pertinent problem (see section 8 below). And conversely, the larger and the more indeterminate the class of participants, and the more frequent the occurrence of the dilemma among them, the more likely it is that a solution, if any, would be in the form of a PD norm.

3.2 *Refinement*

When the class of participants is large, the essential features of a generalized PD-structured situation as stated above are stronger than need be and can be somewhat relaxed. It is a little over-dramatic to formulate the conditions in terms of 'all' and 'all but one'. It should obviously be possible to substitute 'most' for 'all' in some appropriate way. Also, the fact that the dilemma is recurrent should find some expression in any reformulation of the features, possibly by means of time-terms like 'always' and 'sometimes'.

I propose, therefore, the following refined characterization.

A generalized PD-structured situation is any situation involving at least two persons each of whom is repeatedly facing a decision as to whether to do A or non-A, such that

(i) If, in any occurrence of the dilemma among them, most of them do A the outcome is (and is known to them to be) mutually harmful;

(ii) If, in any occurrence of the dilemma among them, most of them do non-A, the outcome is (and is known to them to be)

mutually beneficial—or at any rate better than the outcome
produced when most of them do A;

(iii) Each of the persons involved obtains, at least in some occurrences of the dilemma among them, the highest possible pay-
off in the situation when he himself does A while most of the
others do non-A;

(iv) If, in any occurrence of the dilemma among them, some
do A, the outcome to the non-A doers is less beneficial than
it would have been had everyone done non-A.

Note that in feature (iii) it is not required that in *each* occurrence of the dilemma each participant stands to gain most by
unilaterally doing the 'bad' action. Rather, it states the weaker
requirement that each participant is at least *sometimes* tempted
to do so. The generalized PD case is, consequently, not to be
regarded as an amalgam of discernibly isolated proper (two-
person) PD cases. It is, rather, a situation of complex social
interaction which, when taken in its entirety, displays the four
features just stated. These features clearly constitute a somewhat weakened generalization of the features characterizing
the proper two-person PD case.

Thus, to consider the example of promise-breaking, in order
for it to be a generalized PD-like situation we need not suppose
that every one of us is always tempted to break his/her promises;
it suffices that each of us sometimes finds it to his/her advantage
to do so. Similarly, the situation involving a decision between
truthfulness and mendacity can be construed as a generalized
PD-structured one, in which feature (iii) holds in its weak
version.

It might, furthermore, be possible, in some specific situation,
to make more precise just what is meant by 'most' and 'some'.
One might think, for instance, of the example of the lawn: if
only a few tread it each day, the damage to it might not be
significant. So they themselves gain a short cut and the others
can still derive pleasure from contemplating the still beautiful
lawn. However, once a few more tread it each day, the lawn
might by now be appreciably damaged, a state of affairs which
is assumed, for the sake of the argument, to be repugnant to
all. Similarly, one might think of the case of petty shop-lifting
in a supermarket which, once it transgresses certain limits,

inevitably leads to the collectively undesirable outcome of price-raising due to a decline in profits, extra security precautions, etc.

In general, this further refinement is conceived as being along the following lines:

Let the community of participants be denoted by C. Then, with regard to any occurrences of the dilemma in C, there is some maximal sub-set of C, say D (for defectors, dodgers, deviators, or what have you), which is in general rather small relative to C, such that if all members of D do A while the members of C−D do non-A, the A doers obtain for themselves the highest possible pay-off in the situation, and yet the outcome of the non-A doers is still not significantly affected by the deviators and is in general rather satisfactory. However, if more members of C defect and join the sub-set D, then deterioration takes place. That is, for any D′ such that D′ ⊆ C and D ⊂ D′, if the members of D′ do A then the outcome for all—both A doers and non-A doers—is already harmful.

This is still quite crude. In order to refine it further one would have, for instance, to consider the point that it may not be a certain crucial *number* (or *proportion*) of people who deviate that brings about the jointly harmful consequences; it might also be the *frequency* in which these deviations occur. Also, attention would have to be paid to the fact that in some cases it might be the addition of just one deviator to D which upsets the balance, while in other cases (perhaps in most) it takes a certain *range* of additional deviations to produce that effect. Such further refinements, however, although quite interesting in themselves, are immaterial for the issues in hand.[3]

3.3 *The Condition of Individual Insignificance*

Special attention should now be directed to feature (iv) (pp. 23, 26 above)—that is, to the extent to which one's doing the 'bad' action directly harms the doers of the 'good' action. In the case of the original story about the prisoners, unilateral confession not only brings about freedom for the confessor, but

---

[3] I believe that David Lyons's carefully worked-out notions of the *density* of a practice, of general *v.* universal practices, and in particular of *thresholds* and *threshold effects* are directly applicable to any attempted refinement along the lines suggested above. (Lyons, 1965, pp. 63–75.)

sends his mate to the longest term in prison. That is, in the case of just two participants, unilateral deviation (defection) is directly at the expense of the other, and results in a state of affairs where the former obtains the highest possible pay-off in the situation and the latter the lowest.

However, it stands to reason that the more participants in the situation, the less the damage to the majority by the minority of deviators (provided it is small enough). If, for instance, there are in a large community only very few tax-evaders, the system will go on functioning and no appreciable decrease in the provision of goods and services by the state will occur. To be sure, *some* harm, at least in principle, is always done by such a minority: it would surely be better, even if it is only very slightly better, for the community as a whole were there no tax-evaders at all and as a result were there somewhat more resources in the state treasury. For this feature of the generalized PD-structured situations to obtain, there is one necessary condition which must be fulfilled. It is that the contribution of each participant taken alone be sufficiently small and untraceable as to be practically insignificant to the over-all outcome. The whole point, of course, is that the composition of such near-insignificant contributions is, as from a certain point (or range), quite significant; indeed it is capable of swaying the final outcome.

This condition—call it the *condition of individual insignificance*—implies (but is not implied by) another condition, which we might call the *condition of homogeneity*. It requires that the contribution of each participant has more or less the same weight as that of any other participant relative to the over-all outcome. Jointly they ensure that there be no single participant (or a small group of participants) whose decision whether to do A or non-A tips the scale as to the over-all outcome, regardless of what the others do. (In economics the fulfilment of these two conditions results in a state of *perfect competition* where a large number of small producers compete for the market and there is no leading firm which dominates it.)

Note that in situations where the condition of individual insignificance is satisfied the temptation to do the 'bad' action might persuasively be argued to be greater than it is in PD-structured situations in which it is not satisfied (such as in the original case of the prisoners). The argument is that in situations of the former kind unilateral defection to the tempting, 'bad' action is not at the personal expense of any of the other participants, and is moreover likely to go entirely unnoticed by them. It is an action which, if unilaterally done, gratifies its doer—possibly even highly gratifies him—while not directly and appreciably harming the others. Thus a potential inhibition which might exist in situations of the latter kind, regarding the infliction of direct and personal damage on one's partners, is removed in the cases where the condition of individual insignificance is satisfied. (Regardless of whether the situation is one in which the condition at hand is satisfied or not, though, it holds true that the tempting, 'bad' option dominates the 'good' one, in the sense explained on p. 19.)

Let me finally recall briefly the statement of the main proposition of the present chapter (as put forward in Section 2 above), that generalized PD-structured situations are prone to be norm-generating. The last two sections aimed at clarifying the notion of a 'generalized PD-structured situation'. I would like to add at this point the conjecture that generalized PD-structured situations which satisfy the condition of individual insignificance—and hence the condition of homogeneity too—are more likely to constitute recruiting fields for norm-generating contexts than are those which do not. In generalized PD-structured situations in which the condition of individual insignificance is not satisfied (and the condition of homogeneity is either satisfied or not, as the case may be), I believe that it is more likely that solutions other than (PD) norms might exist, or be devised. This point will be taken up again later (Sections 8 and 8.1 below).

4. *The Solution as a Stabilizing Device*

The problem posed by a situation of the generalized PD variety is clear: it is how to protect a state of affairs which is jointly beneficial yet unstable from deteriorating—via the yielding to temptation by each (or by most) of the participants involved—into a state of affairs which is not only jointly harmful but also highly stable so that the possibility of redemption from it seems at best remote. That is, what is needed is some stabilizing device.

A stabilizing device in the type of situations under consideration would be anything which successfully eliminates the
temptation to deviate from what is obviously the 'good' action.
In terms of the matrix representation (matrix 2.3, p. 19 above)
this means that an adequate stabilizing device would be one
which would change the pay-off structure of the situation in
such a way that the second action—referred to by 'D'—will no
longer dominate the first—'C', and that the jointly beneficial
outcome (represented by the upper-left cell) will become an
equilibrium from which it would pay no one to deviate alone.

All this amounts, very simply, to the statement that what is
required is a reduction in the pay-offs referred to by 'T' at least to
the level of the pay-offs referred to by 'R' but preferably to a considerably lower level than that. A prospective solution characterized in this way is, it seems, just what T. C. Schelling had in mind
when putting forward the following propositions (1964, p. 487):

> Game theory can help to identify solutions, that is, ways that one
> may change the situation so that choices will be made differently. ...
> Game theory can also discover that reducing pay-offs to both
> players, if the reductions are selectively accomplished, to change a
> dominant strategy into one no longer dominant and to provide a new
> equilibrium point, can benefit both players. Though they might
> appear to be worse off from selective reductions in their pay-offs, in
> fact each gains by the resulting change in strategies chosen.

I propose now to construct an imaginary example of a PD-
structured situation and to examine in some detail several ways
out of the dilemma which all fall under the above characterization. I shall then proceed to assess these solutions, and to
examine which of them, if any, is connected with PD norms,
and in what way. The analysis of this example will prove instructive, I believe, for the understanding of the nature and
function of PD norms in general.

5. *The Mortarmen's Dilemma*

5.1 *Presentation*

Let us imagine two mortarmen in two isolated outposts, facing
an enemy attack. Each of them considers that he has two
alternatives open to him: to remain at his post and fight, or to
take to his heels.

Now suppose the possible outcomes are:

1. If both stay in their posts and shell the enemy, the attack is repelled.
2. If both run away there is nothing to hold the enemy up, so the enemy break through right away and manage to take both of them prisoner.
3. If one stays in the post and the other runs away, the one who stays behind manages to hold the enemy up by engaging them in fire just long enough for the other to escape safely, but then gets killed by the enemy who eventually break through.

Suppose too that both mortarmen know these to be the possible outcomes.

Let us further suppose that the mortarmen's preferences among the outcomes are represented by the following 'pay-offs':

To remain in the post and repel the attack: 1
To remain in the post and get killed: -2
To desert successfully: 2
To desert and be taken prisoner by the enemy: -1

The situation may now be summarized in the classical PD matrix (2.4).

Each realizes that, whatever the other does, he is better off deserting: the D-strategy dominates the R-strategy. This leads them to double desertion (D, D), which results in them both being taken prisoner, whereas both would prefer the

	R	D
Remain	1 / 1	-2 / 2
Desert	2 / -2	-1 / -1

2.4

outcome (R, R) which entails their remaining alive and free. The trouble, typically, is that 'not only is a constant temptation [to desert] pressing on each player, but also the *knowledge* that the other player is tempted makes the defection practically compelling' (Rapoport, 1966, p. 129).

We now ask ourselves how can this dilemma be resolved. At the outset, however, we note that it is not only in the interest of the mortarmen's superiors, or their country for that matter, that they both remain in their posts and repel the enemy attack, but it is also in the interest of the mortarmen themselves to do so. The problem, then, is to find some means by which to deprive the desertion strategy of its tempting force; that is, to

change the situation—or the degrees of desirability of the outcomes—in such a way as to cancel the dominance of the D-
choice over the R-choice.

I shall propose and examine three such ways.

5.2 *Minelaying*

The first way of solving the dilemma to be considered looks
like a rather brutal one: mines are to be densely laid all around
the mortarmen's posts.

The possible outcomes and the pay-offs connected with
them are now:

To remain (when the other remains too) and repel the
attack: 1

To remain (when the other deserts) and get killed by the
enemy: -2

To try to desert but get killed by a mine: -2

The matrix of this situation is 2.5.

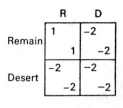

2.5

A rough examination of the matrix
shows clearly that the outcome (R, R)
has all the 'good qualities' of a game-
theoretical solution. It is by far the best
outcome for both parties; there is no
question whatever of even contemplating
the D-choice. It is clear, then, that this
minelaying solution, brutal as it may
appear, turns out to work in the interest of both parties. It
effectively eliminates the possibility of desertion, and consequently each is happy to stay by his mortar and fight, knowing
that the other has in fact no alternative but to fight too, with
the result that the attack is repelled and they both stay alive.
The minelaying changes the situation—more specifically, the
outcomes associated with the D-choice—in such a way as to
endow the outcome preferred by both with the accessibility,
stability, and dominance which it lacked before.

This minelaying device may call to one's mind the famous
story that in World War I German soldiers were in fact chained
to their machine guns, to prevent their running away. In this
connection Schelling points out (1964, p. 476) that 'it is particu-

larly interesting that machine-gunners might volunteer to be chained, each willing to stay on condition his partners be made equally reliable.' In our case we may say that it is not irrational for the mortarmen themselves to ask for the laying of the mines around their posts (provided they are given no map of the location of the mines), thus assuring their solidarity in battle.

5.3 *Discipline*

The second variation on the mortarmen story is this: suppose the two mortarmen belong to a unit in which military discipline is harsh and effective. Whoever gives way under enemy attack is liable to be executed by his officers, if caught.

The possible outcomes and the pay-offs associated with them are now taken to be the following:

To stay with one's weapon (when the other stays too) and repel the attack: 1

To stay with one's weapon (when the other deserts) and get killed by the enemy: -2

To desert (when the other deserts too), get caught and be taken prisoner by the enemy, *and* be liable to execution if eventually handed over to one's own forces: $-1 \cdot 5$

(This pay-off, it will be noted, is better than that for getting killed, which is -2, and worse than that for captivity, which—in the original mortarmen's matrix—was -1; the rationale being that this case involves certain captivity conjoined with probable execution.)

To desert (when the other stays behind) and be liable to execution: -1 or 0

(Here the pay-off depends upon the probability one assigns to one's being caught, and hence executed, by one's own forces. Note that if being caught, and hence executed, is taken to be certain, then the appropriate pay-off will be -2, and we shall be back, for all practical purposes, at the Minelaying variation of the story.)

The matrix of this situation is 2.6.

This matrix is an interesting one: it has two equilibrium points, viz. (R, R) (since -1 and 0 are worse than 1) and (D, D)

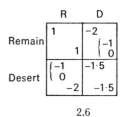

2.6

(since -2 is worse than $-1\cdot5$), the first of which is obviously preferred by both parties. It might seem, then, that the outcome of (R, R) is the natural and straightforward one, and that the desired solution of the dilemma is consequently guaranteed. However, there is a certain complication here. The (D, D) equilibrium, albeit being the worse of the two, is nevertheless the one contained in the plan maximizing both participants' security level (for the worst that may occur when choosing R is -2, whereas the worst that may occur when choosing D is $-1\cdot5$, which is better). So that the situation is such that there are two equilibria: one good and in a sense risky, the other worse but safer.

This means that neither party will find remaining in the post the more rational course of action *whatever the other does*. If there is the slightest suspicion that the other might desert, desertion has to be considered the safe choice. But as long as there is no ground for suspicion, and since each stands to gain from remaining as long as the other remains, there is reason to assume that the choice of both mortarmen will fall on the R-strategy. At least this much is true, that if communication between them is at all possible they should have no difficulty in co-ordinating their choice of actions to bring about their remaining in the posts and repelling the enemy attack, to the advantage of both.

However, if, as we assume, the mortarmen belong to a strongly disciplined unit, they should be *in the habit* of obeying orders, knowing from experience that disobedience is not tolerated. So when they are stationed in their posts with the order to repel the enemy attack with their mortars, even if communication between them is not possible this habit of obedience will serve as the needed ground on which each will expect the other to remain in his post and fight, and therefore he himself will remain and fight too.

Thus we see that the contribution of discipline to the dissolution of the dilemma is two-fold. In the first place its existence and effectiveness change the pay-offs associated with the outcomes in such a way that flight no longer dominates fight, and that the outcome (R, R) becomes an equilibrium. In the second, the knowledge, common to both mortarmen, *that* their unit is disciplined constitutes the necessary ground on which each bases his expectation that the other will not desert. This expectation is decisive at the point where each has to decide which of the two equilibria he is going to aim at by his choice of action, and it is likely to turn the scale in favour of the jointly beneficial outcome.

Note, finally, that discipline functions as a *deterrent device*. It is the threat of punishment which outweighs, and thus cancels out, the temptation to desert.

In a recent paper addressing the issues of morality and rationality with regard to the Prisoners' Dilemma, Amartya Sen urges us to consider a variation of the preference orderings of the two prisoners (1974, pp. 59 ff.) which in essence corresponds to my 'discipline matrix' (no. 2.6, p. 33 above). That is, he proposes to begin by leaving the facts of the original story about the two prisoners (as represented by matrix 2.1, p. 18 above) intact, and then to imagine that the prisoners' preference ranking of the four possible outcomes be such that it will be represented by a matrix like no. 2.6 rather than by the usual PD matrix (i.e. like no. 2.2, p. 18 above). Realizing that in this variant of the 'game' there are two equilibrium points, and that its structure is such that 'a contract of mutual non-confession [non-desertion] does not need any enforcement . . . whereas it is the crux of the matter in the [original] Prisoners' Dilemma' (p. 60), Sen proposes to call it the Assurance Game (or AG): 'Each prisoner [mortarman] will do the right thing if it is simply assured that the other is doing it too and there is no constant temptation to break the contract' (ibid.). Sen then proceeds to argue that a resolution of the prisoners' dilemma will come about if 'every one behaved *as if* they had AG-preferences and had the assurance of similar good behaviour by others' (ibid.), rather than the PD-preferences they actually have.

The idea of acts according to *as if* preferences is mysterious to me. What seems to me somewhat clearer, though, is just where Sen's approach to solving PD-type problems essentially differs from mine—and I would like to point that out. Sen's idea is to leave the reality of the dilemma-ridden situation as it is, and somehow to affect the participants' (moral) *perceptions* of and *attitudes* to it in such a way that they will act on 'as if' (AG) preferences rather than on their real (PD) preferences. What I maintain, on the other hand, is that in such cases certain devices (generally speaking, PD norms) will be generated such that it is the *reality* of the situation which changes (e.g. to one of the discipline, or AG, type), and along with it, of course, the participants' preferences over the (new) outcomes.

(As to the relation between the 'discipline device' and PD norms, see below, Section 6.)

5.4 *Honour*

Suppose now that in the society to which the mortarmen belong honour is all in all. In their unit one is not so much in dread of death, provided it is heroic death, but of denunciation as a deserter and traitor. For these people glory sugars the pill of death, and a mark of disgrace as a traitor makes the prospect of saving one's life by escape, let alone an escape which ends up in captivity, gloomy, if not hideous.

Given this system of values, the pay-offs connected with the four possible outcomes are taken to be the following:

> to stay and fight (when the other stays and fights too), and repel the attack: 1
>
> to stay and fight (when the other deserts), get killed by the enemy and become a (dead) hero: −1
>
> to desert (when the other stays behind and fights), be saved from death, retain freedom, but be denounced as a traitor and people's enemy: 0
>
> to desert (when the other deserts too), be taken prisoner by the enemy, *and* be denounced as a traitor: −2

The essential point here is, then, that these people had rather die as heroes than live in the enemy's captivity, stigmatized as traitors. On the other hand we should not, and in fact for our purposes need not, go to extremes and impute to our mortarmen preference of being dead, even though as heroes, over being alive *and* free, even though as traitors. This is the rationale of the order of preference among the outcomes, as represented by the above pay-offs.

	R	D
Remain	1 1	−1 0
Desert	0 −1	−2 −2

2.7

The matrix of this situation is 2.7.

The (R, R) outcome is here the obvious solution: it is the best outcome for both, it is an equilibrium (the only one), and it is contained in a dominant choice (and hence also in the choice maximizing security level). In other words, one is here better off remaining and fighting *whatever the other does*. It is interesting to note that in this respect the 'honour device' of solving the Mortarmen's Dilemma turns out to be more effective than the discipline device, the choice of R in the latter case being dependent upon the expectation that the other chooses R too.

It is noteworthy that honour, on the foregoing analysis, functions not only as a device of deterrence, but also as something which is rather close to being a *compensative device*. This is so since we have here both *decrease* in pay-offs, where being denounced as a deserter is involved, and *increase* in pay-offs, in terms of esteem, reputation, prestige, and glory, where behaviour which is up to what is considered honourable is involved.

(The latter point might seem to echo, in a sense, Schopenhauer's observation—in *Parerga und Paralipomena*—that since the state cannot afford to pay its officers and officials a high salary, it pays them the second half of it in livery, decorations, and honorary titles.)

Note also that both disgrace and glory are conferred not only on the deserter or the hero (as the case may be) himself, but on his family too. This is of significance since it contributes to the fact that it might after all indeed make a difference to a man whether he dies as a traitor or as a hero.

6. *An Assessment of the Proposed Solutions to the Mortarmen's Dilemma and their Relation to PD Norms*

Three ways out of the Mortarmen's Dilemma have been examined in the last few sections. All of them consist, essentially, of the bringing about of restraints on choices, or of changes in the preference-order among the outcomes which are reflected in pay-off changes. The first way considered, the minelaying, is in fact a sort of technical device; for most practical as well as theoretical purposes it amounts to eliminating an alternative, that is, to a reduction of the matrix into a degenerate one-choice matrix. In this respect this device is similar, as we have seen, to the measure of chaining machine-gunners to their weapons.

Let us now turn to assess the other two means through which the dilemma was shown to be resolved. What is discipline? I

think it is better to ask: What is a disciplined unit? At any rate
the answer to the second question is simpler, and more pertinent
to our present purposes. Very generally, a disciplined military
unit is one whose members regularly obey their commanders'
orders. They might do so out of habit, fear of punishment, or
some inner conviction about the value of obedience; probably
out of some combination of these.

What is the object of military discipline? In order to ap-
proximate an answer to this question, let us start by assuming
that the entire machinery of an army is ultimately geared
towards an encounter of its infantry with the enemy's. When
this takes place, the case is a generalized PD-structured one in
which, moreover, the condition of individual insignificance is
likely to be satisfied. Each soldier's contribution to the final
outcome of the battle can probably be taken to be negligible;[4]
each soldier might reasonably be envisaged as facing a temptation to desert, to 'disappear', to stay behind as soon as the
fighting begins; if too many yield to this temptation the outcome is likely to be disastrous to all; their only chance of
obtaining a collectively satisfactory outcome might lie in their
all storming and fighting together.

This description is, of course, oversimplified. But the over-
simplification helps me make my point. It is that what might be
taken to be one of the most fundamental military norms, that
a soldier ought never to desert in time of battle, can—at least
in part—be construed as a PD norm. It is a norm which, when
supported by sufficiently severe sanctions, is capable of solving,
or indeed dissolving, potential generalized PD-structured problems of the type outlined above. General compliance with it,
conjoined with common knowledge that it is generally complied with, guarantees the desired collective effort and solidarity
in battle.[5]

---

[4] Unless there is an appropriately detailed division of roles and positions among
the soldiers, in which case the picture is changed. On this issue, see below, Sec.
8.1.

[5] Within the context of the military, it might be contended, along the lines of
Urmson (1958), that this PD norm is some kind of a 'basic duty', a minimal requirement of co-operation which prohibits behaviour that is intolerable if an army is to
achieve its primary goal. Furthermore, this norm leaves plenty of room for heroic
actions which go beyond this duty. Indeed, I think that a case can be made that
what falls under Urmson's category of basic duties are in general PD norms.

There is, however, a further point to be considered here. Suppose that it is a long time since the efficacy of this norm has been put to the test. Suppose, that is, that there has not been a battle for a long time, so that at least as far as the younger soldiers are concerned, there are no previous cases to go by. The requirement that the PD norm concerned (prohibiting desertion in time of battle) be effective and be known to be effective is thus not satisfied in such a case. Does it follow that in these cases a state of general desertion would almost inevitably occur?

To be sure, this norm is—and it can safely be assumed that it is known to be—accompanied by the severest sanctions, possibly execution. So that the temptation to desert is considerably diminished. But still, as was shown earlier (p. 34 above), the equilibrium state of collective desertion, although less preferred by all to the equilibrium state of collective fighting, might be considered safer in the sense of being contained in a choice maximizing the security level of each. Consequently, the deterrent effect of the punishment for desertion might nevertheless be outweighed by the consideration of maximum security level. This would be so, provided that the systems of mutual expectations were such that each expected the others to desert rather than to stay on and fight.

But do we in fact have any reason to believe that this would be the nature of the mutual expectations involved?

Let us, at this point, go back to the opening statements of this Section and tie them in here. My argument is that if the units under consideration are, and are known to their members to be, disciplined, then deterioration into the state of general desertion would *not* take place even if there are no recent precedents of behaviour in time of battle, and so the problem would be overcome in these cases too.

The reasoning is this: that the units are disciplined means that they have the propensity to obey orders; and that they are known to their members to be disciplined means that each member thereof may reasonably expect each other to obey orders in any given case. Hence, in the case of the battle in question, even if there is no recent precedent of compliance with the particular (PD) norm not to desert, the fact that the units involved are, and are known to their members to be, disciplined, suffices to make the pertinent systems of mutual expectations such that each will have good reason to expect the others to obey their officers' orders and fight rather than desert. Consequently, the equilibrium state to be aimed at by each would be the better one—that of collective fighting—and the problem would be overcome.

To sum up, then. The fundamental military norm prohibiting desertion in time of battle is, it has been argued, a PD norm. It emerges out of, and applies to new, situations which can be viewed as generalizations of the mortarmen's predicament, that is, situations which are generalized PD-structured ones. The efficacy of this norm, conjoined with the severe punishment for its breach, solves the problem inherent in this type of sitnation: the good outcome is stabilized, the danger of deterioration into the bad state of affairs is eliminated. Furthermore, in cases where the condition of the efficacy of this norm is not satisfied owing to lack of appropriate precedents, it has been argued that the alternative condition—that the units concerned be in general disciplined—is sufficient to guarantee that the pertinent problem would nevertheless be solved.

As to the issue of honour, finally, I think that it might be advisable to make a shift here, similar to the one made above from 'discipline' to 'a disciplined unit', and to proceed to deal with 'honourable behaviour' instead of with 'honour'. It seems that there are certain standards of behaviour associated with, and presumably following in some sense from, the idea (or ideal) of honour. Behaviour which meets these standards—compressed by such injunctions as 'Return from war either with your shield or on it'—is, accordingly, considered honourable. Be the precise content of the concepts of honour and honourable behaviour what it may, however, the essential point concerning the issues in hand is that, under specific circumstances (such as those considered in 5.4 above), they might give rise to certain values which are capable of affecting one's preferences over a given set of alternative outcomes in such a way that dilemmas like the mortarmen's practically dissolve. From the point of view of the military, therefore, it seems that it is worth while to foster and to cultivate the idea of honour among its soldiers, indeed to make them adopt the standards of behaviour connected with it as their own inner ones, for with such soldiers the officers need have no fear of predicaments of the mortarmen's variety, still less of cases of general desertion actually occurring in time of battle.

7. PD and Morality

7.1 Are PD Norms Norms of Morality?

David Gauthier characterizes a moral system, and in a derivative way a moral man too, in terms of behaviour in a PD-structured situation (1967). Practically speaking, a moral system, according to Gauthier, is a system of principles which will make people involved in a PD-structured situation choose the co-operative (dominated) action rather than the alternative (dominating) action of defection. The reasoning is that a moral system must be one which 'requires that some persons perform acts genuinely disadvantageous to themselves as a means to greater mutual advantage'. And since in a PD not to make the defection choice, when one's partner (or opponent, as the case may be) is expected to make the co-operation choice, is indeed genuinely disadvantageous to one, it follows that a system of principles inducing one to choose the co-operative action notwithstanding, in order to increase the mutual advantage, counts as a moral system.

Now the derived behavioural characterization of a moral man is the following. A moral man is one who, in a PD-structured situation, chooses the co-operative action on the assumption that the other is also going to make the same choice, and who, moreover, does not deviate from this choice even if he be certain that the other cannot, for some reason, punish him later by deviating too. The reasoning which leads to this contention starts by noting that the choice of the co-operative action, on the expectation that the other is going to make the same choice is, according to Gauthier, out of *prudence*. It is a choice which involves a sacrifice of some greater personal advantage for a maximum of mutual advantage. When to this is added one's readiness to stick to this choice in spite of a postulated certainty that deviation from it would—with impunity—significantly improve one's own position, then, according to Gauthier, one is shown to be *trustworthy* too. And, finally, one's being both prudent and trustworthy is, for Gauthier, a sufficient condition for being a moral man.

I find it rather curious that Gauthier seems to be oblivious of the fact that the original story of the Prisoners' Dilemma might well be dealing with detained gangsters, or criminals. Suppose that for whatever reason both of them choose the co-operative action of non-confession. Would that be sufficient for them to be considered moral men? I suspect that Gauthier would be constrained to answer this question in the affirmative, whereas to me it appears like an almost rhetorical question requiring an off-hand No for an answer.

My proposed amendment to Gauthier's condition, therefore, would be that choosing the co-operative action in a PD-structured situation, and persevering in this choice, would count as moral behaviour if a further condition is satisfied: that this involves no disadvantage to anyone extraneous to the PD-structured situation under consideration. In default of this stipulation, mobsters of the Mafia and members of an industrial cartel might turn out to provide paradigmatic cases of moral behaviour, a result which surely does not fall into line with Gauthier's intentions.

I believe, incidentally, that Gauthier's faulty condition can be traced back to the fact that in the early discussions of game theory in general, and of the Prisoners' Dilemma in particular, the dominant example of a real-life PD-structured situation was seen by many to be the armaments race between the super-powers. And since a restriction on armaments, achieved through a strategy of co-operation, was taken to constitute a paradigm case of a moral act, there emerged this uncritical identification of the choice of the co-operative action in any PD-structured situation with moral behaviour.

Is my proposed amendment a necessary condition of morality, or is it a stipulation which, in conjunction with Gauthier's condition, makes for sufficiency? I contend that the requirement that an action of co-operation in a PD-structured situation be at the expense of no one who is not involved in the situation is *not* a necessary condition of morality. In order to see this, consider the case of the prisoners, but imagine them to be political prisoners fighting against a tyrannical and immoral ruler, rather than criminals. In such a case their choosing the co-operative action of non-confession is indeed to the disadvantage of the regime, and yet it is clearly not to be condemned as immoral.

As for sufficiency, I take it that the proposed stipulation together with Gauthier's condition do constitute a sufficient condition of morality. The notion of morality, however, should in this context be construed broadly as comprising the realm of everything which is not immoral, as the remarks below bear out.

From the discussion so far it may be concluded, then, that PD norms need not in general be norms of morality. A norm among mobsters to the effect that they ought never to tell on one another when caught by the police,[6] and a norm among oligopolists prohibiting reduction of prices, do qualify as PD norms, their efficacy among the members of the groups concerned ensuring that any potential occurrence of problems of the PD type among them be overcome to their mutual satisfaction. But such norms would not ordinarily be considered moral.

So let us turn our attention to the sub-class of PD norms which consists only of those PD norms adherence to which by the participants concerned does not disadvantage anyone not involved in the pertinent situation. This sub-class certainly excludes such patently immoral norms as those just exemplified. But does it follow that the PD norms contained in this sub-class can all be classified as norms of morality?

I think that on our *ordinary* conception of morality the answer is No, since in it, besides norms prescribing truthfulness and promise-keeping etc., there will also be norms which are generally taken to be morally neutral. Thus, a norm prohibiting treading on a certain lawn, or the norm obliging one to pay one's income tax, are PD norms which would normally be taken to be outside the realm of morality (although the latter one might be argued to have moral undertones associated with the concept of 'good citizenship').

However, on a *utilitarian* conception of morality, it seems that all the PD norms contained in the sub-class under consideration would qualify as norms of morality, since by definition they

[6] Compare the Sicilians' law of *omerta*, 'the law of silence', as described in Mario Puzo's *Godfather* (Pan Books, London, 1970, pp. 102–3, 217).

come to ensure that the state of maximum social advantage is achieved and maintained.

7.2 Norms for Keeping People in a PD Situation

So far we have been dealing with norms whose function was to help avert a deterioration, in PD-structured situations, into the mutually harmful state of affairs denoted by (D, D) in the PD matrix (matrix 2.3, p. 19 above). These norms were supposed to keep the participants in the mutually beneficial state of affairs denoted by (C, C) in the PD matrix.

I shall now proceed to show that there are norms whose function is to maintain social control on certain groups of people through preventing them from solving the problem inherent in the PD-structured situation in which they are placed. That is, these norms are designed to help keep these people in a state of affairs which, while disadvantageous to them (i.e. it is the one represented by the bottom-right cell of the PD matrix), is considered beneficial to society as a whole.

A conspicuous example of norms of this type are anti-trust laws. Let us consider this in some detail. The situation of competition among producers in a market system is a generalized PD-structured one. Concerning each product, its various producers can, somewhat ideally, be taken to face a choice between two alternatives: full production and restricted production. If all of them choose full production then the price the product achieves in the market is low, and individually they fare worse than they would have done had they all restricted production and thus ensured a higher price for their product. (This is so provided that the demand curve of this product is inelastic, i.e. provided that a one-per-cent cut in price will expand its quantity by less than one per cent.) However, with regard to any given producer, the choice of full production dominates the choice of restricted production; that is, each producer would be better off with full production whatever the others do. Yet if all yield to this temptation they all come to suffer.

It would clearly be best for the producers if they were to come to an agreement among themselves to ensure that they all restrict their production and thus maintain a relatively high price for their product. This type of agreement, accompanied by appropriately severe sanctions to be imposed on its breach, amounts to limiting the competition among the producers concerned and hence to the forming of a cartel among them. As said, it is in the interest of each producer that such a cartel be formed and that it be effective.

However, when the community of consumers is brought into the picture, it is evident that it is in its interest that such a cartel *not* be formed and that a state of competition among the producers, possibly leading to price reductions, be maintained. Now in certain countries, led by the United States, the awareness has grown that the interests and welfare of the society as a whole ought to outweigh those of the producers, and, consequently, that the latter are to be prevented from coming into a cartelization agreement. That is, there are cases where a society might decide to devise norms, possibly legal ones, that would serve as means of social control to preserve a desired degree of competition in its market.

This, essentially, is what anti-trust laws (such as the celebrated Sherman's Anti-Trust Act of 1890 in the U.S.A.) are all about. They are—at least on the surface—aimed at preventing producers from improving their own position at the expense of the consumers, or, as a more severe formulation has it, they are a means of social control against certain bodies who might wish to conspire against the economic welfare of the rest of society. In other words, such laws function to preserve the PD problem of the producers and to prevent them from solving it at the expense of others.

This point will be taken up again later (Chapter III, Section 5.5).

8. *Functionally Equivalent Solutions to PD Problems*

In this section I would like to mention briefly a few experimental results regarding factors encouraging people to co-operate with each other in PD-structured situations. There is a large experimental literature on this subject, but I shall be concerned only with the results which have theoretical bearing on the issues in hand. Some of these studies do mention norms, but none investigates them as a factor. What have been investigated experimentally are other factors which I take to be functionally equivalent to PD norms in that they also solve the pertinent

PD problems. That is, they help bring about a choice of the 'good', co-operative action and thus help prevent the menace of deteriorating into the mutually harmful state of affairs. My general argument here is that the more generalized the PD-structured situations (in the sense explained above, pp. 23-4), the less the degree to which the other means investigated are substitutive to PD norms. This is so owing to the nature of these means, which are all dependent on some kind of personal contact among the participants.

The first factor to be considered is friendship. It is reasonable to assume that relations of friendship among the participants would make them tend to co-operate with each other when placed in a PD-structured situation, even when there is no prior communication among them concerning the specific problem they are facing. Some experiments indeed seem to confirm this assumption. (Thus: 'Intragroup dyads showed more co-operation than did intergroup dyads', Wallace and Rothaus, 1969, p. 379.)

There is, however, an interesting study (by Oskamp and Perlman, 1966) in which the influence of friendship on co-operation in PD games was investigated among students of two colleges. The results showed a rather extreme difference between the colleges: in one college the influence of friendship was in the direction of a high degree of co-operation, and in the other in the direction of a high degree of competition. On the other hand, there were no significant differences between the colleges in the degree of co-operation obtained in games played with outsiders. The conclusion drawn by the authors of this study is that there is, contrary to intuitions, no direct link between the degree of friendship and the degree of co-operation in a PD game. Just as it is reasonable to expect good friends to co-operate, it might be argued that it is reasonable to expect them to compete: it is precisely because of the familiarity among them that they can afford to go on an all-out competition without their image, status, or mutual esteem being at stake.

By way of commenting on this interpretation of the results I would venture to suggest that friends would compete with each other in a PD situation only when they are playing a game. It seems to me to be a common-sensical conjecture that when friends find themselves trapped in a real-life PD-structured situation, their friendship would tend to contribute toward an increase in the degree of co-operation among them.

The second and third factors investigated are solidarity and prior communication. There is for instance a finding (again by Oskamp and Perlman, 1965) according to which members of a small college tend to achieve more co-operation in PD games than members of a large university. This is taken by the authors to corroborate the hypothesis that the more intense the 'sense of belonging', or the 'group spirit', or in general the feelings of solidarity among people—even if they are not friends and perhaps are not even acquainted with each other—the greater the degree of co-operation among them.

To this is added the information that communication among the participants, and especially pre-game communication, increases the degree of co-operation among them, even where it is only short and superficial. (It is, however, argued elsewhere that, if a state of conflict and competition is already established in a group, then short communication cannot alter it significantly (Wallace and Rothaus, 1969).) From all these findings it emerges that there are indeed factors, other than PD norms, which help stabilize the mutually beneficial state of affairs in a PD-structured situation and in this sense contribute to the solution of the problem involved.

However, the attainment of co-operation in the cases where these factors operate depends largely on some sort of personal contact among the participants. Also, it seems to depend on the participants' possessing certain properties (such as being one's friend, belonging to a certain group to which one belongs too, etc.) which are capable of forming a basis for the mutual expectations needed in this type of situation as to how the others will act.

Now my contention, I repeat, is that the more difficult (or costly) it is to ensure these types of personal contact, i.e. the larger, the more indeterminate, and the more anonymous the group of participants—the more acute the need for some *impersonal* device, such as social norms, which would induce the desired co-operation.

Let me note, finally, that there are systems of values and social norms, such as the hippies', which induce those subscribing to them to co-operate with each other when placed in

PD-structured situations. Moreover, it is reported (by Pilisuk, Kiritz, and Clampitt, 1971) that hippies tended to persevere in their choice of the co-operative action even when their partners were military cadets who consistently took advantage of them. The values and norms involved in such cases, however, are not, it seems to me, to be in general classified as PD ones: it would be wrong, I suspect, to assume personal connections among them and some past experiences of PD-structured situations in which the members of these communities were placed and from which they might be assumed to have been generated. Rather, they have to do with these people's rejection of materialistic gains, with their altruism and their adherence to such principles as that of 'turning the other cheek'.[7]

8.1 *Division of Labour in PD Situations*

Division of labour might in a sense also be taken as a means —different from PD norms—of solving a PD problem. It is a device which in fact amounts to ensuring that the condition of individual insignificance be not satisfied.

Suppose there is a certain task that has to be carried out by a certain group of people. Suppose further that it is a relatively unpleasant, or difficult, task, say to weed a certain field. Now if the members of the group just scatter around all over the place and start weeding, each might be tempted to put on a show and not to strain himself too much, on the assumption that his own efforts and output do not matter much and that the task would be completed by the group anyhow. However, if they all act on this consideration, then the job might remain unaccomplished—a state of affairs which is assumed to be un-

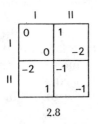

2.8

[7] It might be of some interest to note in this connection that there is an Altruists' Dilemma, analogous to the Prisoners' (egoistic) Dilemma. Consider the situation depicted by matrix 2.8.

If the motive of each is to increase the pay-off of the other, then there is a dominant choice for that, viz. II. The outcome brought about when both make this choice, however, is clearly worse for both than the outcome which would be brought about had they both acted selfishly (viz. (I, I)). See, e.g., Schelling, 1968.

A 'story' which fits this sort of situation might, e.g., be one about an elderly man and a lady who both refrain from approaching the single unoccupied seat on the bus, which *can* seat them both although not too comfortably, with the altruistic intention of leaving it free for the other to occupy.

desired by all. This clearly is yet another version of the PD problems.

But in this sort of case there is a rather simple way out: once the field is divided into strips, and each is allotted a certain strip of land which he/she must weed alone, the situation is altogether different. To be sure, each might still be reluctant to do his/her part, but the assumption that his/her own contribution makes no difference no longer holds. The essential point is that now the contribution of each, however small, cannot any longer be regarded as insignificant, since it is *identifiable* and *traceable*. This in itself is sufficient in many cases to cancel the temptation to dodge (desert, defect).

That is to say, an appropriately detailed division of labour and allotment of tasks in PD-structured situations might serve as a means of social control which ensures co-operation, thereby promoting the general good.

But of course such division of labour is not feasible in all cases of generalized PD-structured situations. My position on this issue is that in those cases where the individual contributions to the over-all outcome are indistinguishable in principle, or, alternatively, where the cost of an appropriate allotment of tasks is too high, the importance of PD norms—and of their efficacy—increases as means of solving the pertinent problem, thereby promoting collective goals and the general good.

A case in point, to which we now turn, is that of public goods.

9. *Public Goods*

Even if you do not pay the municipal fee for street lighting, you might enjoy it nevertheless. Likewise, even if you do not pay for your defence levy, you might still be defended by your country's forces. If, on the other hand, you do not pay for a pair of shoes, you will not be able to enjoy wearing them, and if you do not pay for a cinema ticket you will not be able to watch the film. Street lighting and the security of the state are commonly referred to as *public goods*, shoes and cinema tickets as *private goods*. The former ones are commodities and services provided by the state (or the municipality), the latter ones by the market mechanism.

Even thinkers whose image is that of preachers for *laissez-faire* have acknowledged that certain commodities and services are ones which must be provided by the state to its citizens. Thus, Adam Smith speaks of the 'duties of the sovereign' (1913 (1776), pp. 541–644), which he goes on to divide into three categories: first, security in face of external enemies, second, internal law and order, and third, services concerned with commerce (such as the building of roads, bridges, docks, etc.), with education (schools, professional education), and the like.

The question which must be raised in this connection is: Why did the liberal thinkers not require that the market mechanism provide *all* commodities and services, including those falling under the categories mentioned above? J. S. Mill's answer (1926, p. 978), as well as Keynes's (1926, p. 67), is that while it is not the case that the state ought to interfere where individuals do not, or cannot, act *efficiently*, it ought to interfere where individuals will not act *at all*.

My contention is that the category of public goods covers all those commodities and services regarding which the citizens of a state find themselves in a generalized PD-structured situation. To wit: with regard to every commodity which is a public good each citizen potentially faces a temptation to be a 'free rider', i.e. in the language of the matrix representation, to be a lone deviator from the upper-left, good cell. This is so, provided that the others would not deviate too, that is to say, provided that the others would go on financing this commodity. The situation being one in which the condition of individual insignificance is in general satisfied, the temptation to deviate is further increased owing to the peculiar characteristics of public goods: that they are indivisible, and that once they are provided everyone may enjoy them regardless of whether one paid for them or not. Put otherwise, they are such that if they are at all available, they are *ipso facto* available to all. And, of course, the basic assumption regarding public goods is that they are commodities and services which are important to the general welfare of the public and that all citizens therefore have an interest in their being adequately financed, i.e. in ensuring that there are no deviations from the good state of affairs.

Let us probe this situation somewhat more deeply by trying to put it into a matrix form. It will, for this purpose, be conceived of as a two-person game, the participants being 'I' (Row-Chooser) and 'all the others' (Column-Chooser). The two alternatives each 'player' has to choose from are 'pay' (P) and 'evade payment' (E). The idea, then, is to attempt a representation, in a matrix form, of the situation as *I* see it—that is, of my own deliberations and calculations as to the pending question of whether to pay my share or not.

The situation from my point of view is the following: I find the state of mutual payment (MP)—that is, when I and all the others pay our shares and receive the public goods concerned in return—rather satisfactory (1). However, I find it tempting not to pay, assuming that my contribution to the total sum collected is negligible and won't be missed. That is, unilateral evasion (UE) enables me to enjoy the commodity in question without paying for it (2). On the other hand it is clear to me that if all the others evade and I am the only one who pays (unilateral payment—UP) I fall between two stools: I both give up a sum of money which for me may be quite significant and find myself in a state where the desired goods are not provided after all (−2). Finally, mutual evasion (ME) means that these goods are not provided, and hence implies mutual disadvantage (−1).

My matrix, as a Row-Chooser, then is 2.9. Namely, my matrix is just my PD matrix as a Row-Chooser, with the E-choice dominating the P-choice.

	[P]	[E]
P	1	−2
E	2	−1

2.9

Let us examine now the position, as I see it, of all the rest—that is, the Column-Chooser's matrix from my point of view. MP and ME are as good, or as bad, for all the others as they are for me; namely the pay-offs associated with them are 1 and −1, respectively. But UP, as far as they are concerned, means that all but one (me) pay; and since my share is very small, the total sum collected would still suffice to finance the commodity (or service) in question. And so the pay-off associated with UP is, as far as the others are concerned, practically identical with that for MP (viz. 1).

It could, however, be argued that something *is*, after all, subtracted from this pay-off: suppose, for instance, that the street lighting is *somewhat* less dense (or is on for somewhat shorter hours) than it could have been had my contribution been available, or, say, that the school building lacks some small item of luxury which my contribution could have provided for. So let us conclude that the others' pay-off for **UP** is $1-\epsilon$, where ϵ is a small positive fraction, probably very close to zero.

Likewise UE, as far as all the others are concerned, means that all but one (me) evade payment, and thus its pay-off is identical, for all practical purposes, to that of ME. At best my tiny contribution suffices to do *some* good, changing the pay-off from -1 to $-1+\delta$, δ being a very small (positive) fraction indeed.

The matrix of 'the others' as Column-Choosers, then, is 2.10. This matrix is evidently different from Column-Chooser's PD-matrix. For one thing, note that here it is the P-choice which is dominant.

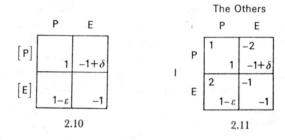

2.10   2.11

Combining the two matrices into the 'game''s complete matrix, we get 2.11. The point to be noted about this matrix is that the outcome (E, P) (bottom-left cell) is an equilibrium. (To be sure, its being an equilibrium was to be expected from the fact that this outcome is the intersection of the two partici-pants' dominant actions.)

To sum up thus far: in analysing my deliberations, regarding the question whether to pay my share or to evade payment as a game between myself and the rest of the citizens, it appears that it rewards me to evade payment, whereas the effect of my evasion is negligible as far as the others are concerned; more-over, it appears that my E-choice and their P-choice are dominant, and as a result the outcome (E, P) is an equilibrium, implying in a way that my tax evasion should actually be favourably looked on! Something must obviously have gone wrong somewhere in the presentation of the situation. And, indeed, there has been a cheat: my 'partner' to the game, viz.

'the rest of the citizens', has been conceived by me as a *collective*. And this, of course, is a fiction.

When the body of people constituting my 'partner' is conceived *distributively*, the picture changes: each member of this body finds it tempting, just as I do, to evade payment (that is, UE is preferred by every one to MP), and the worst that can happen to each member of this body is to end up being a lone payer (that is, UP implies, to each, the worst possible outcome). In other words, the considerations of a given citizen, when *I* am taken by him to be a member of 'all the rest', are just my considerations as presented above, with the E-choice dominating the P-choice. This is true of any given citizen, hence of all of them. So that all might opt for the E-choice with the result that the mutually disadvantageous outcome of ME will be brought about, and will, moreover, be stable (no one will be willing to deviate from it unilaterally—that is, to be a lone payer). So it is in fact in the interest of each citizen that they be somehow coerced, possibly by a law accompanied by legal sanctions, to pay their share—provided that all the others are to be similarly coerced. The norms requiring citizens to contribute their share toward the financing of public goods are, consequently, to be conceived of as PD norms. (See also Section 13.2 below.)

As it happens, in modern states these PD norms are in fact absorbed in part in the income-tax law. So that the norm obliging citizens to pay income-tax can be said to be a PD norm, but it should be recognized that underlying it, at least in part, is the need for financing public goods, regarding each of which the situation of the citizens is a generalized PD-structured one *par excellence*.

10. *The Generalization Argument and PD Norms*

The discussion in the last section may have called to mind the issues involved in the so-called generalization argument, which turns on the question: 'But what if everyone did that?' The argument, which is taken to establish a presumption against acts of certain kinds, is of considerable interest to moral philosophers and has been discussed quite extensively in the last couple of decades. These discussions have usually centred round various attempts to reconstruct the argument in such ways as to render it logically, as well as ethically, valid.

It is of importance for our discussion to realize that the generalization argument is actually used, and quite often too, in everyday life. The formulations it takes in ordinary discourse are admittedly not sophisticated, but I shall not be here concerned with listing, nor with refining, its various possible formulations. For the present purposes let me just represent the argument by one of its most common variants:

(Premiss:) The consequences of everyone's doing A would be undesirable (harmful, destructive).

(Conclusion:) Therefore it would be wrong for anyone to do A.

Alternative formulations employ such notions as 'right' (e.g. '. . . therefore no one has the right to do A'), 'ought' (e.g. '. . . therefore everyone ought not to do A'), and also the notions of duty and obligation.[8] The most frequent examples in the literature of cases to which the generalization argument is applied relate to potential tax-dodgers, conscription-evaders, lazy voters, promise-breakers, lawn-crossers, apple-pickers, and so on.

Now when taken as an inference—as it often is—the validity of the generalization argument is doubtful: denying the conclusion, on various grounds, is not incompatible with accepting the premiss. As Colin Strang points out '. . . the validity of the argument cannot depend on its form alone' (1968, p. 152), since many arguments of the very same form are plainly absurd. (The standard examples are well known: the consequences of everyone's producing food whole-time would be undesirable—we would, for one thing, all die of exposure in winter. Would it therefore be wrong for anyone to do so? And conversely: if no one ever produced food we would all starve. Ought we all to produce food always, then? For further examples, see Strang, ibid.)

That is to say, the argument as it stands cannot be said to be *logically* valid; at best it may be argued that it is *analytically* valid, viz. valid in virtue of the meaning of the non-logical terms occurring in it. This, however, means that a lot is called for: first, some extra assumptions are needed, indeed a whole theory is needed, concerning, e.g., the interdefinability of the

[8] For the most detailed and perhaps exhaustive discussion of the variety of the possible formulations the generalization argument can take and of the dimensions of the distinctions among them, see Lyons, 1965 (esp. ch. I). Note, however, that Lyons treats it as a *principle* based on a *generalization test*, and not as an *argument* composed of a premiss and a conclusion.

terms 'wrong' and 'undesirable', or the soundness of principles like Marcus Singer's Generalization Principle which states that 'If not everyone has the right to do x, then not anyone (no one) has the right to do x' (1960, p. 66). And secondly, there is need to specify the restrictions to be imposed on the conditions for the appropriate application of the argument (e.g. the restriction against 'invertibility'—see Singer, ibid., p. 72 and Lyons, p. 43 —i.e. a restriction to the effect that 'valid' applications of the argument cannot be 'inverted', as in the food-producing example, to establish a presumption both against an act and against its complementary act).

I do not propose, however, to supply these missing elements. My point so far is merely to draw attention to the debatability of the argument's validity. Having realized this, it seems all the more remarkable that the generalization argument is, as a matter of fact, of considerable persuasive power. That it is psychologically effective, notwithstanding its logical defects, is, I think, evident—or else we would not have been that familiar with it, from ordinary discourse as well as from philosophical discussions.

The question to which we now turn, then, is: what does this apparent force consist of and whence does it derive?

My answer to this question is the following:

The generalization argument is ('validly') applied to those cases only where the situation is such that its analysis is bound to reveal an underlying (generalized) PD structure. The common denominator—not usually sought after—of the numerous examples of cases to which the argument is (convincingly) applied consists, I submit, of the identical pattern of the situations involved. To wit:

(i) A potential defaulter considers doing A, when doing A is in some sense tempting for him (rewarding him).

(ii) He is put right about the fact that if everyone were to do the same (where the 'if' is usually taken in its hypothetical rather than in its causal sense),[9] the result would be a state of affairs undesirable to all, himself included.

[9] The causal form of the generalization argument takes into account the likelihood that the example of one's doing A will as a matter of fact influence others and hence cause them to do A too. To those who accept the argument in its hypothetical form, on the other hand, this causal influence is totally irrelevant: what matters to them is only the question of what would happen *if* everyone did the same. The distinction, as far as I know, is A. K. Stout's (1954).

(iii) The generalized consequences of non-A (that is, the state of affairs resulting from everyone's *not* doing A) are assumed to be desirable on the whole—or at least less undesirable than those of everyone's doing A.

The potential defaulter is then supposed to take the hint and realize that it would be wrong for him to do A, or that he ought (it is his duty, he is obliged) to refrain from doing A (or to do non-A). These roughly sketched features of the situation to which the generalization argument is commonly applied, as indeed some of the cases which exemplify these situations, are of course familiar to us from the foregoing analysis of generalized PD-structured situations. The claim, once more, is that this argument gives a common, ordinary expression, in 'ethical' terms, to the problematics of situations the 'game-like' analysis of which invariably reveals them to be of the generalized PD variety.

Let us examine the significance of this claim a little further. Among the difficulties the generalization argument encounters, there are rebuttals such as the following:

(1) 'But of course the others will not (or—few others will) do the same (viz. A). Therefore the evil will not be produced anyway, regardless of what I do, so why not let me enjoy my doing A?'

(2) 'But of course most others will do A. Therefore the evil will be produced anyway, regardless of what I do, so my act cannot matter' (compare Lyons, 1965, pp. 6–7).

(A hilarious example of rebuttals of this kind is provided, of course, by the dialogue between Yossarian and Major Major, concerning the former's refusal to fly any more combat missions. It ends as follows:

'I don't want to fly milk runs. I don't want to be in the war any more.'

'Would you like to see our country lose?' Major Major asked.

'We won't lose. . . . Some people are getting killed and a lot more are making money and having fun. Let somebody else get killed.'

'But suppose everybody on our side felt that way.'

'Then I'd certainly be a damned fool to feel any other way. Wouldn't I?')[10]

These objections pose considerable problems for those who wish to defend the generalization argument. They lead them, for example, to complicated discussions concerning the 'relevance of the behaviour of others'. Now what I suggest is that once it is realized that the situations to which the argument applies are (generalized) PD-structured ones, much is already gained. We may, first, be put right about the fact that the generalization argument, as it stands, relates explicitly to only one of the four states of affairs constituting the entire composite set-up—namely to the one where everyone does A (represented in matrix 2.11 (p. 52 above) by the bottom-right cell), and implicitly to one more—namely to the one where nobody does A (top-left cell in the matrix). (By the way, if the argument is in its comparative formulation—along the lines suggested by Lyons, p. 23—then this second state of affairs is also quite explicitly referred to by the argument.)

Secondly, with regard to the above objections for instance, we shall be clear about the fact that they simply describe the *remaining* two states of affairs: the one where only I do A and all (or most of) the others do not (corresponding to the bottom-left cell in matrix 2.11) and the one where everyone but me does A (corresponding to the top-right cell), respectively. Furthermore, it will become apparent that all that these objections amount to is the statement that the 'bad' action A dominates the 'good' action non-A.

It seems to me that were it realized precisely what the composite situation consists of, what role in it is played by strategies—and by dominant strategies in particular, and such-like prominent structural traits of these situations—the significance and relevance of many a puzzling aspect of the generalization argument would clear up; indeed much of the fog surrounding it would lift. To be sure, no forthright solution is automatically guaranteed by such recognition, but the problematic, and seemingly paradoxical, aspects involved would be instructively pinpointed.

[10] Joseph Heller, *Catch-22* (1955). New York, Dell Publishing Co., p. 107.

Furthermore, considerable effort has been directed, by various writers on the subject, toward devising restrictions, which would not seem patently *ad hoc*, to be placed on the use of this argument so as to allow only 'valid' (convincing, appropriate) applications of it. However, much of this effort could have been saved, I think, had it been clear that it is only PD-structured situations that the generalization argument can meaningfully be applied to. For example, take the restriction against invertibility referred to above. Regardless of the extent to which it appears *ad hoc*, this restriction would be superfluous were it realized that the situations to which it pertains (e.g. whole-time occupations) lack feature (iii) (above, p. 56). (In the food-producing case: it is *not* the case that the consequences of everyone's producing food whole-time are desirable on the whole, nor even that they are less undesirable than those of nobody ever producing food; and the converse holds too.) These situations, therefore, do not qualify as PD-structured situations to begin with.

Now in order to resolve the quandaries inherent in the generalized PD-structured situations, it has been my contention that norms are generated; norms the function of which is to protect the better-yet-weak state of affairs from deterioration—via the yielding to temptation by each of the individuals involved in the situation—into the worse-yet-stable state of affairs. However, this is precisely what the generalization argument is all about: it constitutes an appeal to norms, obedience to which would prevent the menacing undesirable state of affairs from materializing.

To sum up. We addressed ourselves to the question: Of what does the persuasive force of the generalization argument consist, in view of its dubious logical status? My answer is that this argument is applicable to generalized PD-structured situations, and to such situations only. Its power derives from the facts that it points to the genuine dilemma inherent in these situations, and that it appeals to means of solving it, e.g. to (PD) norms prohibiting the doing of actions of type A.[11]

[11] I offer a fuller treatment of the generalization argument in an article which was written while the book was in press: 'The Generalization Argument: Where Does the Obligation Lie?', *The Journal of Philosophy*, Vol. 73, No. 15 (2 Sept. 1976), pp. 511–22.

10.1 *The Modified Generalization Argument*

In his article 'The Refutation of the Generalization Argument' (1964) Neil Dorman attempts to show that Marcus Singer's derivation (1960) of the generalization argument from two other principles is invalid. For the purposes in hand let the formulation of the generalization argument be:

(GA) If the consequences of everyone's doing x would be undesirable, then each person has the obligation not to do x.

The details of Dorman's criticism are unimportant to the point I wish to make in this section; it might just be mentioned that they have to do with an alleged fallacy of equivocation concerning the collective v. the distributive senses of 'everyone'. What is important for us here is Dorman's proposal to substitute for the (GA) another principle, which he regards as a modification of it and which he takes to be sound:

(MGA) If the consequences of not having a rule against x would be undesirable, then there ought to be a rule against x.

In the light of the foregoing discussions it might be said that PD norms in fact constitute an explication of these rules of Dorman's. I would like to emphasize at this point once again that I, in distinction from Dorman and Singer, was not concerned with the logical validity of inferences which establish the (GA), or principles akin to it, as their conclusion. I was concerned, instead, with an analysis of the main features of situations which underlie, so I believe, the cases where an application of the (GA) is warrantable. The conclusion I came up with is that such situations are generalized PD-structured ones, and that therefore they 'call for' norms; the norms corresponding to these situations and capable of solving the stabilization problem inherent in them having been introduced as PD norms. Hence I take it that a PD norm more or less explicates what Dorman had in mind when postulating his 'rule against x'. (Incidentally, Dorman does *not* specify the grounds on which he arrives at his (MGA); it is not a conclusion of any valid argument the premises of which have previously been shown to be sound. He just states that as it stands it is sound, and that its justification is that it works.)

There is a difference, though, between Dorman's (MGA) and my thesis concerning PD norms. It can be put thus. The consequent of Dorman's (MGA) is *normative*: 'there ought to be a rule.' (It is in fact a *second* order, 'ought-to-be' norm.) My conclusion, on the other hand, is *predictive*. It is to the effect that in the type of situation concerned it is likely that there will as a matter of fact be (PD) norms. I do not say that a norm ought to emerge in order to serve as a solution. What I say is that the situations of the type characterized in this chapter are prone to generate (PD) norms.

The idea of explicating Dorman's rules in predictive rather than in normative terms is not new. It has in fact been proposed by the welfare economists Buchanan and Tullock in their paper entitled 'Economic Analogues to the Generalization Argument' (1964). There are, however, considerable differences between their result and mine, and I deem it important as well as instructive to grasp the essence of these differences. For purposes of representation I shall take the liberty of rearranging Buchanan and Tullock's line of reasoning.

The starting-point is that in which it is noted that there are social situations where if everyone does x the consequences are socially undesirable, and if everyone does not do x the consequences are socially undesirable too. We have seen that cases in point are, e.g., those where x stands for a choice of a particular occupation. Many of these problems, however, are solved in practice through differences between people—differences in temperament, ability, ambition, etc. So that the state of affairs achieved in practice is what Buchanan and Tullock call that of *private adjustment*, in which some do x and some do not.

In the next step it is noted that the solution obtained through private adjustment might well be an equilibrium which qualifies as a Pareto optimum: i.e. the private interaction of individuals might produce a state of affairs which is optimal in the sense that no individual in it can improve his/her own position without it being at the expense of at least one other individual. This private-adjustment equilibrium is likely to be achieved where the issue concerned belongs within the framework of a market mechanism in perfect competition.

However, Buchanan and Tullock proceed to point out that there are cases where the private adjustment achieved through the private, and to some extent haphazard, interaction of individuals is *not* a Pareto-optimal equilibrium. Their example is that of inoculation against a communicable disease, where the optimal proportion of people to be inoculated is less than 100 per cent: if none gets immunized the entire population is in danger of contracting the disease, and if all get immunized the social outlay involved is excessive since at least one person should be exempt from the inoculation (for if all but one get immunized, there is no one from whom the non-immunized person might contract the disease: the additional assumption needed is, of course, that the disease can be contracted only from another human and not, say, from an animal).

This case, typically, is not governed by the market mechanism of supply and demand. It is likely, therefore, that the private adjustment obtained here, in which some individuals get inoculated and some remain not inoculated (possibly according to how much weight each assigns to the chances of contracting the disease as opposed to the cost and inconvenience involved in getting inoculated) would be (Pareto) non-optimal. That is to say, it would be possible to improve the position of at least one person in the community concerned without damaging that of anyone else.

Now it is with regard to such cases, where the private adjustment achieved is non-optimal, that Buchanan and Tullock point at the need for some social solution of public adjustment which would affect the transition into the Pareto-optimal state of affairs. Their argument, then, is that in these cases 'there will be forces [note: not "there *ought* to be forces"] tending to the establishment' of some general rules of behaviour which would achieve the desired transition. These rules, I take it, might in general be characterized as edicts of rationing and allotment.[12]

[12] It seems to me that Smart's example (1956, p. 180) of watering one's garden during hot weather when there is shortage of water belongs here: the Pareto-optimal state of affairs in this case would involve less than a hundred per cent of the garden-owners not watering their gardens; the private adjustment produced by unrestrained private behaviour is likely to be non-optimal; a municipal edict would probably be issued, therefore, specifying in which districts and at what times garden-watering is allowed.

(I find Smart's own treatment of his example, however, unsatisfactory. Its essence is that each person assigns himself a probability of watering his garden. He then proceeds to give the equation from which this probability can be calculated. I find both the approach to the problem and the equation itself erroneous.)

It is these rules which Buchanan and Tullock offer as an explication of the rules mentioned in Dorman's (MGA). Or, more
precisely, the norm affecting the transition from the non-
optimal private adjustment to the Pareto-optimal state of affairs
is offered by Buchanan and Tullock as the economic analogue
to Dorman's 'rule against x'.

To sum up. Both my PD norms and Buchanan and Tullock's
rules are proposed as predictive interpretations of the rules
referred to in Dorman's (MGA). It is clear that these two sets
of norms are not coextensive, and that each of them covers a
good many of the norms (rules) encountered in ordinary
human affairs. Is there, however, anything to choose between
them as interpretations to Dorman? That is, is one of the proposed interpretations to be preferred over the other *as an interpretation* of Dorman's rules?

I submit that, as an interpretation, mine is to be preferred to
Buchanan and Tullock's. The reason is, simply, that I believe
I have shown that the situations in which the generalization
argument is in fact applied and in which, moreover, its application tends to be successful and persuasive are generalized
PD-structured ones—the ones which are prone to generate
PD norms. I believe that they are *not* in general the type of
situations Buchanan and Tullock are concerned with, in which
there is need for public adjustment to replace a non-optimal
state of affairs brought about by private adjustment.

11. *Hobbes and the Prisoners' Dilemma*

It is quite commonplace to regard Hobbes's original situation
of mankind as a version of the Prisoners' Dilemma (e.g. Barry,
1965, pp. 253–4; Rawls, 1971, p. 269).[13] It has recently, however, been challenged (Gauthier, 1969) whether it is indeed
warrantable to do so.

In this section I propose, first, to show that the original
situation of mankind according to Hobbes does possess the

---

[13] Rawls, as well as others, makes the mistake of taking Hobbes's *state of nature*
to exemplify the Prisoners' Dilemma, whereas in truth the state of nature, as we
shall presently see, is but *one* of the several states of affairs (represented, in the two-
person case, by the four cells of the PD matrix) of which the entire PD-like situation
is comprised. It is for this reason that I speak of Hobbes's 'original situation of
mankind', rather than of his state of nature, as being a version of the Prisoners'
Dilemma.

essential features of a generalized PD-structured one; second, to examine Hobbes's solution to the pertinent problem and its relation—if any—to PD norms; and third, to offer a rebuttal to Gauthier's challenge.

11.1 *The Original Situation of Mankind as PD-structured*

The state of nature is, according to Hobbes (1948), that of 'war of everyone against everyone'. It is a state which no one enjoys, which is uniformly bad for all: '. . . and the life of man, solitary, poor, nasty, brutish, and short' (p. 82). On the other hand we then learn that 'All other time [other than "that condition which is called war"] is *peace*' (p. 82), from which are implied its advantages. The state of peace is uniformly good for all, and indeed Hobbes states 'that every man ought to endeavour peace—to seek peace and follow it' (p. 85).

But here emerges the problematic aspect of the situation: it is dangerous, and against the Hobbesian 'laws of nature', to be a lone peace-keeper: 'For he that should be modest, and tractable, and perform all his promises, in such time and place, where no man else should do so, should but make himself a prey to others, and procure his own certain ruin' (p. 103). This means that, once in the state of nature, no one will have an incentive to pursue a peaceful policy, if all the rest stick to their belligerent policy. And this in turn means that the state of nature, notwithstanding its 'incommodities' (p. 82), is stable. Furthermore, the purpose of every one in this war of all against all is, of course, to win: first and foremost to survive, and also to reap such fruits of winning as gain, safety, and reputation (p. 81). Hence it is clear that, whenever some 'make themselves a prey' to others, that is, unilaterally withdraw from the policy of war, the others thereby gain the upper hand over them and profit by it.

Hobbes recognizes the dilemma. When one has no hope of obtaining peace—and obtaining it on one's own is impossible— one may, says Hobbes, 'seek, and use all help, and advantages of war' (p. 85). This is in accordance with the fundamental right of nature, which is 'by all means we can, to defend ourselves' (p. 85). This right of nature is in fact closely akin to the principle of maximizing security level, viz.: make sure the worst, i.e., in our case, being defeated in war, does not happen to you;

that is, do not adopt a peaceful policy which will result in such a defeat if the others do not adopt it too.[14] Consequently, a possibility of achieving the peaceful state preferred by all, while existing, is conditional. Hobbes's 'second law of nature' requires that a man be willing to lay down his 'right to all things'—which inevitably leads to war—*'when others are so too'* (p. 85, Hobbes's emphasis). That is to say, Hobbes realizes that the nature of this 'game' is such that one would not choose to keep the peace unless one knows that the others' choice would be the same.

The essential features of generalized PD-structured situations are evidently present here. Notice, however, that whereas in ordinary situations of that type the emphasis is on the advantages implied by lone deviation from the mutually beneficial state of affairs (represented by the top-left cell in the PD matrix), the emphasis here is on the disadvantages implied by lone deviation from the mutually destructive state of affairs (represented by the bottom-right cell).

This is so since in ordinary PD-structured situations, like the ones which served as examples throughout this chapter, the assumption is that the *status quo* in which the participants are placed is the good state, their problem being to stabilize it so as to avert the danger of deterioration into the bad state. In the Hobbesian original situation of mankind, on the other hand, the assumption is that the *status quo* is the bad state of war of all against all. (I believe that it is only in games, as opposed to real-life situations, that the participants are extraneous, so to speak, to the situation. In a game, therefore, the problem of the participants is which course of action they are to choose from the two alternative ones. In the type of situation with which we are here concerned, on the other hand, the problem of the participants is whether to remain in the *status quo*— whether it be the good or the bad one—or to deviate from it.)

The problem inherent in the Hobbesian situation of mankind, then, is two-fold. In the first place it is to find some means of deliverance, i.e. some means of 'lifting' from the bad state to the good one, and in the second place it is the usual problem of how to protect and stabilize the latter.

[14] Notice, however, that this of course is no *guarantee* against defeat: in the state of nature resulting from the belligerence of all the strong will win, the weak will lose.

11.2 *Hobbes's Solution*

The gist of Hobbes's solution is that people get together and covenant with each other to keep the peace. This covenant is then presumed to provide the needed ground on which everyone may reasonably suppose the others to choose a peaceful policy. But this, as Hobbes recognizes, is still far from being an adequate solution to the problem at hand. It seems that in Hobbes's view the following point cannot be overemphasized: that 'the bonds of words are too weak to bridle man's ambition, avarice, anger, and other passions without the fear of some coercive power' (p. 89), and that 'covenants, without the sword, are but words and of no strength to secure a man at all' (p. 109).[15]

It is not enough, then, that people covenant with each other and promise each other to keep the peace. They have to keep their promises too (cf. p. 21 above). And if there is reason to suspect they (or some of them) would not, then they have to be made to keep them. To this end Hobbes proposes a procedure whereby a sovereign is installed over the people—through an act of authorization made by every one of them—who is the representative of each person and is responsible for all matters of peace and security among them. This is achieved by means of mutual contracts, between each and every other person, in which all commit themselves to transfer their natural right to defend themselves to the sovereign, this commitment being conditional upon its being mutual ('on this condition that thou give up thy right to him, and authorize all his actions in like manner'; p. 112). Thus the sovereign becomes possessed of unlimited right of sanction. His word is the law ('. . . whereas law, properly, is the word of him, that by right hath command over others'; p. 105), and they who disobey the law, thereby threatening the maintenance of peace, are liable to as severe a punishment as the sovereign 'shall think expedient'.

The central point, however, in this procedure, is that the sovereign himself is not a party to any contract: 'the right of bearing the person of them all, is given to him they make sovereign, by covenant only of one to another, and not of him

---

[15] See also p. 115: 'understanding this easy truth, that covenants being but words and breath, have no force to oblige, contain, constrain, or protect any man'.

to any of them' (p. 114). He stands outside this network of mutual contracts. As a result there is no arguing with him, no threatening him, and no disposing of him. Moreover, all this is taken to be, and to be known by everyone to be, very much in the interest of every individual in the community, since it guarantees that the sovereign, who has the responsibility of keeping the peace, would also have 'untied hands' (p. 115) to maintain it. In practice this is achieved through punishments for peace-breaking which are severe enough to outweigh any prospective profit to be gained from it ('. . . some coercive power, to compel men equally to the performance of their covenants, by the terror of some punishment, greater than the benefit they expect by the breach of their covenant'; p. 94).

To sum up thus far: The original situation of mankind, as conceived by Hobbes, belongs to the PD variety. It is given that people are in the state of nature, as represented by the bottom-right cell in the PD matrix. Now a mechanism is proposed, consisting of a network of mutual contracts, which leads to the installation of a sovereign who is responsible for peace and who has—owing to the content of the contracts and to the fact that he himself is no party to them—the means of keeping it. Through this mechanism, when adopted, two things are achieved simultaneously: the much-desired 'lifting' from the state of nature (bottom-right cell) to the state of peace (top-left cell) takes place, and—at the same time—the situation of mankind (represented by the PD matrix as a whole) changes into a new and different situation.

In the new situation the state of peace, which is now the *status quo*, is good, as before, and the state of war is bad, as before. But deviation toward a belligerent policy is now going to be severely punished (whether it be unilateral or general: remember that the sovereign who inflicts the penalties is not a 'player' in this 'game' but controls it from without), so that there is now a deterrence against it, whereas the peaceful policy pays—even if it be unilateral, since its chooser enjoys the protection of the sovereign. (The last statement may perhaps be modified by taking into account the probability that the sovereign will in fact intervene to protect the peace-keeper before his belligerent neighbour manages to get the upper hand of him.)

That is to say, the installation of a Hobbesian sovereign resolves at once the two parts of the problem. In the first place it affects the needed transition from the bad *status quo*—the state of nature—to the good state of peace, thereby serving as a means of deliverance. In the second place, owing to the sovereign's unlimited right of sanction, the pay-off structure of the situation changes in such a way that once the transition into the state of peace takes place, the situation is no longer PD-structured. The belligerent policy no longer dominates the peaceful one; the state of peace is rendered stable.

Is Hobbes's two-fold solution related in any way to PD norms? I think that it is. Quite obviously it makes no sense to speak of the installation of a sovereign as a PD norm; nor, for that matter, can the mutual contracts be, in any straight-forward sense, regarded as PD norms. However, I submit that it is because he is the originator of law in general, and of peace-promoting PD norms in particular, that a Hobbesian sovereign, empowered as he is by the mutual contracts, consti-tutes a solution to the pertinent double problem of transition and stabilization. To elaborate: the responsibility of such a sovereign is keeping peace and security; the law is his word. The principal norms he would issue, therefore, are such as would prohibit belligerence. These norms, accompanied by the threat of appro-priate punishments—which the sovereign himself is entitled to administer—are those which in effect transform the situation into one no longer PD-structured; hence they qualify as PD norms.

Essentially, then, my point is that Hobbes's solution of the problem inherent in the original situation of mankind consists primarily of providing an originator of (peace promoting) PD norms.

11.3 *An Answer to Gauthier*

In his book *The Logic of Leviathan* (1969, pp. 77–85) David Gauthier raises the question of whether violation of a covenant can, according to Hobbes, be more rational (or, to use Hobbes's term, reasonable) than keeping it. In Gauthier's formulation: is it possible, within the Hobbesian system, that it is the case that $R(A\&B)e$—which is read 'it is reasonable for A and B to enter the covenant', and yet it is not the case that $R(A\&B)k$—which is read 'it is reasonable for A and B to keep the covenant'?

In order to show that it is *in principle* possible, in some situation, for R(A&B)*k* not to hold although R(A&B)*e* holds, Gauthier presents the Prisoners' Dilemma situation. It is presented through the familiar matrix, where it is assumed that the players (only two, for simplicity) have entered into a covenant. The alternatives, accordingly, are labelled A—for adherence, and V—for violation.

Let us, for convenience of reference, reproduce the matrix (see 2.12).

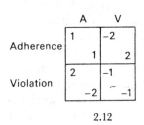

2.12

In this situation, as we know, even if there be an agreement between the participants to adhere to the covenant (that is, if they agree on the (A, A) outcome)—and each indeed has reason to enter into such an agreement—each of them nevertheless cannot fail to realize that it pays him, and hence is reasonable, or rational, for him, to deviate to V.

However, Gauthier claims that this is not possible within Hobbes's system. That is, he claims that, according to Hobbes, whenever R(A&B)*e* holds, R(A&B)*k* holds too: that breach of covenant is not reasonable. In other words, according to Gauthier the basic Hobbesian situation is *not* PD-structured, for as soon as people covenant to keep the peace, it is not reasonable for any of them to violate the covenant, that is, to resort to a belligerent policy. In terms of the matrix this means that Gauthier, in the name of Hobbes, denies that the pay-off for Unilateral Violation is higher than that for Mutual Adherence. (In fact Gauthier does not deal with pay-offs but with 'degrees of reasonableness', so that, in his terminology, the claim is that according to Hobbes the degree of reasonableness of Unilateral Violation is not higher than that of Mutual Adherence.)

The arguments Gauthier presents to establish this claim rely on Hobbes's 'reply to the fool'. As this is the key passage concerning the question in hand, and as my interpretation of it will be somewhat different from Gauthier's, I would like to quote it in full:

For the question is not of promises mutual, where there is no security of performance on either side; as when there is no civil power erected over the parties promising; for such promises are no covenants: but either where one of the parties has performed already; or where there is a power to make him perform; there is the question whether it be against reason, that is, against the benefit of the other to perform, or not. And I say it is not against reason. For the manifestation whereof, we are to consider; first, that when a man doth a thing, which notwithstanding any thing can be foreseen, and reckoned on, tendeth to his own destruction, howsoever some accident which he could not expect, arriving may turn it to his benefit; yet such events do not make it reasonably or wisely done. Secondly, that in condition of war, wherein every man to every man, for want of a common power to keep them all in awe, is an enemy, there is no man who can hope by his own strength, or wit, to defend himself from destruction, without the help of confederates; where every one expects the same defence by the confederation, that any one else does: and that therefore he which declares he thinks it reason to deceive those that help him, can in reason expect no other means of safety, than what can be had from his own single power. He therefore that breaketh his covenant, and consequently declareth that he thinks he may with reason do so, cannot be received into any society, that unite themselves for peace and defence, but by the error of them that receive him; nor when he is received, be retained in it, without seeing the danger of their error; which errors a man cannot reasonably reckon upon as the means of his security: and therefore if he be left, or cast out of society, he perisheth; and if he live in society, it is by the errors of other men, which he could not foresee, nor reckon upon; and consequently against the reason of his preservation. (pp. 95–6)

The two arguments Gauthier extracts from this passage to establish the point that breach of the peace-covenant is not reasonable are the following:

(i) 'Violation of covenant cannot be expected to be advantageous, although it may actually *be* advantageous'—for the advantage of violation can only be a consequence of the *error* of other people, and it is not reasonable to count on other people's committing an error (pp. 84–5).

(ii) Even if violation may, in the short run, be advantageous, 'the long-term effects of such violation must always be expected to be sufficiently adverse to outweigh any short-term benefits' (p. 85).

It seems to me that this is not the best way of interpreting the quoted passage. However, in order to understand Hobbes's position it is important to realize that he makes a clear distinction between two cases (both in the quoted passage and elsewhere, e.g. pp. 85, 103):

(a) The case when one of the covenanting parties has no reason to believe that the other party has already honoured his promise or will do so in the future; or, for that matter, when one has reason to believe that the other party has already violated the agreement or will do so in the future.

(b) The case when one of the covenanting parties knows that the other party has already honoured his promise, or when he has sufficient ground on which to assume that he will do so in the future (e.g. when he knows that 'there is a power to make him perform').[16]

Regarding the first case, Hobbes states categorically that it is not reasonable to keep one's covenants where the others do not or would not so do, since it runs counter to the 'law of nature' concerning one's preservation (see above, p. 63). As to the second case, it should first of all be pointed out that the passage quoted above relates to it and to it only. It seems that Gauthier has not realized this. He takes the passage to answer the general question, whether it is reasonable to adhere to covenants reasonably entered into, whereas in truth the passage deals with the question whether it is reasonable to adhere to covenants upon the knowledge that the other party does.

Now Hobbes's answer to *this* question is, indeed, that in the given circumstances it is 'not against reason', that is, not 'against the benefit of the other' to perform one's covenants. However, I would like to reconstruct Hobbes's arguments establishing this answer in a manner somewhat different from Gauthier's, and with some shift of emphasis.

First, in the quoted passage Hobbes says that in a state of war, when everyone needs allies for self-defence, whoever deceives his allies cannot in the end rely on anyone but himself. It seems to me that this point can be explicated in a way which will render it subtler and more precise than it is in Gauthier's rather simple-minded talk about the short-term as opposed to

---

[16] Note that there may be a third case: when one does *not* know whether to expect the other party to keep his covenant or to violate it. Hobbes in fact does not take up this case, but I think it quite safe to assume he would include it in case (a), in accordance with his generally pessimistic view of human nature.

the long-term effects (see argument (ii) p. 69 above). The idea is to make use of the notion of recurrence, and to regard the 'Hobbesian Game' as a recurrent, or even continuous, rather than as a 'one-shot' game.

When viewed in this way, the reasoning then proceeds as follows: If you know that the other party has chosen (or that there is a power which will compel him to choose) A—that is, adherence to the covenant—it is rational for you to choose A too. This is so because if you are tempted to take advantage of the other by choosing V—that is, violation of the covenant— you ensure by this the other's vengeance, namely his choosing V in the very next instance of the 'game' among you; in which case you will *have* to choose V too, in which case you will both be deadlocked in what is for both of you a grim state of affairs from which, moreover, you will have no means of escape.

What Luce and Raiffa say in connection with the temporal repetition of the PD game turns out to be nicely relevant here: '. . . in the repeated game the repeated selection of (a_1, b_1) [in our case—(A, A)] is in a sort of quasi-equilibrium: it is not to the advantage of either player to initiate the chaos that results from not conforming, even though the non-conforming strategy is profitable in the short run (one trial)' (1957, p. 98).

Furthermore, your choice of V when you know your opponent chooses A is eventually worse for you than just a bad and undesired deadlock. It should be kept in mind that your opponent in this case is a *confederation*, and that the revenge of the confederation in the following trial of the 'game' means that it sees itself released from its obligation to protect you and turns to fight against you. And this in turn means that you have brought upon yourself a battle in which you stand alone against a confederation which will be stronger than you, and so it is with certainty that you bring upon yourself ruin and destruction.

The second point I wish to make relates to the issue of relying upon the others' error (see Gauthier's argument (i), p. 69 above). To sum up Hobbes's argument by saying that violation of covenant cannot be *expected* to be advantageous seems to me again to leave much to be desired. I would rather put it thus: if one regards oneself as playing one against many, and thinks it clever to make allies, enter into a protection-covenant with them, and then violate the covenant and enjoy both the advantages of violation and the alliance's continuing protection—one must be relying on their *not noticing one's violation*, reasoning that one is but one while they are many.

But putting reliance on such an assumption amounts, as we know, to the proposition that the present case is one in which the condition of individual insignificance is satisfied. Namely, it amounts to the proposition that the effect on the over-all outcome of a single person's decision whether to adhere to the covenant or to violate it is negligible. In the present case, however, it is a mistake to rely on this assumption. The mistake is due to the *nature of the violation* which must be self-defeating; for violation of the covenant in our case means opting for a belligerent rather than for a peaceful policy, and such policy cannot fail to be discovered by the others, who must be hurt by it, sooner or later: '. . . nor when he is received [into a society, can he] be retained in it, without seeing the danger of their error'.

To sum up Hobbes's reconstructed arguments, then: when one knows that the other party keeps the covenant (or will be compelled to do so) it is rational for one to keep it too, for violation on one's part will result in one's destruction *either* on the very next occasion the situation comes up—when the Hobbesian Game is conceived as a recurrent one, *or* as soon as the others have discovered one's violation—which cannot be very far off because of the aggressive nature of the violation.

Let us now turn back to the question whether the basic Hobbesian situation is a PD-structured situation or not. It turns out, as we saw, that this question cannot be given a single answer, for it turns on the distinction between the case in which one expects the others not to conform to the covenant and the case in which one expects the others to conform. In the first case it is clear that the analysis of the situation undertaken above (Section 11.1) holds, and hence the situation *is* PD-structured. In the second case, however, the discussion in the present section seems to imply that the situation is not PD-structured, since we have come to the conclusion that the V-choice does *not* dominate the A-choice: Unilateral Violation should not, we learned, be preferred to Mutual Adherence.

But here we have to ask ourselves a further question: when does it happen, or rather when *can* it happen, that one can with certainty expect the others to adhere to the peace-keeping covenant? The other party is, after all, also guided by considerations of self-preservation! There is only one possible answer: that this cannot happen unless the covenant is already strongly protected by severe sanctions which will with certainty be imposed on those who violate it; namely, when a sovereign has already been installed.

However, as the foregoing discussion shows, when a sovereign exists, in whose power it is to hold people to their covenants, the situation is no longer the original one, but a new situation which is no longer PD-structured. The upshot is clear: Hobbes's distinction between the two cases, as well as the long quoted passage in which he deals with the second of these cases are, strictly speaking, redundant.[17] There is only one original situation, the one which constitutes the 'Hobbesian Game' and which is undoubtedly PD-structured. It is a situation in which $R(A\&B)e$ holds and yet $R(A\&B)k$ does not hold: although it is reasonable for all parties concerned to enter into a covenant to keep the peace, it is common knowledge among them that it is not reasonable for any of them to keep this covenant, for 'covenants, without the sword, are but words, and of no strength to secure a man at all'. However, as soon as this 'sword' is supplied and a sovereign is installed, the situation is transformed into an altogether different one. In the new situation there is no longer any temptation to violate one's covenants: it is common knowledge among all concerned that the sanctions ensuing violation outweigh any gain expected from it, and so everyone will keep his covenants, and everyone will expect the others to keep their covenants too.

[17] It seems to me that the source of the confusion may lie in Hobbes's inconsistency in the quoted passage: he starts by saying that he confines his present discussion to 'where one of the parties has performed already or where *there is a power to make him perform*', but a few sentences later, in his 'manifestation', he makes a point implied by the 'condition of war, wherein every man to every man, *for want of a common power to keep them all in awe*, is an enemy' (my italics).

III

CO-ORDINATION NORMS

Introduction

A CENTRAL problem faced by Hobbes can be put thus: given that society is composed of extremely self-interested individuals, who are in permanent conflict over goods which are in scarcity, how is social integration at all possible? Hobbes's answer is based on the concept of social covenant; the individuals being driven to covenant with each other by the dominant element of fear common to them all. Although each individual is postulated by Hobbes to be a covenanter with each other, it is possible to speak of *the* social covenant, since the contents of all these covenants are identical.

Herbert Spencer's answer to a closely related problem can be summarized as follows: each of the permanently competing and conflicting egoists, of which society is composed, knows that his own personal interests would best be served in a state of specialization and division of labour. However, a state of specialization and division of labour creates relations of dependence among the members of society, in the sense that the provision of goods and services to each depends upon the behaviour of others. In order to secure the egoistic advantages concomitant to a state of division of labour, therefore, the members of society are postulated by Spencer to enter into a network of binding mutual contracts.

In a nutshell, then: given that society is composed of extreme egoists, social integration is guaranteed by the advantages to each from a state of specialization and division of labour, these advantages being in turn secured by a system of mutual contracts. Here it makes no sense to speak of *the* contract: there is here a large number of mutual contracts, their contents depending on the roles of the parties to them in the particular state of division of labour concerned.

In objection to this contractual approach, Durkheim, Parsons, and others have argued that the concept of a contract (covenant) cannot be taken as primitive, since it presupposes norms: norms which would determine what makes a contract valid, what are the constraints on possible contents of the contract (e.g. Spencer: one cannot enter into a contract of a kind that would enslave oneself), what are—or can be—the sanctions for breach of contract, and so on. In other words, these authors have maintained that it is social norms rather than contracts which should be postulated as primitives in explaining how social integration comes about.

This criticism of the contractual approach is largely based on the apparent inability of the latter approach to explain how a contract can come into existence without there having been an explicit agreement among the parties to it; the assumption being that any explanation of contracts in terms of explicit agreements presupposes norms. To be sure, proponents of the contractual approach have always been careful to emphasize that their contracts are but historical fiction and that they should not be construed so as to be based on explicit agreements. But they have in fact failed in accounting for this basic concept of an 'implicit' agreement, so that their concept of a social contract can at best be taken to be merely a metaphorical extension of the concept of a legal contract.

It might be mentioned in this connection that Russell's and Quine's argument against the conception of Language as convention falls into line with this criticism of the contractual approach: in order for Language to be a system of conventions one must postulate some 'primary language' in which the (explicit) agreements constituting these conventions could be formulated. That is, given that the concept of convention presupposes an explicit act of convening and agreeing, Language cannot ultimately be reduced to convention.

It is against this background, I contend, that the works of Schelling and Lewis—referred to in the ensuing text—should be appreciated. I take their analyses of the type of situations called co-ordination problems, and Lewis's analysis of convention, to constitute a breakthrough in that they give a systematic and precise account of the concept of convention (or, for that matter, of that of covenant or contract) in terms of tacit rather than explicit agreements. Using a largely game-theoretical apparatus, and assuming only individual interests, they have demonstrated that conventions do not presuppose explicit agreements, nor do they depend upon them; more precisely, they have shown that an explicit agreement is not a necessary condition for convention.

Given, then, that the basic intuitions of Hobbes and Spencer concerning the concept of contracts among egoists can be given adequate explication without recourse to social norms as primitives, this much is nevertheless to be conceded to Durkheim and Parsons: that norms are indeed pertinent and important to the issue of social contracts (conventions).

What I undertake in this chapter is to try and show that with the aid of the apparatus developed by Schelling and Lewis a certain type of context, the second so far, can be shown to be prone to generate a large group of norms.

The chapter begins with an introduction of the concept of a co-ordination problem. It is then claimed that norms solve recurrent co-ordination problems; these norms are referred to as co-ordination norms.

Two types of such norms are distinguished: (1) accepted and established solutions to past recurrent co-ordination problems which—with time—assume the status of norms; (2) solutions to novel recurrent co-ordination problems which from the outset are being decreed as norms. The first type is then called 'conventions', the second 'decrees'.

The characteristics of the two types of co-ordination norms are compared; in spite of the obvious differences between them they are shown to resemble each other in several basic respects, e.g. in their source of effectiveness and in their both serving the individual as well as the collective interests of those involved. It is further claimed that the social role of co-ordination norms, besides that of contributing to social integration, is that of being a method for social choice. The question of rationality is discussed in this connection.

A rather detailed comparison between the co-ordination and the Prisoners' Dilemma problems and respective norms is then undertaken. Among the points which emerge from the comparison: in both cases the maxim to the actor, 'choose what you prefer most', breaks down, but for different reasons; an explicit agreement is a sufficient condition for solving a co-ordination but not a PD problem; conformity to co-ordination norms is in the best interests of those concerned whereas compliance with PD norms serves only their 'second best' interests; sanctions play a primary role in the case of PD norms but only a secondary one in the case of co-ordination norms. Two cases are presented of problems which partake of the features of both co-ordination and PD situations. Finally, an analysis of the concept of co-operation and its relation to that of co-ordination—and to co-ordination norms—is offered.

1. Co-ordination Problems

The following is a co-ordination problem:

Suppose you and I are on separate trains, neither directly in touch with the other. We both want to meet each other, and each of us has to choose at which station to get off. It matters little to either of us at which station he or she gets off, as long as we meet each other there. So each has to choose at which station to get off according to his or her expectation as to which station the other is likely to choose. If I succeed, so do you; if I fail, we both fail.

Another example of a co-ordination problem is the following (cf. Schelling, 1960, p. 94; Lewis, 1969, p. 5):

You and I are unexpectedly cut off in a telephone conversation. We both want to continue the conversation, and each of us has to choose whether to call back or to wait. It matters little to either of us whether he or she in fact calls back or waits, as long as the connection is immediately restored. So each has to choose according to his expectation as to what the other will do: to call back if—and only if—the other is likely to wait. And again, the success or failure of either of us is the success or failure of us both.

Let us now go on to discuss the general characteristics of co-ordination problems. The two examples given above are of course too few to generalize from. However, it might be useful to keep them in mind and check their concrete features against the rather more formal and abstract comments relating to the general case of co-ordination problems. The following exposition relies in the main on Schelling's and Lewis's respective analyses of co-ordination problems.

Co-ordination problems are interaction situations distinguished by their being situations of interdependent decision. That is, they are situations involving two or more persons, in which each has to choose one from among several alternative actions, and in which the outcome of any person's action depends upon the action chosen by each of the others. So that the best choice for each depends upon what he expects the others to do, knowing that each of the others is trying to guess what *he* is likely to do.

What has been said thus far can be summarized by saying that situations (problems, games) of co-ordination are a species of the genus of situations (problems, games) of strategy in the strict technical sense of this term; the interdependence of decisions—and hence of expectations—being the feature which distinguishes these problems from those of chance or skill. The specific difference of co-ordination problems within this class is that in them the interests of the parties coincide. When the coincidence of interests is perfect we speak of a *pure* co-ordination problem. In the non-pure co-ordination problems the convergence of the parties' interests is less than perfect, but still outweighs any possible clash of interests. A non-pure co-ordination version of the first example given above would be obtained if we supposed that both you and I care *somewhat* where we get off the train—I preferring one station, you another —but these conflicting preferences are overwhelmed by our desire to meet each other and hence by the need to concert our choices on some one of the stations. In either case, though, whether the problem is one of pure or of non-pure co-ordination, the success (gain) of any of the participants is the success (gain) of all of them, and the same goes for failure (loss).

It is worth noting that within the large class of problems of strategy (i.e. problems of interdependent decision), the problems of co-ordination stand in opposition to problems of conflict, the contrast being particularly acute between the extreme cases of pure co-ordination on the one hand and of pure conflict (the so-called zero-sum problems) on the other. Whereas in the pure co-ordination case the parties' interests converge completely, and the agents win or lose together, in the pure conflict case the parties' interests diverge completely, and one person's gain is the other's loss.

Indeed, it has been just this observation which led Schelling to argue for a 'reorientation of game theory' (1960, pp. 83–9). He advocates there abandoning the traditional twofold division of games of strategy into zero-sum and non-zero-sum, and adopting instead the view that games of strategy range over a continuum with games of pure conflict (i.e. zero-sum games) and games of pure co-ordination as opposite limits. All other games, located between these limiting cases, involve mixtures in varying proportions of conflict and co-ordination, of competition and partnership, and are referred to as *mixed-motive games*.

It will prove useful in what follows to be acquainted with the matrix representation of co-ordination problems. The essential feature of co-ordination problems is, as we have seen, the coincidence of the parties' interests. This feature finds its expression in the pay-off matrix of these problems in that the parties' pay-offs are equal in every cell (perhaps only after a suitable linear transformation).

Typically, a matrix depicting a two-person co-ordination problem is of the form 3.1.

	C1	C2	C3
R1	1	0	0
	1	0	0
R2	0	1	0
	0	1	0
R3	0	0	1
	0	0	1

3.1

If we take my (Row-Chooser's) choices of rows 1, 2, and 3 to stand for my choices of getting off the train at stations A, B, and C respectively, and similarly with regard to your (Column-Chooser's) choices of columns 1, 2, and 3, matrix 3.1 will represent our first example given above. We meet—and gain—when we succeed in concerting our choices, that is, when the combinations of our actions are those represented by the cells R1–C1, R2–C2, or R3–C3; otherwise we fail to meet and we both lose.

For the sake of contrast: the perfect opposition of interests in the pure conflict (zero-sum) situations finds its expression in the matrix representation in that the parties' pay-offs (perhaps only after a suitable linear transformation) sum to zero in every cell. Thus, a matrix depicting a two-person pure conflict which serves to bring out the contrast with the pure co-ordination matrix given above will be 3.2.

	C1	C2
R1	1	0
	-1	0
R2	0	-1
	0	1

3.2

Perfect coincidence of interests does not in itself guarantee there being a co-ordination *problem*. The identical ranking of all possible outcomes by the persons involved, in their separate preference scales, might result in a quite trivial interaction situation which poses no problem of co-ordinating expectations, intentions, and actions. Thus, in the situations depicted by the matrices 3.3 and 3.4

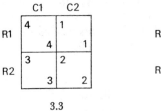
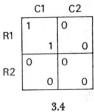

3.3   3.4

there is perfect coincidence of interests but no genuine problem of co-ordination: in both there is just one state of affairs most preferred by both participants (namely the one represented by R1–C1), and once they both aim at it—Row-Chooser by choosing row 1 and Column-Chooser by choosing column 1— it is achieved without further ado.

It is quite clear, then, that mere coincidence of interests does not suffice to create a problem. However, the main thesis of this work being that norms are generated to resolve situational problems, it is of paramount importance to single out that feature of co-ordination problems responsible for there *being* a problem of co-ordination. The missing element—which was, however, present in the two examples given at the outset—is that of *ambiguity*. In a co-ordination problem there are several outcomes most preferred by all concerned, and the problem is which of them is to be aimed at by them all. In matrix 3.1 (p. 79 above), for instance, there is no difference of interests between the two parties in their choice of actions; there is simply cause for confusion. This is what truly lies at the heart of co-ordination problems.

To capture this element formally, and at the same time to rule out unwanted trivial cases, it is necessary to introduce the concept of a *proper co-ordination equilibrium* (see Lewis, 1969, pp. 8, 14, 22).

An *equilibrium*, we recall, is a combination of the agents' chosen actions such that, once reached, no one agent wishes he had acted otherwise given the choice of the others; that is, no one agent would have gained had he *alone* acted differently.

A *proper equilibrium* is in fact an equilibrium in the strong sense. That is, it is a combination of the agents' chosen actions such that each agent would have lost—and not merely not have gained—had he alone acted differently. (Thus, the combinations R1–C1, R2–C2, and R3–C3 in matrix 3.1, R1–C2 in matrix 3.2, R1–C1 in matrix 3.3, and R1–C1 in matrix 3.4 are all proper equilibria. The combination R2–C2 in matrix 3.4, though, is an *improper* equilibrium.) In general, a proper equilibrium in a two-person matrix is such that Row-Chooser prefers it in the strong sense to all other combinations in its column, and Column-Chooser to all other combinations in its row.

A *co-ordination equilibrium* is a combination such that once reached, no agent wishes *any one* agent—either himself *or* someone else—to have alone acted differently; that is, no one would have been better off had any one agent chosen a different action.

And a *proper co-ordination equilibrium*, finally, is a co-ordination equilibrium in the strong sense; that is, a co-ordination equilibrium such that at least one agent would have been *worse* off had any one alone acted differently. (Of the various matrices given so far, the combination R1–C1, R2–C2, and R3–C3 in matrix 3.1, R1–C1 in matrix 3.3, and R1–C1 in matrix 3.4 are proper co-ordination equilibria. R2–C2 in matrix 3.4 is an improper co-ordination equilibrium, and R1–C2 in matrix 3.2 is a proper equilibrium which is *not* a co-ordination equilibrium.)

We are now in a position to state the requirement which comes closest to ensuring that situations of interdependent decision with coincidence of interests pose a genuine problem of co-ordination: it is that they should have at least two proper co-ordination equilibria. (Of the above-given matrices only matrix 3.1, appropriately, satisfies this requirement and thus deserves to be classified as representing a co-ordination problem.) This requirement is necessary[1] for the presence of an element of

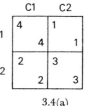

3.4(a)

---

[1] It is not sufficient though. Consider for instance the following variation on matrix 3.4. Here there are two proper co-ordination equilibria (viz. R1–C1 and R2–C2), and yet the problem of co-ordinating choices—if it can be called a problem—is trivial.

ambiguity, or 'embarras de richesse', essential for there being a problem of concerting expectations and hence choices of actions.

Finally, we recall that co-ordination problems need not be pure co-ordination problems; they might involve less than perfect coincidence of interests. In terms of the matrix representation this means that the pay-offs need not be precisely equal in every cell. The agents might not be wholly indifferent between the various co-ordination equilibria, and there might even be some conflict between them in this respect. Thus, in the situation depicted by matrix 3.5, the agents' interests do

	C1	C2	C3
R1	6 5	0 0	0 0
R2	0 0	4 4	0 0
R3	0 0	0 0	5 6

3.5

	C1	C2
R1	2 1	0 0
R2	0 0	1 2

3.6

not coincide perfectly, the agents caring somewhat as to which of the three co-ordination equilibria (R1–C1, R2–C2, and R3–C3) is to be aimed at. And yet coincidence of interests still predominates: each of these co-ordination equilibria is still much preferred by the parties to any of the non-co-ordination equilibrium combinations. The differences in pay-offs making for conflict between them are small enough compared with their common interest in concerting their choices on some one of the three co-ordination equilibria. So such situations do present genuine co-ordination problems.

It should, at the same time, be pointed out that there is no clear borderline between imperfect co-ordination situations of the type just discussed and situations which can be regarded as ones of favouritism, or partiality. Take a situation depicted by matrix 3.6. Ought we to suppose that coincidence of interests predominates here? Or could this represent, rather, a case of the favoured v. the deprived, where it does matter a great deal to the parties which of the co-ordination equilibria is in fact the outcome? (Indeed, Chapter IV uses just this matrix as a paradigm for the generation of norms of partiality.)

That the borderline between these types of cases is fuzzy is, of course, not surprising, since it is the participants' strength of preferences for the various outcomes *relative to each other* which ultimately determines whether a given situation is one of imperfect co-ordination or one of conflict of favouritism (inequality). Moreover, it is quite possible that there be some trade-off between these two types of cases, such that some progressive changes in the 'prizes' involved might turn one into the other. Think, for example, of two youth gangs, co-ordinating their hang-out in one neighbourhood rather than in the other. The situation might start out as one in which the mere achievement of co-ordination matters to the members of both groups more than where it is achieved. With rising transportation costs, however, or with rising crime rates in the area, it might come to matter a lot to them where they actually meet: the feelings of resentment and of being exploited might develop in the outside group *vis-à-vis* the local one. This situation is already close to the cases of inequality dealt with in the next chapter.

Such dynamics serve to emphasize, therefore, that the classification of given cases of social interaction cannot always be simply read off their matrix representation.

2. Co-ordination Problems and Norms

Having introduced the concept of a co-ordination problem I now proceed to raise the question where norms do, or can, enter the picture.

Very generally, my answer will be twofold:

(1) In a recurrent co-ordination problem a successful solution, once arrived at and thence repeated, becomes a norm.

(2) In certain novel co-ordination problems a solution is likely to be dictated by a norm issued specifically for that purpose by some authority.

Let us examine in detail these two types of connection between co-ordination problems and norms.

2.1 An Established Solution Turned Norm

As Schelling and Lewis have shown, co-ordination problems are, very generally, solved through *salience*: one of the co-ordination equilibria might appear conspicuous to the people involved, owing to some specific feature it possesses, and might hence serve as a focal point for the convergence of their choice of actions. The salience of the co-ordination equilibrium need not be, and in general is not, a result of its being in any obvious sense better than the other co-ordination equilibria; i.e. in terms of the matrix representation, it need not be the case that its pay-offs are higher than those of the other co-ordination equilibria—since this would mean that the parties would have preferred this outcome *un*conditionally, whereas we are concerned with those genuine co-ordination problems where the parties' preferences are always conditional upon the actions of the others. Rather, a certain co-ordination equilibrium might be salient owing to some specific feature of the circumstances in which the problem is set, or to the parties' being acquainted with the associations, imagination, or even the obsessions of each other. It is, in short, the connotations of the problem rather than its bare mathematical features which are likely to point to a solution.

Precedent and agreement also solve recurrent co-ordination problems. They can, however, be viewed as special cases—albeit important ones—of salience. And since our prime concern at present is not with the precise way a solution was arrived at in the first place, but with what character it assumes after it has been achieved, repeated, and established, they will not here be further dwelt upon.

Many regularities in everyday life might be conceived of as having become established and accepted solutions to recurrent co-ordination problems. Type of dress for formal occasions—and fashion items in general, driving on the right (or on the left, as the case may be), some of the practices connected with the concept of the gold standard, the acceptance of, and trade in, a particular legal tender, and in general many rules of etiquette—all of these can be thought of as specific solutions to what were originally recurrent co-ordination problems among the members of certain communities.

The nature of a co-ordination problem, we saw, is such that the parties involved in it either win or lose together. Conformity to a regularity which solves a recurrent co-ordination problem, therefore, answers to the interests of all involved (even though, perhaps, not to the *best* interests of each: some might wish there were a different regularity, leading to an alternative co-ordination equilibrium. See below, Section 4.3). Naturally, everyone involved must be pretty anxious to cling to whatever clue of salience one might perceive, and expect the others to perceive, and expect the others to expect one to perceive, and so on. An established regularity, which points to one of the available co-ordination equilibria in the situation as *the* solution, is likely therefore to be welcomed by everyone as possibly the best source of salience they might wish for. The reward for conformity to a regularity in these circumstances, then, consists in the very act of conforming, since it guarantees what is desired by all—the achievement of *a* co-ordination equilibrium. A regularity which produced convergence on an alternative co-ordination equilibrium would, in the nature of things, have been just about as useful and therefore just about as welcome; conformity to it would, within limits, have served the interests of all just as well.

From the above account it appears that, conceptually, there is nothing normative about a regularity which solves a recurrent co-ordination problem. Moreover, it is noteworthy that a complete description and an adequate explanation can be given the type of regularity in question without resort to any normative terms like 'ought', 'right', or 'duty'. And yet I maintain that such a regularity is apt to become a norm. This clearly calls for an explanation. The question to be tackled, then, is why should a regularity which successfully solves a recurrent co-ordination problem and hence answers—within limits—the interests of all concerned, turn into a norm? In other words, what is there to require that a *repeated* pattern of behaviour of the type here under study turn into a *binding* pattern of behaviour?

I shall offer a number of arguments in defence of my contention.

First, a norm is capable of regulating and channelling the expectations—and hence the choice of actions—of anonymous participants. A regularity which successfully solves a recurrent co-ordination problem is established when the same pattern of behaviour is repeated in each instance of the co-ordination problem among the members of a certain community. This repetition is, however, likely to develop only when the people involved are the same ones on each occurrence of the problem, or at least—if they are not—when the members of the community concerned can rely on their sharing some common background knowledge and common inductive standards. Newcomers to the community, or in general people concerning whom there can be no definite expectations, pose a problem, if not a threat, to the continuing existence of this type of regularity. But once future behaviour in accordance with the established pattern is normatively prescribed, anonymity can be accommodated. The existence of a norm, rather than merely of a discernible regularity, will alleviate the burden of searching for specific clues in the specific context of each instance of the co-ordination problem; it will prescribe—and hence provide— a uniform solution to the problem-type, thus circumventing the difficulties of solving anew, and possibly with strangers, the varying problem-tokens.

To illustrate this point it seems to me worth while elaborating a little on the second example of a co-ordination problem given at the outset (p. 77 above). Suppose that in a certain town for some reason all telephone calls are cut off without warning soon after they have begun. We, as residents of this town, will find ourselves facing frequent co-ordination problems of the same type. In the first few instances, however, still unaware of the proportion of this natural disaster which has hit us, we might treat each occurrence of this problem on its own merits: both partners to the call, that is, will try to look for some specific feature in the circumstances of the specific telephone conversation between them which might indicate to both who is to call back and who is to wait. For instance, if one of the parties is talking from his office, where it is usually difficult to reach him, it might be evident to both that he is the one to call back, regardless of whether he was the original caller or not. Or when the called party is known to both to be clumsy in remembering or finding telephone numbers, it might be clear to both that the original caller should call back; and so on.

However, while it gradually dawns on us all that this co-ordination problem is here to stay, we are likely soon to abandon our *ad hoc* efforts to try for some clue which will point to a particular solution in each particular case, and a regularity might emerge among us instead: say, that always the original caller calls back while the called party waits. General conformity to this regularity, and the system of convergent mutual expectations produced by it, ensure the smooth achievement of a solution in each instance of the problem, even among people who are strangers to each other. The regularity's assuming the status of a norm entails its being taught to the young and told to newcomers, and hence its being more widely known and adhered to, and more securely perpetuated.

Secondly, while a regularity extracted from past events might sometimes be continued in more than one way, a norm will provide the principle of continuation which will resolve potential ambiguities in most future events. To wit: a chain of past solutions to a recurrent co-ordination problem might fall under several regularity descriptions that fit, but which might guide to different actions in a given new instance. A norm, by fixing on a unique fitting description of the regularity, provides a unique guidance for action in normal future cases.

To take a simple example: a young housewife might wrongly extrapolate from her past experiences and come to the conclusion that in laying the table for an elaborate dinner all the knives are to be placed at the right of each plate, the forks at the left, and the spoons in front, their size increasing the closer they are to the plate. An embarrassing blunder will be committed, of course, whenever this principle clashes with the correct rule of etiquette which requires that the type and order of the silver be determined by the type and order of the courses to be served, the dessert cutlery being placed in front.

Thirdly, there is a higher degree of articulation and explicitness associated with a norm than with a mere regularity of behaviour. In this respect a norm is closer to an agreement than is a regularity, and an explicit agreement affords the best and safest solution to any co-ordination problem. Furthermore, the fact that a norm is taught and told, and its being supported by social pressure, enhance the salience of the particular co-ordination equilibrium it points to; in a sense it even slightly changes the corresponding pay-off matrix so as to make this particular co-ordination equilibrium a somewhat more worthwhile outcome to be aimed at than it would otherwise have been.

In addition to these three considerations there are two more points, of a different nature, which deserve attention.

In the first place, a regularity which solves a recurrent co-ordination problem is almost by definition more than a merely regular pattern of behaviour. From the nature of a co-ordination problem it follows that an action in conformity with such a regularity is one that gratifies the preferences of the actor, and also the expectations as well as the preferences of (most of) the others involved with him in any instance of the problem. One who for some reason fails to conform, therefore, is likely to be taken by the others to be acting in the first place contrary to what is in one's own interest, and also contrary to what one ought to know are *their* preferences, as well as contrary to what one should be aware of as their reasonable expectations of one. Such an action tends to be explained discreditably and to evoke unfavourable responses, which is not usually the case with an action not conforming to a pattern of behaviour which merely *happens* to be regular. So the very concept of a regularity of the type under study in a sense includes its being socially enforced, or, if you will, its exerting a normative pressure on those involved in any instance of the recurrent co-ordination problem concerned.

The second, and last, point to be made in this connection involves a distinction between two types of expectations: *theoretical* ones, as expressed in 'ground frost is expected to develop during the night in low-lying areas', and *deontic* ones, as expressed in 'I shall expect you here tomorrow at eight o'clock sharp.' Now a co-ordination problem, we know, is one in which the interdependence of expectations plays a major role. A good reason—the only good reason—for my taking the decision to do A rather than to do B in a co-ordination problem is my expectation that you will do A, my expectation that you'll expect me to do A, my expectation that you'll expect me to expect you to do A, and so on. What sort of expectations are these?

I contend that however theoretical, or 'neutral', the systems of mutual expectations in any isolated co-ordination problem might be, matters change once we are dealing with a *recurrent* co-ordination problem. Where a co-ordination problem is recurrent, and where there emerges a regularity which solves it, and where there is room for speaking of precedents, these expectations tend rapidly to assume the character of deontic ones; i.e. to be more than mere predictions: to constitute mutual demands. When such expectations fail to be satisfied, the reaction is more likely to be a reproach to the ones who frustrated them than an acknowledgement by the others of their simply having made a mistake in their prediction.

The claim that expectations upholding regularities tend to become deontic is, as such, an empirical generalization. But conjoin to it the previous point made, namely that an action in conformity with a regularity which solves a recurrent co-ordination problem is one that gratifies both the actor's and the other participants' interests, and you will have an independent justification why this will be so, in the case of the specific type of regularities we are here concerned with.

To sum up: quite apart from the question of why it is needful that regularities which solve recurrent co-ordination problems be norms, I have in the last two points endeavoured to show why and in what sense it is in the nature of these regularities that they are normative.[2] This, then, is the first type of connection between co-ordination problems and norms. In view of the consideration that these 'don't rock the boat' norms, to be referred to as Co-ordination Norms, answer, within limits, the interests of all concerned, I would propose, finally, to talk of *conformity to them*, as distinct from *compliance with* other types of norms, the source of effectiveness of which is primarily the fear of sanctions combined with respect for some authority.

2.2 *Norms as Solutions to Novel Co-ordination Problems*

Suppose a certain region in some country becomes militarily occupied by a neighbouring country. A clear-cut, well defined, and rather sudden co-ordination problem might then present itself to the residents of this region: which currency had they better use—their own country's, the occupying country's, or perhaps both? The assumption is that each of them cares little which currency they use, so long as (most of) the others use

---

[2] Note, however, that the logical form of the sentence stating such a regularity will nevertheless be that of a descriptive sentence, in contrast to the form of a sentence expressing the corresponding *norm*. (I am indebted for this point to Carl G. Hempel.)

it and accept it too. It is possible to imagine that for a while there will be confusion and hesitation, perhaps even a temporary regress to barter, until things clear up and a new regularity establishes itself.

However, it is more likely, I suggest, that this type of problem will be solved 'from above': that an edict, issued by the occupying authorities, will specify that as from a certain date this or that currency (or possibly both) holds as legal tender in this region. Note that, supposing it is decreed that it is the occupying country's currency which is to hold, even if some may resent this on patriotic grounds, their resentment will be overwhelmed by the preference of each of them to conform to whatever regularity is likely to be adhered to by the others. That is, even if one wishes a different co-ordination equilibrium to have been the solution, one still prefers to stick to the established (decreed) one rather than achieve no co-ordination equilibrium at all (which in our case would mean to refuse what others take and to pile up useless coins).

A similar example will be obtained if we take England to be the occupying country, France the occupied, and the problem of whether to drive on the left or on the right on French roads as the pertinent co-ordination problem. It might be mentioned that historically this was a problem which arose from the 1938 Anschluss of Austria. (Only here of course there will be precisely two possible co-ordination equilibria: the third one, that of driving *either* on the right *or* on the left will obviously not do.) Incidentally, in this case the point about the possible resentment of the decree being outweighed by the sheer need to achieve a co-ordination equilibrium is especially pertinent.

As a further variation on this type of example it might be mentioned that on passing the roadblock on the road leading to the British Headquarters in the British Sector of Berlin, the first thing which meets the eye is a large signpost KEEP RIGHT. Is it an order? a prescription? an advice? I suggest that it is precisely a decree of the type we are after. It directly resolves an ambiguity, neatly demarcated in terms of time and space, whether to consider oneself as driving on German or on British territory—which in fact constitutes a co-ordination problem.

Or take a different type of example. Suppose a communication satellite is put into orbit. A certain number of countries can benefit from it, provided the available frequencies are appropriately distributed among them. Again, the situation is such that each broadcasting service does not care much which range of frequency bands it uses, as long as no other service uses it at the same time. This is a co-ordination problem. Again, it is possible to imagine that regularities which solve it develop only after an initial period of general scramble, where each broadcasting service tries to 'conquer' a certain range by sheer persistence and obstinacy. However, it is much more likely that this problem will be solved in a different manner: some international communication authority (a U.N. agency, presumably) will convene and decide on the matter, allotting frequency bands and times of use thereof to all the relevant broadcasting services. This, again, is an arrangement, or decree, 'from above'; it establishes regularities among the users of the satellite by fixing on one particular co-ordination equilibrium out of the numerous possible alternative ones.

With these examples in mind we may proceed to make the general point. Quite apart from the fact, argued for in the previous section, that regularities of behaviour—originating no matter how or when—which successfully solve recurrent co-ordination problems are normative in character, there are cases of co-ordination problems the solutions of which are from the outset decreed by norms issued specifically for that purpose by some authority. Further, the examples seem to suggest what is typical of the situations where this is apt to happen. They will be situations which involve a clash between two existing arrangements (concerning, e.g., a medium of exchange or the side of the driving lane) in an ambiguous 'no man's land'; or, alternatively, which call for a projection of existing arrangements (concerning, e.g., the allotment of frequency bands for broadcasting) to new areas, where this projection is not sufficiently straightforward and is inherently ambiguous. The arrangements which thus clash, or which are to be projected, may or may not themselves constitute established solutions to situations which on analysis might feasibly be shown to be recurrent co-ordination problems. But once they clash, or once the need for projection arises, a rather acute and sharply defined co-ordination problem might present itself, as from a quite specific point of time and extending into the future. These problems, I submit, are in principle susceptible to solutions—and are in practice often solved—by decree-type norms issued specifically for that purpose.

These norms, then, constitute the second type of what will hence be referred to as co-ordination norms. Note that from the above examples, as well as from the ensuing discussion, it appears that it is reasonable to expect such norms to be generated in situations of intercourse between distinct communities, their size ranging from small groups to whole nations (or states). Very generally, where communities which have their own ways of going about things—their own arrangements, regularities, conventions—come into contact, and where the situation demands that barriers between them be dropped, or that one—*any* one—of them absorb the other, various co-ordination problems are likely to crop up and to call for these decree-type co-ordination norms to solve them.

When the authority called upon to issue the appropriate decree-type co-ordination norm is on the level of the state, an interesting relation between law and custom is brought to light. In such situations, which involve novel co-ordination problems, the legislature will find it necessary to *extend* existing arrangements—roughly falling under the heading 'customs'—to novel areas. I find this interesting since it appears to my mind to constitute a significant addition to the two prominent and generally recognized types of interrelation between law and custom (the last term being pretty loosely used). These two occur, briefly, (1) when the legislature recognizes traditional practices or customary norms—e.g. in Israeli law, several matrimonial practices and the practice of paying severance pay—adopts them, and incorporates them into the legal system of the state; and (2) when the law interferes with prevailing traditions and usages on purpose to change them or actually to annul them. Cases in point are the compulsory abandonment of Arabic script in Turkey and the introduction (in 1925) of the Roman alphabet instead, the outlawing in the state of Israel of marriages between minors formerly practised among some oriental Jewish communities, and the steps taken by Indian law to void some of the traditional caste taboos and practices. Now in contrast with and in addition to these two, in the case of novel co-ordination problems, as said, it will be incumbent upon the law to extend existing practices and usages, or to reconcile clashing ones, rather than either to adopt or to cancel them.

Often, though, the inter-community intercourse producing novel co-ordination problems will not be intrastate but will involve whole states (or nations), the decree-type co-ordination norms which are issued to solve them forming the substance of international treaties, conventions, and law.

2.3 On Conformism

Armed with the conceptual framework propounded so far, let me now touch on the phenomenon of conformism. Technically this will be a digression from the continuous flow of the exposition, but I take it to be of material importance for the clarification of the approach undertaken in this chapter.

To begin with, consider the individual conformist. My basic argument here is that a conformist is one who regards the majority of the situations in which he has to make a decision about action *as if* they were co-ordination problems. That is to say, instead of possessing his own preference system according to which he will order the alternatives open to him and then take that course of action which leads to the most desired one, the conformist perceives his preferences as conditional upon the actions of the others: instead of its being a case of 'I prefer A to B and B to C and therefore I shall choose A', with the conformist it is a case of 'I shall choose A if and only if the others (will) choose A, choose B if and only if the others (will) choose B', and so on. 'The others' in this sort of deliberation might refer either to all, or most, of the other people involved with him in the situation, or to a certain leading group thereof considered to be setting the tone, or, finally, to a certain relevant group of reference such as neighbours or colleagues. The same point might also be made about the extreme non-conformist, non-joiner. He too turns all decision problems into co-ordination ones: he wants to be wherever the others are not. (This was pointed out to me by John Mackie.)

The point, then, is that, the conformist's main motive being to meet the others in their choices, any decision situation might present itself to him as a co-ordination problem; which fact will owe little to the objective structural features of the situation itself and everything to the conformist's own disposition and state of mind. But it will constitute a co-ordination problem only from *his* personal viewpoint; it will constitute what might rather be termed a *unilateral co-ordination problem*. Namely, the situation concerned does not have to be such that *each* of those involved with him in it considers it a co-ordination problem; coincidence of interests in it does not necessarily outweigh conflicting personal preferences; and it does not have to be the case that those involved either win or lose together. Indeed it does not even have to be an interaction situation with interdependence of individual choices (see p. 78 above). It is a co-ordination problem only to the individual conformist who suppresses whatever personal opinions and desires he might have to yield a conditional preference pattern. If he knows the others' choices—concerning dress, opinions, vacation resort, or what not—he will just do the same. If he does not know them, or if they haven't yet taken shape, he will have to look for clues and to apply guesswork so as to make his own choice compatible with what the others' will prove to be. The latter case, then, appears to constitute a unilateral co-ordination problem the participants in which are the conformist on the one hand and 'the others', as a body, on the other.

But the difference between this case and a genuine co-ordination problem is in fact more substantial. To realize this, recall the system of expectations involved in a genuine co-ordination problem: I shall choose that action which I expect you to choose, and which I expect you to expect me to choose, and which I expect you to expect me to expect you to choose, and so on. In the most general case of a single, isolated genuine co-ordination problem there are two things to be noted about these expectations:

a. that this chain of high order expectations may in principle go on indefinitely (although in practice it will stop after a few steps).

b. that they are expectations of the *theoretical* kind (see p. 88 above), i.e. they do not involve more than just having ground to believe that some future event will take place, and they are not much different from ordinary predictions.

In the case of the conformist, on the other hand, the situation is different. The conformist will just make that choice he expects the others to make. This expectation will again be theoretical, but it will not constitute the terminal link in any chain of high order theoretical expectations: the conformist need not consider the others' choice as dependent in any sense upon his own, nor need he consider the others' choice as dependent upon his expectation of them. Indeed the suppression of whatever personal preferences he might have is proof enough of the conformist's lack of regard for them and in general for the effect of his own choices of action.

But there is a sense in which the conformist's *second* order expectations, i.e. those concerning the others' expectations of him, are of primary importance to his deliberations. And that is when the conformist takes the others to expect something of him in a sense closer to the deontic than to the theoretical. One is concerned here with a 'quasi-deontic' domain, where the conformist cannot afford not to do what others in the peer-group do since he considers his status and 'face' to be at stake. (See Goffman (1969), 'On Face-Work'.) Thus, the conformist's expectation of the others' chosen course of action influences and guides his own behaviour; it is virtually taken by him to constitute a demand upon him—the penalty for non-conformity being the pain of conspicuousness.

Turning now to a society composed entirely of conformists, to all of whom conformity matters more than anything else, the question which is naturally posed is whether in *it* any decision problem might not be a genuine co-ordination problem. Given a situation which requires every one to make a choice of action from among a certain set of alternative ones, it is granted that each of the conformists will try to guess what the others are likely to choose, each will look for sufficiently salient clues, each will have a conditional preference pattern. However, this is not sufficient for this type of situation to qualify as a genuine co-ordination problem. An additional assumption is needed, on which it is common knowledge in this society that they are all avowed conformists who are, moreover, quite content to remain that way. Only when this is assumed can the spirals of mutual expectations necessary for it to be considered a genuine co-ordination problem get off the ground; without it the situation can more accurately be described as being constituted of many unilateral co-ordination problems with the expectations reaching at most the second step, the first being theoretical and the second quasi-deontic.

I have not, in this discussion of conformism, explained what makes a conformist tick. I did try to show, though, in what sense the phenomenon of conformism can be accounted for as parasitic on the notion of co-ordination problems. To be sure, cases of conformism are much more abundant and familiar to us than cases of genuine co-ordination problems. But the concept of a co-ordination problem, unlike that of conformism, does not involve dispositions and states of mind, and, in its purity, lends itself to a more systematic analysis on what I consider firmer ground. It is for this reason that I have introduced and explicated the concept of co-ordination norms in terms of co-ordination problems, and only then indicated in what way the phenomenon of conformism and its normative aspects might be seen to be derivative from it. This constitutes somewhat of a reversal of a procedure quite common in the social sciences, where many discussions purporting to be of social norms slip right away into discussions of conformism. (See, for instance, (1) K. Davis, *Human Society*, New York, 1950 (esp. ch. 11); (2) Ely Chinoy, *Society: An Introduction to Sociology*, New York, 1967 (ch. 18); (3) S. Wheeler, 'Deviant Behaviour', in: *Sociology*, W. J. Smelser (ed.), New York, 1967.)

3. *The Distinguishing Features of Co-ordination Norms*

3.1 *General*

Two types of connections between co-ordination problems and norms have been pointed out. We now turn to ask what are the distinguishing features of the norms thus connected with co-ordination problems. In particular, we shall be interested in the relations, if any, between the two groups of norms associated with co-ordination problems in the two distinct ways indicated.

To facilitate the discussion, let us first introduce a shorthand terminology. Following Lewis, let us agree to refer as *conventions* to norms of the first group; that is, to those regularities of behaviour which owe either their origin or their durability to their being solutions to recurrent (or continuous) co-ordination problems and which, with time, turn normative. Let us further agree to refer as *decrees* to norms of the second type; that is, to those norms which are issued specifically for the purpose of solving novel and acute recurrent (or continuous) co-ordination problems.

There is a set of distinctions more or less generally accepted as a useful tool for the analysis and classification of norms.[3] When examined in the light of these distinctions our two groups of norms appear to be very different in their main features, as their shorthand titles—conventions v. decrees—indeed suggest. From the account given above of what we termed conventions and decrees we are justified, it seems, in putting forward the following somewhat rough and schematic claims concerning their characteristic features.

Conventions are, typically:

(1) Non-statutory norms, which need not be enacted, formulated, and promulgated.

(2) They are neither issued nor promulgated by any identifiable authority, and are hence what is usually called impersonal, or anonymous norms.

(3) They involve in the main non-institutionalized, non-organized, and informal sanctions (i.e. punishments or rewards).

Decrees, in contrast, are, typically:

(1) Statutory;

(2) Issued and promulgated by some appropriately endowed authority (not necessarily on the level of the state);

(3) The sanctions they involve might be organized, institutionalized, and formal, even physical.

These differences are considerable, no doubt. However, there are two considerations when viewed in the light of which the common aspects of these two groups of norms are readily seen. As might be expected, they have to do with the fact that both groups of norms are inherently connected with co-ordination problems. They are the considerations of (1) the source of effectiveness of the norms; and (2) whose interests are served by conformity to the norms.

[3] In what follows I rely partly on: (1) Hart, 1961; (2) von Wright, 1963; (3) Shwayder, 1965; (4) Ross, 1968.

Let us consider each of them in turn.

3.2 *The Source of Effectiveness*

By the phrase 'the source of effectiveness' of a norm is usually meant the main reason, or motive, for conformity to (compliance with) it. In contrast to the motives for observance of personal norms (such as commands, requests, advice), and that of technical norms (or directions for use), with which we are *not* concerned, there are a few rather generally recognized motives for observance of impersonal norms of the types here under study. These include mainly apprehension of sanctions (including, possibly, a desire to be rewarded—even where the reward consists of non-punishment only), respect for some (impersonal) authority, or, what is usually the case, some combination thereof.

However, from the account given above of co-ordination problems and of the senses in which the norms under consideration might be regarded as solving them, it should be quite clear what is peculiar to these norms' source of effectiveness. Since a co-ordination problem is a situation such that any of its co-ordination equilibria is preferred, by all involved, to any combination of actions which is not a co-ordination equilibrium, each of those involved is interested in there being *something* which will point—in a way conspicuous to all and perceived to be conspicuous to all—to one particular co-ordination equilibrium as *the* solution. This precisely is what our co-ordination norms, whether conventions or decrees, do. They serve as indicators, as devices to help focus attention, and hence as rallying points for the systems of (conditional) preferences and expectations built into any co-ordination problem. Such a norm provides not so much a general rule for behaviour as a rule for selecting one particular course of behaviour (action) out of a rather well demarcated set of alternative ones in a rather well defined type of situations. It is possible to say, therefore, that one is *using* a co-ordination norm, or that one is taking advantage of its existence by acting in accordance with it, rather than that one is just conforming to (complying with) it. (This should not be taken to suggest, however, that co-ordination norms are *always* conformed to by *everyone*: in any particular co-ordination problem there might be a source of salience which outweighs, or which might seem to someone involved to outweigh, that of the relevant norm, and which points to a different co-ordination equilibrium than does the norm.) In other words, it is to the advantage of all concerned to conform to a co-ordination norm; this advantage, however, being distinguished in that it does not stem from external sanctions but from the inherent structure of co-ordination problems. To repeat the formula used earlier, the reward for conformity to co-ordination norms consists in the very act of conforming; hence the source of effectiveness of these norms.

This does not mean, of course, that there are no sanctions at all for non-conformity to co-ordination norms. Indeed, the type of sanctions employed was taken to be one of the features that account for the differences between what we termed conventions on the one hand and decrees on the other. Apprehension of sanctions contributes to the effectiveness of co-ordination norms no doubt. However, and this is the essential point, at least primarily the motive to conform to co-ordination norms has to do with the peculiar nature of co-ordination situations, with the intrinsic reward concomitant to the achievement of co-ordination; the fear of sanctions being only a secondary and subsidiary element in this motive.

The question of why people conform to norms is dealt with in a study of John W. Thibaut and Harold H. Kelley (1959). Their position (concerning social norms in general) appears to be rather close to the one developed above (concerning the smaller class of co-ordination norms) when they state that 'conformity to agreements [their definition of norm being based on the notion of an agreement] becomes rewarding in and of itself' (ibid., p. 128). Being familiar neither with the notion nor with the analysis of co-ordination situations, however, their explanation of this 'intrinsic reward' is fundamentally different from the one offered here. In their view, an agreement between parties, which forms the basis of a norm, must have been initiated, at some point in the past, by an external third party, who also saw to it that conformity to the agreement was rewarded and its breach punished. So there was a good (external) reason for the parties to keep the agreement; conformity to it was 'reinforced': 'For example, two brothers disagree about what to play because they prefer different games. Their mother steps in and says, "play what Jimmy wants for a while, and, after you've done that, give Johnny a chance", and rewards them if they follow her rule' (p. 128). Conformity to such an agreement is supposed to become a sort of a habit, and to assume, with time, an 'intrinsic value' capable of perpetuating the conformity even after the original sanctions have long ceased to be applied.

The source of effectiveness Thibaut and Kelley attribute to their norms, then, is primarily the force of external sanctions, and in the second place, in a derivative and to my mind rather mysterious sense, the 'intrinsic value' of habit and precedence. This is very different, of course, from the source of effectiveness here attributed to co-ordination norms. I suspect, however, that the concept of a co-ordination problem, and the idea—connected with it—of the possibility of there being *tacit* agreements which need not be 'reinforced' by external sanctions, would have served Thibaut and Kelley better than their own paradigmatic conception of an agreement[4] (see pp. 127–30)—quite apart from its demonstrating to them that their approach can at best apply to *some* social norms, but not to all.

Finally, let it be noted that the source of effectiveness of co-ordination norms, as propounded above, has something in common with that of advice and technical norms. The source of effectiveness of advice is similar to that of co-ordination norms in that it is oriented towards the interests of the person about to take action. In both cases there is no real need to create a motivation for observance (through external positive or negative sanctions), since it already exists. Rather, the person concerned might be pictured as using the given piece of advice in the one case, and the existence of a co-ordination norm in the other, as items of information likely to guide him towards the choice of that action which will best serve his interests.

Secondly, co-ordination norms have this much in common with technical norms, that conformity to them is in truth

---

[4] They define norm (in a two-person relation) as a 'behavioral rule which is accepted . . . by both members'. This they take to presuppose that there must be some degree of *conflict* between the members which can be settled only by an imposed agreement, reinforced by external sanctions, which—with time—turns into a norm. But the existence of co-ordination situations, with their characteristic features, demonstrates that this 'agreement-presupposes-conflict' assumption is not necessarily true.

a means for attaining a certain desired end. The end in the case of co-ordination norms is, of course, the achievement of co-ordination, the successful meeting—in the broadest sense—of all involved at one particular point (combination of chosen actions). Here, then, there is a common element in the source of effectiveness of two types of norms which otherwise belong to completely distinct categories, in any conceivable classification of norms.

3.3 *Whose Interests Are Served by the Conformity to Co-ordination Norms?*

The consideration of whose interests are served by conformity to the norm is yet another consideration when examined in the light of which a feature common to the two types of co-ordination norms—termed conventions and decrees—is revealed. This feature, at the same time, is one which distinguishes co-ordination norms—the two types taken together—from other norms.

To the extent that norms have been evaluated from the angle of whose interests are served by the conformity to them,[5] the answers given this question in the literature tend to be general and somewhat vague. It is usually held that it is 'society's' interests or 'no one's' interests which are served, according to the type of norms considered. 'Society's interests', however, is ambiguous: is it meant in a distributive sense, i.e. that the interests of each and every one in the society are served by the conformity to the norm in question? Or is it meant in an aggregative sense, i.e. that the joint, collective interest of society is served—whatever interpretation *that* might be given? And 'no one's interests' is strange; unless what it really means is that with certain types of norms the consideration of interests is simply *irrelevant*—as, perhaps, in the case of rules of games and in the case of some of the principles of morality (although even here it is, to my mind, debatable).

In the case of co-ordination norms, however, it is quite clear that, in so far as conformity to them ensures the achievement of co-ordination, it is the interests of each and every one involved which are served by the conformity. It is in the nature

[5] Von Wright and Shwayder, for instance, all but ignore this consideration in their respective classifications of norms (rules).

of co-ordination problems, we know, that everyone involved in them is interested in the achievement of some *one* of its (two or more) co-ordination equilibria. So, to the extent that a co-ordination norm helps the agents converge on one particular co-ordination equilibrium, it answers the interests of all, distributively. Further, since a state of *proper* equilibrium is achieved, through conformity to the norm, every one stands to lose were he to deviate alone (i.e. were he not to conform to the norm). Further still, since this state is a proper *co-ordination* equilibrium, every one stands to lose were any one *else* to act differently (i.e. not to conform to the norm). So the sense in which the claim that it is the interests of each and every one concerned that are served by the conformity to co-ordination norms, has, I believe, been made sufficiently explicit.

But of course it is also the interest of 'society', or, more precisely, of the community of agents involved in the co-ordination problem as a whole, that are served by the conformity to the corresponding co-ordination norm. To see this, let us note that the total amount of want-satisfaction (represented in the matrix by the pay-offs) among those involved in a co-ordination problem is high in all of its equilibria (allowing for small differences among them; see p. 82 above) and ¦low in all combinations of chosen actions which are not co-ordination equilibria. So again, a norm which helps converge on any one of the co-ordination equilibria, thereby averting the possibility of a failure to co-ordinate, serves the joint collective interests of the community in question.[6]

It has been established, then, that a feature common to both types of co-ordination norms (that is, to the so-called conventions and decrees) is that by conformity to them it is the interests of each and every one involved in the corresponding co-ordination problems which are served, as well as the interests of the community they form as a whole. Attention must now be directed to the fact that it is by no means always (and 'automatically') the case that what seems to answer the interests of all distributively will also answer the interests of all collectively.

---

[6] To employ the language of Brian Barry's Political Argument (1965), we might say, I think, that the achievement of co-ordination (in situations classified as co-ordination problems) is a want-regarding principle which is both distributive and aggregative (see esp. pp. 38–47).

The prominent example is, of course, the Prisoners' Dilemma situation, with which we are already familiar. In it, were every one to pursue his own interests single-mindedly, the result of the distributively rational choice is bad for all, jointly as well as severally. It ought to be mentioned in this connection that although compliance with a PD norm (that protects the good-yet-unstable state of affairs from deteriorating) also serves the interests of all involved, it is nevertheless significantly different from the case of co-ordination norms. That a PD norm is, in a sense, welcomed by those trapped in a PD situation, inherently involves an element of renunciation, of coming to terms with the grim fact that they have to settle for a second best if they are to avert a disaster. This partly finds an expression in the fact that the state protected by the norm is *not* an equilibrium (let alone a co-ordination equilibrium); that is, that every one stands to gain should he alone have acted differently (not conformed to the norm). In the case of co-ordination problems, on the other hand, owing to the perfect (or near-perfect) coincidence of interests, the attainment of each individual's most preferred state is perfectly compatible with the attainment of the state best for 'society'. Hence it might be assumed that a co-ordination norm, which helps single out and achieve such a desired state, is much more genuinely welcomed by the persons concerned, with no element of renunciation or of 'second best' involved. (We shall have occasion below (p. 119) to return to this issue when a comprehensive comparison between PD norms and co-ordination norms will be taken up.)

Having mentioned that it is not always the case that gratification of the interests of all distributively coincides with gratification of the interests of all collectively, attention must also be directed to the fact that there are situations other than co-ordination problems in which the pursuit of individual interests is compatible with—or is even conducive to—the promotion of the interests of society as a whole. Consider what might be termed the 'liberal matrix' which, for two persons, is of the type 3.7.

This matrix is supposed to represent, in an extremely oversimplified fashion, the

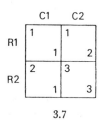

3.7

classical liberal–utilitarian outlook: were every one to mind his own business and to pursue his own personal interests, the interests of society as a whole would be promoted as well. (For a more detailed discussion of this position seen Chapter IV below, Sec. 3.) In the realm of economics this outlook of harmony finds an expression in the concept of the 'hidden hand of the market'. According to this conception, then, what is good for all distributively is good for all collectively.

In spite of this apparent similarity between 'the liberal situation' (as represented by matrices like the one above) and situations of the co-ordination problem type (as represented by the familiar co-ordination matrices), however, there is an essential difference between them. The difference consists in the fact that whereas a co-ordination problem is inherently a situation of interdependent decision, the liberal situation is not really so. According to the liberal conception (in the version adopted here for our illustrative purposes) everyone has to work in one's own interests *as if one were acting in isolation*, the (optimistic) assumption being that society's best interests are somehow being taken care of in the process. This type of situation, though veritably an *interaction* situation (since it involves many acting agents), is not a situation of strategic interaction: it is by no means necessarily a situation of interdependent decision, since the outcome for society does not depend on the mutual expectations of the persons involved, and each of them can make his choice of action wisely without regard to what the others are likely to do (see p. 7 above).

The case is very different, as we know, with co-ordination problems. In a co-ordination problem, where the interests of the agents coincide, and where they all either gain or lose together, there is no 'hidden hand' to take care of the outcome. What is needed here is a source of salience which will enable the agents to concert their actions so as to achieve one of the alternative states (co-ordination equilibria) which gratifies at one and the same time their distributive as well as their collective interests.

4. *The Social Role of Co-ordination Norms*

4.1 *The So-called Integrative Function*

It is quite customary among philosophers and social scientists to speak of the 'integrative function' of social norms. The norms they have in mind are those falling under the rough categories of conventions, customs, tradition, and even etiquette.[7] There is usually a whole semantic field evoked in the discussions of this topic, comprising, besides 'integration', such terms as 'consensus', 'cohesion', 'social control', 'group solidarity', and the like. Thus, Peter Blau (1967) says that 'Integrative bonds of social cohesion strengthen the group in the pursuit of common goals. Group cohesion promotes the development of consensus on normative standards and the effective enforcement of these shared norms. . . . Cohesion, therefore, increases social control and coordination' (p. 60). (He also cites a number of studies which corroborate this hypothesis experimentally.)

Thibaut and Kelley note that norms 'will develop more rapidly and more surely in highly cohesive groups than in less cohesive groups'—assuming that the majority of the members have about the same degree of dependence on the group (1959, p. 133). Later on they sum up, in their usual jargon, their position on the social function of group norms: 'To the extent that norms reduce interference, cut communication costs, heighten value similarity and insure the interaction sequence necessary for task performance, norms improve the reward-cost positions attained by the members of a dyad and thus increase the cohesiveness of the dyad' (pp. 138–9).

Alf Ross also points out (1968) the connection between the homogeneity of a group, the degree of consensus among its members, and the effectiveness in it of norms of the conventional type: 'In primitive societies, where living conditions and social functions vary only slightly between individuals, fundamental values, attitudes and religious beliefs are for the most part uniform and harmonious. Tradition and custom, therefore, forcefully rule the life of the members in all its aspects' (p. 94). He then goes on to contrast this situation with modern, non-homogeneous societies, where the degree of consensus is much lower and hence social customs lose their force and are replaced by legal regulations.

We see, then, that sometimes it is claimed that the existence of social norms contributes to and increases social integration, cohesion, etc., and that sometimes it is the group cohesion etc. which is conducive to the development, maintenance, and

---

[7] See, for instance, Goffman, 1969, pp. 21–2(n.).

effectiveness of social norms. Whatever the precise claim, though, there is no detailed account given of just *how* it is that these things influence each other, the impression created by the quoted passages being that they rely quite heavily on the suggestive power of the terms belonging to the semantic field in question. However, the minimum content of the received view which does emerge from the quoted passages is that there is a cluster of group properties which are all closely interrelated, that each of them bears upon and is conducive to the others, and that all of them are somehow or other related to group norms.

Co-ordination norms contribute, no doubt, to social integration. Conformity to them, as we know, serves at one and the same time the interests of the relevant society and those of its individual members. Hence co-ordination norms tend to maintain and perpetuate (and sometimes cause) regularities in behaviour. Such regularities afford rather good and reliable bases for the systems of mutual expectations concerning behaviour among members of the society in question. All this is undoubtedly at least part of what is meant by saying that co-ordination norms have an 'integrative function'. What I wish to do in the next section, however, is to point at another role of co-ordination norms, which is quite distinct from that connected with the 'integrative cluster' discussed above.

4.2 *An Instrument for Social Choice*

My contention, in a nutshell, is this: to the extent that co-ordination norms solve co-ordination problems, they function as a method for social choice. Let me explain and elaborate.

On a very elementary level we may say that 'social choice' means a preference ordering of society, concerning a set of alternatives, which is obtained by some rule from the preference orderings of the individual members of that society over the same set of alternatives. The crucial element in this procedure is of course the rule of aggregation (or the 'social decision function') which specifies just *how* to pass from the various—possibly incompatible—individual choices (preference ordering) to the one which is to be the social choice.

For example: a certain village receives a large endowment from a visiting Old Lady. Suppose the three alternative ways of spending the money are agreed to be the renovation of the old village church, the arrangement of a pop festival, or the distribution of the money equally between the villagers. Each villager is then supposed to order these alternatives according to his own preferences, and the question is what will the social choice be. A democratic rule of aggregation might determine, for instance, that the alternative ranked first by the majority of villagers will be the first in the social ordering, the second second, and the third third. (There can be *other* democratic rules of aggregation—e.g. by using weights.) A dictatorial rule of aggregation will determine that there is a certain individual in the community such that his preference ranking is the social choice, regardless of the rankings of the others. And so on.

Kenneth Arrow points out (1963, p. 2) that it is only dictatorship and convention which, when viewed as methods for social choice, are immune from clashes of wills: 'In ideal dictatorship there is but one will involved in choice, in an ideal society ruled by convention there is but the divine will or perhaps, by assumption, a common will of all individuals concerning social decisions, so in either case no conflict of individual wills is involved.'[8] Just why it is that conventional societies are free from conflicts of wills is only vaguely suggested: in such a society, presumably, there is a high degree of consensus among its members regarding attitudes, values, and beliefs. This consensus, it is assumed, produces similar preference orderings of any set of alternatives presented to the members of this society; hence the accord of individual wills and the triviality of passing from them to a social decision.

In the case of conventions which are co-ordination norms, however, there is no need to understand by 'common will' some kind of an unaccounted-for consensus regarding attitudes, values, and beliefs. Rather, we may stay in the safer realm of self-interest and understand by it something more like *common interest*. A convention which is a co-ordination norm expresses,

---

[8] A similar note is struck by Murakami, when he summarizes his discussion of the so-called Voting Paradox: 'A paradox inheres in any nontrivial piecemeal attempt to aggregate individual decisions. Immune from this paradox are only such extraordinary societies as dictatorial, persecutional or traditional societies, all of which may be regarded as trivial aggregations of individual decisions.' (Yasusuke Murakami, *Logic and Social Choice* (Monographs in Modern Logic, ed. G. B. Keene). London: Routledge & Kegan Paul, 1968, p. 130.)

or represents, a common will in the sense that it constitutes a solution to a general co-ordination problem. It thus answers the interests of the individual members, and conformity to it rather than taking any other course of action open in the co-ordination situation in question constitutes the choice of the society concerned.

For instance: when invited to a formal occasion, it can be supposed that the guests care little what they wear as long as they will 'meet' the others in their dress; i.e. as long as their dress turns out sufficiently similar to that of the others. (Incidentally, what counts as *sufficiently* similar in such cases is also a matter of convention; e.g. is a turtle neck with no tie more 'acceptable' than a wild-coloured tie as a substitute for black tie?) The social choice on the type of dress can in principle be made by a 'dictator' whose will and authority are decisive in the society in question. A case in point: delegates to the first Zionist Congress in 1897 were made to appear in tail coats and bowlers by a decree of Theodor Herzl, the founder of the movement, whose aim was to lend the congress an air of respectability in the eyes of the gentile world.[9] Or the social choice can be obtained by a process of voting, democratic or otherwise; but this method is likely to be too cumbersome for such a matter, and to involve unnecessary conflicts of wills. The convention which fixes on the solution to this problem (say, tail coats), therefore, is a short cut to social choice. Owing to the nature of a co-ordination problem, this social choice will be accepted by all involved since it answers the interests of all, both collectively and individually.

It is important to realize, though, that there is something peculiar about co-ordination norms as a method of social choice. As explained above, by a 'method of social choice' is meant a method for passing from many individual members' preference orderings to one preference ordering which is, in some specified sense, society's. In the case of situations classified as co-ordination problems, however, it is impossible to speak of the individual members' separate preference orderings over the alternatives open to them, since their preferences in these

---

[9] Another example, not connected with co-ordination problems, is the abolition in 1925 of the traditional fez in Turkey, by a decree of Ataturk (Mustafa Kemal), and the introduction of European head-dress instead.

situations are *conditional*. It is the factor of *interdependence* of decision which is crucially involved here, and which is in fact absent from the (elementary) theories of deliberation.

With regard to any one action from among the given set of alternative ones in a co-ordination problem, each prefers to take it if—and only if—he expects to 'meet' the others there;[10] hence, there is no such thing as an independent unconditional individual preference ordering of the available alternatives; hence the social choice cannot be an aggregation, in one way or another, of the individual orderings.

What we do have in the case of co-ordination problems, then, is a floating system of mutually conditional preferences: 'I prefer to do A on condition that (most of) the others will do A; I prefer to do B on condition——' and so on, where the 'I' stands in turn for each one of those involved in the situation. And, to continue the metaphor, what this floating system needs is some *anchorage*; some pre-eminently conspicuous indication as to what action is *likely* to be taken by (most of) the others— or at least what action is likely to be expected by everyone to be taken by (most of) the others. Such an indication will help everyone pin down one—he hopes the same one—of the links in the chain of his conditional preferences, and attach an almost unconditional preference to this particular link. Clearly, a co-ordination norm provides just such an indication. Due to its existence the agents involved are likely to be able to make their (unconditional) choice of one of the alternative actions (though it does not in general enable them to rank-order the rest of the alternative actions). The individual members having made their choice of action—and provided the co-ordination norm was conspicuous and unambiguous enough for it to have been an appropriately co-ordinated choice—society's choice is thereby being taken too. That is to say, co-ordination norms function as an instrument for the attainment of social choice in situations classified as co-ordination problems.

[10] I feel it incumbent upon myself to call attention to the fact that the expression 'one expects to "meet" the others there' does not necessarily mean that one expects the others to do the *same* action: recall the telephone example, where I prefer to call if and only if I expect you to wait. So the intended meaning of this 'meeting' is broader than just doing the same one of several alternative actions: it refers to the achievement of a co-ordination equilibrium.

4.3 *The Problem of Rationality*

An interesting question arises: is the method of social choice, to which co-ordination norms are instrumental, a rational one? Rationality in decision-making is usually defined in terms of (1) the consistency of the agents' systems of preferences (i.e. that the relation of preference in the set of available alternatives be connected and transitive: that it be a weak ordering); and (2) a maximization principle of some sort. It usually boils down to some maxim such as 'Act so as to achieve the state of affairs which ranks highest in your preference ordering.' In the case of the situations of interdependent decision we called co-ordination problems, however, we know that no such 'isolated' ranking of the available alternatives is possible. So a question before the one just posed would have to be: What is to count as a rational decision in this case anyway?

Let us consider the set of all possible outcomes, rather than the set of the alternative courses of action in a co-ordination problem. In the language of the matrix representation, let us consider the set comprising all the cells of the matrix, not just its rows (columns). And let us examine what sort of preference ordering an agent involved in the co-ordination problem would impose on this set.

Clearly, he would divide the set of outcomes into two distinct groups: unwanted ones and wanted ones, the latter comprising those combinations of actions which are co-ordination equilibria. In some co-ordination problems one will be completely indifferent between the outcomes within each group, in others one might be able to order them according to preference. But always each outcome in the 'wanted' group will be strongly preferred to any outcome in the other group. We may safely lay down, then, that it would be rational for an agent involved in a co-ordination problem to choose that action which he believes most likely to result in an outcome which belongs to the group of preferred outcomes; i.e. to do what he believes to be his part of a co-ordination equilibrium. In other words, to act rationally in such a case is to choose from among the actions which are believed to be the ones most likely to result in a 'meeting' of the others.

In order for one to be able to have a basis for one's beliefs, however, one has to turn to all the special features of the particular co-ordination problem one faces. A clue capable of co-ordinating mutual expectations—and hence choices of action—is often to be found in the connotations of the problem, in its contextual details, in the participants' shared background knowledge and associations rather than in the bare mathematical structure of the pay-off distribution function. Thus, it would not be rational for one involved in a co-ordination problem to use a chance device to arrive at his choice of action even though he might be completely indifferent between the available co-ordination equilibria. Similarly, it would not be rational for him to choose the action corresponding to the co-ordination equilibrium he prefers (in the case that he *is* able to order the co-ordination equilibria according to preference— or at least to determine which is his most preferred one) if it is done without regard to what he actually expects the others to do and to expect him to do (and so on). The only strictly rational thing for him to do is to try hard to look for a co-ordinating signal sufficiently powerful to indicate to him, and to indicate to the others, and to indicate to him that it (probably) indicates to the others, and so on, which solution is going to be fixed upon.

A co-ordination norm, according to our foregoing analysis, functions as such a signal; to the extent that conformity to it ensures the achievement of a co-ordination equilibrium, therefore, it is rational for those involved to conform to it (provided, of course, that there is no overriding signal in some particular co-ordination problem, like, say, an explicit agreement which fixes on a *different* co-ordination equilibrium as the solution in that particular instance). To wit: in so far as conformity to a co-ordination norm ensures the achievement of some co-ordination equilibrium, which for everyone involved in the corresponding co-ordination problem belongs of necessity to the group of preferred outcomes, it is rational for everyone to conform to it. Are we to conclude from this, however, that the social choice to which the co-ordination norm is instrumental is itself rational?

My answer to this question is that although it is rational to conform to a prevailing co-ordination norm, the social choice resulting from it is not necessarily rational. What I mean by this is merely that the social choice associated with any co-ordination norm need not be *optimal* for some—or even for all—involved. Thus it is rational for all involved to aim at what is obviously a uniquely salient co-ordination equilibrium, but the salience may be due to its being the *least* desired outcome to all when compared to the other co-ordination equilibria.[11] Or sometimes external circumstances change in such a way as to render the conformity to a certain prevailing co-ordination norm less expedient or more costly as compared with conformity to some alternative co-ordination norm concerting choices on to a different co-ordination equilibrium from among the available ones. In such cases the prevailing norm might be taken to be sub-optimal or obsolete; however, it would be perfectly rational for anyone to conform to it as long as it is effectively in existence.

Cases in point are driving on the left and using non-decimal measurements. These conventions are perfectly legitimate solutions to obvious co-ordination problems. Being in England it is fully rational to conform to them; indeed it would be downright madness for one to drive there on the right just because one thinks it a more sensible or more rational convention to conform to. However, given the realities of the modern, shrinking world, it might be felt that these conventions are outdated and too costly, and that the rational thing to do is to strive to replace them with the optimal alternative ones. Note that there is nothing inherently wrong with the conventions themselves as solutions to the co-ordination problems concerned;[12] it is only the external circumstances of the world—or at least of the business world—which, pressing towards ever more uniformity in these matters, render them sub-optimal and hence, in a sense, irrational.

	C1	C2	C3	C4
R1	10/10	0	0	0
R2	0	10/10	0	0
R3	0	0	9/9	0
R4	0	0	0	10/10

3.8

[11] For example, take the situation depicted by Schelling's matrix (3.8): it is quite obvious that the uniquely salient co-ordination equilibrium in it is the one which results from the combination R3–C3. So, in default of any other clue to concert choices it is reasonable to assume that the participants will aim at it—although it is the least desired of the available equilibria. (See Schelling, 1960, pp. 295–6.)

[12] It is perhaps questionable whether this statement holds in the case of non-decimal measurements, which are less convenient to work with than the decimal ones. (Or is it my own educational bias?) Note: it is clearly assumed here that considerations such as convenience, simplicity, uniformity of usage, etc. play a role in determining what is to be considered an optimal (or rational) social choice.

It is of course possible to change such a convention. But it might be quite a complicated business. It is not only a matter of making me drive on the right instead of on the left: it involves supplying me with a good reason to believe that the driver coming toward me will also drive on the right, and, further, that he will expect me to drive on the right, and so on. So changing a convention of this type involves bringing about a shift of whole systems of mutual first- and higher-order expectations from their focus on one co-ordination equilibrium to an alternative one. I suggest in this connection that the purpose of the long months the Swedish Ministry of Transport took to propagandize its plan to change driving lanes as from a particular date was just to achieve this shift in people's expectations. If all it did was announce the plan a number of times on the radio, then even a threat of a heavy penalty for non-compliance would not have done the trick: since if I had the slightest suspicion that the driver coming up toward me had not heard the news I would still stick to the left, penalty or no penalty.

The changing of an existing convention in favour of a 'better', more rational one, has to be *explicit*. It can be achieved through an explicit agreement of all concerned, or through a regulation (decree) issued and properly promulgated by some appropriately endowed authority. Where communication, or promulgation, is impossible, it is difficult to see how an existing convention (which is a co-ordination norm) might be changed. It is of some interest to note that whereas an 'act of convening' is not necessary for a convention to *form*, it might be necessary for an existing convention to be *exchanged* for an alternative one.

To sum up: a co-ordination norm makes a particular outcome such that any rational participant in the corresponding co-ordination problem concerned will recognize that any rational participant would recognize it as the indicated 'solution'. The solution itself, however, or what we termed the social choice associated with the given co-ordination norm, is not necessarily rational in the sense that it may not be optimal, for some or for all involved. It can in principle be changed into a better one, only this involves an explicit process which is not always feasible.

5. *Co-ordination Norms and PD Norms*

5.1 *Structural Differences*

Let us start the comparison between co-ordination norms and PD (Prisoners' Dilemma)-type norms by contrasting the structural features of the corresponding problems.

First, a reminder of the typical two-person matrices involved (see 3.9 and 3.10).

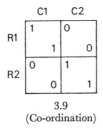

	3.9
	(Co-ordination)

	3.10
	(PD)

Summing up the differences, with which we are by now familiar, we get the following list:

1. A co-ordination problem is an interaction situation of interdependent decision in which the interests of the participants coincide. A PD problem, in contrast, is an interaction situation of interdependent decision in which the interests of the participants both conflict and coincide; it is a 'mixed motive' problem.

2. In a co-ordination problem there are at least two equilibrium points, which are further characterized as (proper) co-ordination equilibria. In a PD problem, in contrast, there is exactly one equilibrium point (represented by R2–C2 in the above PD matrix), and it is *not* a co-ordination equilibrium (that is, when reached, each participant wishes the other had acted differently).

3. In a co-ordination problem the outcomes which are (more or less) jointly satisfactory to all coincide with the set of (co-ordination) equilibria. In a PD problem, in contrast, the unique outcome which is jointly satisfactory (represented by R1–C1 in the above PD matrix) is not an equilibrium; it is unstable.

4. In a co-ordination problem no choice of action is dominant and no choice of action guarantees maximum security level (i.e. no choice of action is preferred to the others regardless of what the other participant chooses, and no choice of action is safe either in the sense that it guarantees at least *some* fixed return or in the sense that it prevents the worst outcome from being brought about). In a PD problem, in contrast, there *is* a dominant choice of action (represented by R2 for Row-Chooser and C2 for Column-Chooser in the PD matrix 3.10), which *a fortiori* is a maximum security level choice.

5.2 *Implications of Structural Differences—General*

Next, let us consider some implications of these structural differences regarding the nature of the corresponding problems. In the first place, recall that the essential point regarding the preferences over actions of the agents involved in a co-ordination problem is, as has been repeatedly emphasized, that they are conditional. I prefer any co-ordination equilibrium— and there are at least two co-ordination equilibria—to any combination of actions which is not a co-ordination equilibrium; I prefer to do X on condition that (or if and only if) the others will do X too. The conditionality is upon the actions of the others, and ultimately upon one's expectations concerning the others' actions. Put differently, the situation here is essentially not one of *choosing* the best alternative available; rather, it is a situation calling for *picking* one out of several alternatives with regard to which one is basically indifferent (in much the same way as one arbitrarily *picks*—rather than *chooses*—a piece of candy from among the more or less identical ones offered to one on a plate). The situation, then, is not one in which it is the case that there is a reason for one to choose x_1 rather than x_2, ..., x_n. Instead, it is the case that there is a reason for one to have to pick from among x_1, x_2, ..., x_n.[13] The problem posed, therefore, is that of concerting the agents' expectations, thereby co-ordinating their picked—rather than their chosen— actions.

Given the alternative courses of action open in a PD-type problem, on the other hand, the agents' preferences over them are unconditional. There is, as was pointed out above (Point 4), one action the choice of which dominates the choice of the other; hence this action is unconditionally preferred to the

[13] I am indebted to Sidney Morgenbesser for calling my attention to the picking–choosing distinction and to its relevance here.

alternative one, regardless of the choice of the other agents. The problem posed here, however, arises from the fact that the outcome obtained when all act on their unconditional preferences is collectively destructive.

The upshot of this is that there is this much in common between the two types of cases under consideration, that in both of them the maxim 'Choose what you prefer' (or, rather, 'choose that action which will produce the result you prefer'), as it stands, breaks down. They differ, however, with regard to the reason: in the co-ordination case it is because of the ambiguity of the situation and the conditionality of preferences; in the PD case it is because of the inherent paradox involved.

A further point of contrast implied by the structural differences between the two types of problems at hand can be appreciated on considering the potential role an explicit agreement might play in solving these problems. So for the sake of bringing out the contrast it will for a moment be assumed that in both of these problem-types communication among the participants is possible. In the case of a co-ordination problem an explicit agreement among the participants as to which of the co-ordination equilibria is to be aimed at directly solves the problem. Indeed it is perhaps the best method of solving co-ordination problems that can be wished for: an explicit agreement is undoubtedly the firmest rallier of the participants' expectations regarding each other's actions. Moreover, it is quite clear that such an agreement has a self-enforcing character, since its breach entails failure to meet the others at the co-ordination equilibrium agreed upon, and hence entails loss of some sort.

The point, then, is that an explicit agreement is a sufficient condition for solving a co-ordination problem. At the same time it is of course far from being a necessary one. A tacit agreement, or 'meeting of minds', is all that is needed; and I take Schelling's work to have shown most convincingly that its achievement, where *no* communication is possible, is not only feasible in principle but a matter of fact in everyday practice.

In a PD problem, on the other hand, it takes *more* than an explicit agreement— supposing, as we do, that communication among the participants is possible—to secure the achievement of the unique jointly satisfactory outcome. Due to the instability of this outcome, if an explicit agreement is to guarantee its coming about, it has to be backed by sanctions so severe as to outweigh the temptation to violate it which each participant must experience. In some cases the sanctions will be internal, finding expression in feelings of guilt, remorse, and shame; an explicit agreement supplemented by *trust* suffices to secure the achievement of the satisfactory outcome. In other cases the sanctions will have to be administered externally, and to involve material pains and penalties. In either event, however, it is the supplement of sanctions which is decisive; an explicit agreement which is not binding in the sense that it is not backed by appropriate sanctions is an insufficient condition for solving a PD problem satisfactorily.

To sum up: where an explicit agreement is feasible, the problematic aspect of the co-ordination case all but vanishes,[14] whereas in the PD case it may very well persist. It must be emphasized, though, that it is only with regard to an explicit agreement as a *sufficient* condition for solution that the difference between the two types of problems is brought out; in both cases alike an explicit agreement is not a necessary condition for a satisfactory solution.

5.3 *Implications of Structural Differences—Norms*

It is the basic contention of this study that norms are generated to solve such problems as those posed by situations of the Prisoners' Dilemma (PD-) and co-ordination variety. Having reviewed the structural differences between these two types of cases, as well as some of their implications regarding the nature of the problems involved, I shall now proceed to consider some differences between the corresponding norms themselves.

A co-ordination norm prescribes an action, or a type of action, such that, when performed by all of those involved in the pertinent recurrent co-ordination problem, a co-ordination equilibrium is achieved, to the (more or less) equal satisfaction of them all. Due to the characteristics of co-ordination problems, it is true of each of those involved that they desire to conform to the norm on condition that (almost) all the others do. Hence, *given* that the others will conform, each

---

[14] There might, however, be problems in arriving at an explicit agreement, especially where the number of persons involved is large. But these are costs of the agreement, not problems of co-ordination.

participant desires to conform too. Put in terms of preference rather than desire, each participant prefers a state where all conform, himself included, over a state where all conform, himself excepted. Also, each participant prefers the state of general conformity over the state of general non-conformity, in which no co-ordination equilibrium is achieved. There is, however, this much arbitrariness here, that the norm could have been different. It could have prescribed an alternative action open in the same recurrent co-ordination problem, such that, when it is performed by all, a (different) co-ordination equilibrium would still have been achieved: recall that in a co-ordination problem there are at least two (proper) co-ordination equilibria (Point 2 in the above list). The conditional desire of the participants to conform, or their preference for general conformity, would not be affected by this change at all.

Drawing the parallel argument for the PD case, we start by recalling that a PD norm prescribes an action, or a type of action, such that, when performed by those involved in the pertinent PD problem, the (unique) jointly satisfactory outcome is achieved. Due to the characteristics of PD problems, however, this outcome is unstable (it is not an equilibrium: Point 3 in the above list): each participant stands to gain should he alone violate the norm. Hence, in contrast with the co-ordination case, *given* that the others will comply with the norm, each participant desires—or at least is very much tempted—to violate it. Put in terms of preference rather than desire, each participant prefers a state where all comply, himself *excepted*, over a state where all comply, himself included. This preference is of course in strict contrast to the corresponding one in the co-ordination case. However, in the second preference considered above there is similarity rather than contrast: here, as well as in the co-ordination case, each participant prefers the state of general compliance over the state of general non-compliance which, in the PD case, brings about the outcome of joint loss.

Lastly, there is nothing arbitrary in a PD norm. It could not have been different in the sense of prescribing an alternative action, since, as said, it is such that, if complied with, it secures the achievement of the *unique* jointly satisfactory outcome.

The difference in the role played by the two types of norms might now be formulated thus: a co-ordination norm helps those involved 'meet' each other; a PD norm helps those involved protect themselves from damaging, even ruining, each other.

This formulation serves to bring out quite clearly the point that norms of the two types alike promote the interests of all the participants in the corresponding situations. Yet, on probing somewhat deeper, a considerable difference between them on this issue (alluded to on p. 103 above) comes to the surface. Suppose 'we' are the agents involved in turn in a co-ordination and in a PD problem. Conformity to a co-ordination norm is, within limits, in our individual as well as collective best interest. The qualification 'within limits' refers to the non-pure co-ordination cases where some of us might prefer a different co-ordination equilibrium to have been the actual outcome. We know, however, that these differences in preference are slight compared with the over-all preference of all of us for any co-ordination equilibrium over a state of no co-ordination equilibrium at all.

Compliance with a PD norm, on the other hand, while being in our collective best interest, necessarily secures an outcome which is only second best individually. The outcome which is each individual's first best, viz. that achieved through lone violation of the norm, is collectively unfeasible: in order to be a lone violator one can do no more than not comply with the norm in the hope that the others will. But if everyone does that the result is a state of general non-compliance which brings about the jointly ruinous outcome.

This point, in turn, serves to bring out another, familiar, one: that a co-ordination norm has a self-enforcing character which a PD norm totally lacks. It is the convergence of the individual and collective best interests which accounts for the presence of the self-enforcing property in the co-ordination case, and their divergence which accounts for its absence from the PD case. Compliance with a PD norm involves an element of renunciation: one gives up the prospect of attaining a state which is for one first best, and settles for an outcome which, although collectively best, is for one only second best. Let it be emphasized, though, that this renunciation should by no means be mistaken for *sacrifice*. By complying with the norm one does not sacrifice one's personal interests for those of the collective; one only averts a personal as well as a collective loss by giving up a prospect which, given the structure of the entire interaction situation, one must realize is not feasible. It seems that William Graham Summer's interesting concept of 'antagonistic co-operation' is of some pertinence here. Summer maintains that human agents, for ever motivated solely by self-interest, will nevertheless sometimes find it either necessary or beneficial to co-operate with each other, albeit reluctantly. He even maintains, furthermore, that this essentially is what lays the foundation to human society, rather than the existence in human beings of some (to him fictional) 'social instinct'. I would speculate that the occasions on which this 'antagonistic co-operation' occurs are PD-structured. I would also venture to speculate that these same situations correspond to those in which J. O. Urmson's 'basic duties' arise (see p. 38 n., above).

However, the temptation to violate a PD norm—with the hope of being a lone violator—is of necessity always there. This state of affairs is, as said, in marked contrast with the case of co-ordination norms. Hence the inherently different role of sanctions in backing the two types of norms. In the co-ordination case sanctions play only a secondary role. Their existence, and the general awareness of their existence, might enhance the salience of the particular co-ordination equilibrium the norm is aimed at attaining, thereby increasing the effectiveness of the norm itself. But above all the mere act of non-conformity to a co-ordination norm (when the others do conform) is its own punishment, since it entails failure to meet the others at the prescribed co-ordination equilibrium.

In the PD case, on the other hand, sanctions play a more important and primary role. Their existence, their effective application, and the general awareness of their existence and their being effectively applied are essential for the dissolution of the PD problem in that they amount to eliminating the temptation to violate the norm by making violation too costly.

The terminological distinction, used throughout the foregoing discussion, between conformity to a co-ordination norm and compliance with a PD norm, was intended to underline the contrast between the two types of norms with regard to the issues of self-enforcement and the role of sanctions (see p. 89 above).

5.4 *Intermediary Case—The Stag Hunt*

So far the focus of the comparison between the co-ordination and the PD cases has been that of contrast. But can these two cases also meet on some common ground? I shall argue that they can. Recall that the first point on the list of structural differences between the two types of problems (p. 114 above) was in fact that they lie in different areas of the spectrum of interdependent-decision problems. Being more or less a continuum, however, this spectrum must allow, at least in principle, for intermediary problems: cases which lie somewhere between the strict PD problems and the strict common-interest problems of the co-ordination variety, and which can therefore be expected to partake of the features of both.

An interesting case in point, which merits discussion in some detail, is provided by Rousseau's story of the stag-hunt.[15] This is how David Lewis presents it as a co-ordination problem:

Suppose we are in the wilderness without food. Separately we can catch rabbits and eat badly. Together we can catch stags and eat well. But if even one of us deserts the stag hunt to catch a rabbit, the stag will get away; so the other stag hunters will not eat unless they desert too. Each must choose whether to stay with the stag hunt or desert according to his expectations about the others, staying if and only if no one else will desert. (1969, p. 7.)

Although Lewis treats this example on a par with his other paradigm cases of co-ordination problems, it is nevertheless a co-ordination problem with a difference. To appreciate the structure of this situation, let us first draw its two-person matrix representation (3.11) (where 's' stands for 'stag-hunt' and 'r' for 'rabbit-catching').

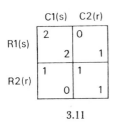

3.11

However, since the two-person case is a somewhat distorted version of the given story, I deem it

---

[15] 'If a deer was to be taken, everyone saw that, in order to succeed, he must abide faithfully by his post; but if a hare happened to come within the reach of them, it is not to be doubted that he pursued it without scruple, and, having seized his prey, cared very little, if by so doing he caused his companions to miss theirs' (p. 349).

appropriate to draw a matrix representation for the three-person case too (3.12) (where the third person's choices are called *levels* L1 and L2, and his pay-offs are indicated in the centres of the cells. Row-Chooser's pay-offs are, as usual, at the top left and Column-Chooser's at the bottom right of each cell).[16]

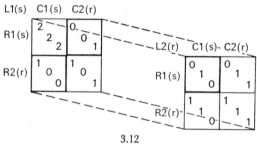

3.12

The difference between this case and ordinary co-ordination problems can be pinned down to Point 4 on the above-given list of structural features (p. 114) : there is here a choice of action, viz. rabbit-catching, which offers a maximum security level. Note, though, that this maximum security level choice is not a dominant choice of action, since in the eventuality that all the others choose to go on a stag-hunt, one had best hunt stags too. The existence of such a safe choice of action is what accounts for the fact that the present case is not a co-ordination problem proper. Although it has, formally, two proper co-ordination equilibria, the achievement of only one of them, i.e. the stag-hunt, requires co-ordination of expectations and actions in the familiar sense. A rabbit, on the other hand, can be caught by each on his own. That is, the pay-off secured by the second co-ordination equilibrium can be had independently of the others' actions and hence independently of one's expectations of the others' actions.

So in spite of the fact that the present case differs from a PD problem in that the choice of maximum security level here is not a dominant choice of action, it nevertheless bears a strong similarity to it. In both cases it makes sense to speak of a strategy

[16] The three-person representation serves to bring out the distinguishing feature of this case: that co-ordination can be achieved only when *all* (in this case all three) co-operate. All minus one will not do, as is clearly depicted by the thick cells.

of co-operation versus a strategy of desertion; in both cases joint co-operation results in an outcome good for all and joint desertion results in an outcome bad (or worse) for all; in both cases being the only one to choose co-operation results in the worst outcome available. The paramount difference between the two cases seems to be that in the stag-hunt case, unlike the PD case, joint co-operation produces an outcome which, being a (proper co-ordination) equilibrium, is stable. In other words, in the present case there is no temptation to deviate from the outcome produced by general co-operation; indeed each stands actually to lose by being a lone deviator.

However, this difference diminishes considerably once the stag-hunt case is compared to a recurrent (or continuous) PD problem rather than to discrete ones. In a recurrent PD problem joint co-operation is an equilibrium. More precisely, an equilibrium is produced when all involved act on the following contingency plan: stick to your co-operative choice of action unless—and until—your opponent defects, in which case you defect too in the next occurrence of the problem among you. When all act on this contingency plan the combination of the agents' chosen actions is stable: no one wishes he had chosen differently, given the others' choice. But note that this contingency plan does not necessarily perpetuate co-operation: there is always the chance that joint defection would, for some reason, be triggered off by someone; and joint defection *is*, on the contingency plan in question, self-perpetuating. So the strongest claim that can be made in this connection is that in a recurrent (continuous) PD problem joint co-operation enjoys what might be termed *precarious stability*: it is stable pending any one's defection.

But this is also very much the case with the stag-hunt situation. As said above, joint co-operation here is, formally, a (proper co-ordination) equilibrium and hence stable in the sense that no one is tempted to desert. But this stability is in fact precarious too. For if anyone suspects, justifiably or not, that even one of the others might opt for the safe choice of desertion, he will desert too. So here joint co-operation is stable pending not just anyone's actual desertion, but pending anyone's belief, or even suspicion, that someone will desert.

The close relation between the recurrent PD situation and

the stag-hunt case may be further clarified by pointing out
that the former can in fact turn into the latter given, first,
a general belief that people's choices will display some habitual
stability and, second, a favourable starting-point where co-
operation has somehow been initially established.

We are now in a position to realize that what the stag-hunt
case essentially has in common with PD problems is that in both
the jointly satisfactory outcome produced by joint co-operation
stands in need of some assistance. Whether achieved through
explicit or through tacit agreement, joint co-operation has in
both cases to be sustained either by the existence of trust among
those involved, or by their feeling themselves under some kind
of obligation to keep co-operating (such as keeping a promise—
explicit or tacit, reciprocating fair play, etc.), or, alternatively,
by effective external sanctions.

So in situations of the stag-hunt type, too, it might be expected
that norms will be generated, which would help fortify the
state of social optimum produced by general co-operation.
Such norms are likely to be closer, in nature and function, to
PD norms than to co-ordination norms. Note however that
whereas a PD norm is there to outweigh the dominance of an
alternative course of action and to eliminate temptation,
a norm of the stag-hunt type has the more modest task of
countervailing the lesser advantage enjoyed by the pertinent
alternative course of action, i.e. its guaranteeing a maximum
security level. That is to say, in stag-hunt cases a weaker norm
will do the trick than would be required in a pure PD case.

It seems worth while to recall at this point the situation of
a disciplined army unit discussed above (Ch. II Sec. 5.3) and
to realize that it is in fact a stag-hunt case, from the point of
view of its structure. And indeed, it was shown there that the
mere knowledge that the members of the unit are disciplined
served to eliminate effectively the option of desertion, whereas
in the pure PD version of the same story the rather harsher
devices of mine-laying, or of chaining gunners to their guns,
were required to achieve the same objective.

5.4.1 *An Example*

I would like at this point to offer an example, putting forward
the claim that the liberal argument for free trade *vis-à-vis*

autarky is underlain by a conception of the macro-economic situation as essentially analogous to the stag-hunt case. On this conception, each economy is ideally supposed to face a choice between two very crude alternatives: either to be autarkic, i.e., to produce on its own all—or almost all—of its needs, or to specialize in those products only in which it enjoys a comparative advantage over other economies and to rely on free trade for the selling of its products and the purchasing of its needs. To opt for autarky means for an economy to go it alone; it is thus analogous to individual rabbit-catching. To opt for specialization and free trade means dependence on other economies and requires co-operation with them. The liberal assumption is that the general level of welfare is higher in the state of specialization based on unhindered trade than in the autarkic state. This option, then, is analogous to that of going on a stag-hunt together.

But in order for the analogy to really hold, it must be shown why it is not trivially and obviously the case that the state of free trade always prevails. In other words, it has to be pointed out what can possibly weigh in favour of autarky in such a way as would account for there being a *problem* here similar in kind to that of the stag-hunt case.

Well, for one thing there is the consideration that while an economy geared to free trade might fare well in times of peace, an autarkic or near-autarkic economy is *safer* once the eventuality of hostilities and war is taken into account. This falls neatly into line with the consideration of maximum security level which weighs in favour of individual rabbit-catching.

But there is another point to which there is no parallel in the stag-hunt case. Whereas in the stag-hunt case the persons involved are envisaged as making their deliberation *before* entering the game, in the present case the starting-point is already from *within*, so to speak. That is, it happens to be historically the case that manors and states have been managing autarkic rather than specialized economies: there has already been, then, a *status quo* from the outset—that of 'catching rabbits'. And a stable *status quo* always enjoys an advantage over any alternative state, even where an alternative one should—at least in the long run—prove to be better.

Furthermore, 'an economy' is a unit composed of a large

number of individuals, among which the 'stags' or the 'rabbits' have to be distributed. And while it might be true that a state of free trade is better, for the economy as a whole, than a state of autarky, there will be those whose share of the 'rabbits' is larger—at least in the short or the middle term—than their prospective share of the 'stag', and who will have therefore considerable vested interests in maintaining the *status quo*.

This in fact accounts for the complicated arrays of customs barriers and legislation, aimed at protecting local products, which have evolved with the years in principalities and states. A prominent case in point is the English Corn Laws, which protected the high price of the English corn by imposing enormous customs duty on imported grains, thus working in the interests of the minority of powerful landowners.

And of course the successful Manchester League campaign in the 1840s to change these laws, indeed to annul them, might be taken as a prominent example of an actual piece of legislation aimed at putting into practice that segment of the liberal ideology of *laissez-faire* which required trade to be free from restrictions of tax and customs. It is noteworthy that this case is peculiar in that the norms (in this case laws) intended to achieve and to fortify the state of free trade, assumed here to be analogous to the state of collective stag-hunting, have historically had to be ones which come about to annul existing laws and regulations which restricted trade. In this respect it might be argued that these particular norms are derivative norms rather than original ones.[17]

[There is however an important point on which the proposed analogy breaks down. In the stag and rabbits case if even one of the group abandons the stag-hunt, the stag gets away. Thus, while one's best choice is to hunt—and catch—a stag, if one has a reasonably well-founded suspicion that at least one of the others will indeed abandon the stag-hunt, one's second-best choice is clearly defined by the situation: to abandon the stag-hunt and chase a rabbit on one's own instead. In the present case, on the other hand, the situation is different. According to the liberal theoreticians (Friedman, Samuelson), even if some economies insist on producing autarkically and on protecting their own products by customs barriers, the second-best choice

<hr>

[17] For the distinction see Hart (1961), pp. 78 f. and Raz (1970), p. 61.

for the other economies would be to act *as if* everyone was pursuing the policy of specialization and free trade; i.e. to pursue it none the less rather than to abandon it altogether.

In other words, the liberal assumption here falls into line with the one tacitly underlying many discussions in ethics: even where it is clear that a certain ideal (moral or otherwise) cannot, owing to our limitations as humans, be attained, the 'second best' for us is to behave *as if* we were angels free from these limitations and to approach the ideal as much as we can. There is, however, an opposing approach[18] according to which it is not necessarily the case that the optimal approximation to an ideal will always be achieved through the 'as if' strategy. Rather, there will be cases in which employing an altogether *different* strategy would carry us closer to the unattainable goal than would the 'as if' strategy. To take a crude example: suppose you have two barometers, A and B, and that A is usually more accurate than B. When you know A to be out of order, however, it is reasonable to assume that you will consider it wiser to use B rather than to rely on the approximation yielded by A.

The realm of morality is, admittedly, more complicated than that, and it is difficult to generalize as to a 'second-best strategy' pertinent to it. But I think that there is a rather good case for the claim that the 'as if' strategy should not be uncritically taken for granted, and that wherever it is employed it should be given an independent and explicit justification.]

5.5 *The Oligopolists' Problem*

The importance of the stag-hunt case lay in its being an intermediary case between PD and co-ordination problems. I would like, finally, to discuss briefly a case which is also connected with both of these problem-types, but in a different way; roughly: it presents a co-ordination problem which is underlain by an unresolved PD problem.

Consider the case of oligopolists, a relatively small number of producers who dominate the supply of a certain product.

---

[18] See (1) Lipsey, R. G. & K. J. Lancaster, 'The General Theory of Second Best'; *Review of Economic Studies*, 1956–7. (2) Bohm, P., 'On the Theory of "Second Best" '; *Review of Economic Studies*, 1967.

Assuming that the demand curve is inelastic, and somewhat idealizing, we may consider each of the oligopolists to be essentially facing a choice between the following two alternatives: to maintain prices at their current level, or to reduce them. He who is alone in reducing his prices gains the lion's share of the market and profits at the expense of the others. If all of them reduce prices, however, then individually they fare worse than they would have had they maintained the original price level. (It is at this point that the inelasticity of the demand is essential.)

The oligopolists' situation is basically, then, of the Prisoners' Dilemma type (see Chapter II, Section 7.2, above). Their dilemma will quite obviously be resolved once they form a cartel, i.e. once there is a binding agreement among them to maintain their prices at a certain fixed level. But such an agreement, which is a PD norm among the oligopolists, goes against the interests of the community of consumers, and is forbidden, by means of various anti-trust laws, in many Western countries. In other words, in these countries oligopolists are prevented, by explicit state laws, from coming into an explicit binding agreement among themselves which would solve their PD problem.

What they cannot be prevented from, though, is the achievement of some kind of an implicit understanding, the reaching of some kind of a *tacit* agreement, as to a certain range of what would be considered by them permissible price fluctuations, instead of explicitly fixing on a precise uniform price for their product. When to this is added the complication that as prices of raw materials vary each of the oligopolists has to set his prices anew, it is quite clear that what we have on our hands is a recurrent co-ordination problem: each must set his prices according to his expectations of the others' range of prices, and, also, each must reconsider his prices whenever he expects the others to be reconsidering theirs. (Indeed, the co-ordination version of the oligopolists' problem is one of David Lewis's paradigm cases of co-ordination problems (1969, pp. 6–7, 46–7).)

To sum up, then: the oligopolists' case points out the possibility of a PD problem being transformed into a co-ordination problem. When an explicit agreement which would solve the

PD problem is not feasible—in the present case outlawed—the persons involved, rather than lock themselves in a ruinous price war, can do much better by coming to a tacit understanding, that is, by perceiving their situation to be in effect posing a co-ordination problem. Note that this case also helps underline another point: that a co-ordination problem need not involve the entire society but might be confined to a limited section thereof, and, moreover, that the (normative) solution to it does not necessarily promote integration, harmony, and in general the good of society as a whole. In other words, social integration and harmony are not, on the present analysis, part of the connotations of co-ordination norms.

6. *Co-ordination and Co-operation*

The concepts of co-operation and co-ordination are commonly linked, and frequently treated as interchangeable. My aim in this section is to straighten out what I conceive to be the relation between these two concepts. My account of co-ordination norms will thereby gain, I believe, a further perspective it lacked so far.

Let us begin by examining the following simple case.[19] Inside a large bottle there are several cone-shaped objects. Each of a group of participants holds a string tied to one such cone. Their aim is to withdraw the cones from the bottle, the shape of the objects being such that only one cone can be drawn out at a time. In order to underline the features of the co-operative version of this game let us first consider a competitive version thereof. The discussion will be confined to the two-person cases which lend themselves most readily to a convenient matrix representation; the generalization to the n-person cases, where n is larger than two, is straightforward. In the two-person competitive version, the one who withdraws his cone first wins, and the other has to pay him a penny. If both pull together there is a 'traffic jam' in the neck of the bottle and neither wins; a stalemate also results when both wait. The situation, then, is one of pure conflict, and can be presented by the zero-sum matrix (3.13).

19 This case is based on an experiment by A. Mintz (1951). The experiment is discussed by Thibaut and Kelley in a section called 'Correspondence Versus Non-correspondence of Outcomes' (1959, pp. 165–6).

In the co-operation version of the game, on the other hand, each of the participants is rewarded if they all succeed in removing all the cones from the bottle within a certain time limit (or if they succeed in beating the time record of another group). This is a co-operative goal, the attainment of which is within the participants' collective power and in the interest of each. The situation is thus directly transformed into a (pure) co-ordination problem. Each will decide whether to wait or to pull according to his expectations of what the others will do: to pull if and only if all the others will wait, to wait otherwise.[20]

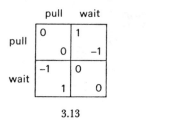

3.13

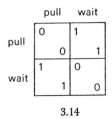

3.14

The matrix representation for the two-person case will be 3.14. A closer-to-life example of the same case is that of escaping from a theatre caught on fire. If the fire spreads at such a speed that only a few will get out, it is a case of competition; if it is such that all will get out provided the evacuation is orderly, it is a case of co-operation (co-ordination). There are also mixed cases: (a) where even if the evacuation is orderly most but not all will escape (Dunkirk comes readily to mind); (b) where one does not know which of the above descriptions holds.[21]

With this example in mind I shall now make explicit what I mean by a co-operative goal. A *co-operative goal*, with respect to a certain group of agents, is a goal G such that

    (1) it is in the interest of each agent that G be attained;
    (2) G is attainable by none of the agents alone;

---

[20] In the general, *n*-person case, the situation turns in fact into a sequence of *n*−1 co-ordination problems: in the first there are *n* co-ordination equilibria in each of which *n*−1 persons wait and one person pulls; in the second there are already *n*−1 participants left, and hence *n*−1 co-ordination equilibria in each of which *n*−2 persons wait and one pulls, and so on. The last member of the sequence will always be the two-person problem represented by matrix 3.14. Once *it* is solved, the last person just pulls out his cone.

[21] For this example I am indebted to John Mackie.

(3) G is attainable by all the agents together, given appropriate planning and division of roles among them.

An attempt by a group of agents to take joint action so as to attain a co-operative goal will be referred to as a *case of co-operation*.

On examining the above conditions, a few clarifying remarks are in order. First, with regard to condition (1), it should be made clear that the agents' motives for being interested in the attainment of G need not be identical; they might be diverse. When the residents of a certain neighbourhood, say, join action with the local police in laying traps for the thieves who plague the area, the former are presumably motivated by a desire to sleep in peace while the latter might be driven by a desire to restore their (independently) damaged reputation; the case will nevertheless qualify as one of co-operation. Where the agents' motives *are* identical—as in the above example of the cones in the bottle—one might wish to speak of a *collective goal*, collective goals thus constituting a special case of co-operative ones.

Secondly, with regard to condition (2), a distinction should be made between the case where G is such that it is *logically* impossible for any single agent to attain it on his own, e.g. when G is a meeting of all the persons involved, or the removing of all the cones from the bottle, and the case where G is such that it is *physically* (or technically) impossible for any single agent to attain it on his own, e.g. where G is the rolling of a big stone off the mouth of a well (see Genesis 29:1–9).

But even the requirement that the attainment of G be absolutely beyond the power of any single agent is certainly too strong. It should be hedged to allow for the task being merely too difficult, or too costly (in terms of time, for instance), for any one agent to attempt its performance on his own.

We come now upon condition (3), and this is where co-ordination enters the picture. This condition amounts in effect to stating that appropriate co-ordination of the agents' actions, in the most common non-technical sense of the term 'co-ordination', is a prerequisite for the successful attainment of a co-operative goal. Or, in other words, that co-ordination of actions is a condition of success for co-operation.

Admittedly, however, not *all* the cases of co-operation one can think of involve co-ordination problems the structure of which is revealed on analysis to fit naturally into the structural pattern of the rather specific co-ordination problem—call them co-ordination problems proper—dealt with in this study. Furthermore, of those that *do*, the co-ordination problems concerned are not always recurrent, or even potentially recurrent, ones. And since our co-ordination norms have to do only with recurrent co-ordination problems proper, the conclusion is that by no means do all cases of co-operation involve co-ordination norms.

But there will be cases of repetitive co-operation, where a prerequisite for the successful attainment of a repetitive co-operative goal is the achievement of a solution to problems which direction each is to take, what fire-hose each is to use recurrent co-ordination problems proper. In such cases a co-ordination norm, in so far as it guarantees concerted action, is conducive to the attainment of the co-operative goal concerned. I am thinking of cases such as the conventions among, or standing orders to, air-raid wardens who seek to co-ordinate their actions so as to attain the objective of getting everyone into the air-raid shelters as soon as the sirens are sounded; the conventions among, or standing orders to, firemen with regard to which direction each is to take, what fire-hose each is to use etc. so as to put the fire out as quickly as possible, and the like.

To the charge that these examples are not entirely convincing, and perhaps somewhat trivial, I shall reply thus: co-ordination norms are more interesting the larger the community within which they hold. But as the size of the community increases, so does the degree of vagueness of its co-operative goals. So that with regard to any concrete example one is likely to feel either that what is taken to be a co-operative goal is questionable, or that the instrumental co-ordination norms are trivial. And yet, in spite of the inherent difficulty in providing a convincing, clear-cut example, the conceptual relation between the two as outlined above is, in my opinion, worth upholding.

It has been pointed out above (p. 100) that co-ordination norms bear an affinity with technical norms in that they serve as means to an end, the end being the achievement of co-ordination (i.e. the convergence of everyone's choice of action on one particular co-ordination equilibrium). We are now in a position to go one step further and observe that often the achievement of co-ordination is itself but a means to a further, ultimate end: that of attaining a co-operative goal. Thus, safety on the road, speedy restoration of communication, maintenance of a monetary rather than a barter system—such will be the co-operative goals served by the existence and effectiveness of the appropriate co-ordination norms familiar to us from the various examples given throughout this chapter.

The temptation to strengthen the claim just made, by saying that any co-ordination equilibrium, pointed at by some co-ordination norm, is of necessity a means to the attainment of some co-operative goal should, however, be resisted. A co-ordination norm prescribing type of dress for formal (or, for that matter, any other) social occasions might serve as a counter-example: the co-ordination equilibria will in this case be the various states in which all are dressed alike and no one is embarrassed, and the co-ordination achieved in each of them seems to be an end in itself. It would require too long a stretch of imagination, or of the ordinary sense of the relevant terms, were it to be maintained that there is some distinct co-operative goal promoted by this particular case of co-ordination. Norms of co-ordination, then, are norms concerning means to certain ends, whether the ends be the attainment of some distinct co-operative goal, or the mere achievement of the peculiar sort of harmony and accord concurrent with a state of co-ordination equilibrium.

IV

NORMS OF PARTIALITY

1. *Status Quo of Inequality*

1.1 *Presentation*

T H E starting-point for the discussion is a *status quo* involving two parties (persons or aggregates of persons) such that one party is more favourably placed than the other. It will be referred to as a *status quo of inequality*. Alternative ways of describing it: one party to the situation is privileged and the other under-privileged; one party 'gets more out of' the situation than does the other; the benefits of the situation are unequally distributed between the two parties. It will be left open just what is un-equally distributed in the *status quo* of inequality. It might be anything which is desirable, competed for, and scarce. Thus, it might be economic resources, authority positions, or access to sources of force, power, or information.

Two things are to be noted about a *status quo* of inequality thus characterized. First, the distinction between the favoured party and the underdog is relative, not absolute; it concerns those who have (derive, enjoy) more versus those who have (derive, enjoy) less, rather than 'haves' versus 'have nots'. Second, the two parties are not assumed from the outset to stand in any particular relation to each other: no relation of exploita-tion, or of authority and subordination, or of domination and subjection, or the like, is presupposed by the notion of a *status quo* of inequality. Indeed it is not even presupposed that the two parties are in conflict. This, then, is the concept, based on minimal assumptions, of a *status quo* of inequality with which we shall start. The question of the existence of such inequality states is left open: we may regard it as a hypothesis. My con-cern is an analysis of these states, hypothetical or otherwise, which will, with the introduction of further assumptions along the way, lead us to such notions as conflict, coercion, and norms. The question of how such states come about in the first place, or from what such states result, is however of no concern to us here.

Of course, this is not to argue that such a question is without its point. Indeed it can be argued (see, e.g., Dahrendorf, 1962) that the question of the origins of inequality has historically been the first question asked by social thinkers, and, furthermore, that 'by surveying the various attempts to answer it a whole history of sociological thought might be written' (ibid., p. 89). In attempting to answer it, however, these thinkers had variously fallen back on such notions as private property (Rousseau, Marx), the division of labour (Lorenz von Stein, and again Marx), functional imperatives (Parsons), and even on the very notions of norms and sanctions (Dahrendorf). The last attempt, that of accounting for the origin of inequality in terms of norms and sanctions, has direct bearing on the present study and therefore deserves our attention.

1.2 *Dahrendorf's Derivation of Social Inequality*

In his article 'On the Origin of Social Inequality' (cited above) Ralf Dahrendorf purports to 'derive' social inequality from the existence of social norms backed by sanctions. The steps of the derivation are the following:

(i) Every human society (following Durkheim) is a moral community.

(ii) The conduct of its members is therefore regulated by 'established and inescapable' expectations, or norms (the latter terms are often used by Dahrendorf as interchangeable).

(iii) To guarantee the obligatory character of these norms there have to be sanctions which reward conformism and punish deviance.

(iv) Wherever behaviour is regulated by and measured in terms of established norms, and wherever these norms are backed by sanctions, 'a rank order of social status is bound to emerge' (p. 102).

The crucial step in the derivation is, clearly, the last one. Let us examine a little closer Dahrendorf's formulations of this almost analytic ('necessary', 'immediate'—p. 103) connection between the sanctioning of human behaviour in terms of social norms on the one hand, and the emergence of a system of inequality of rank on the other. When he first introduces the idea, Dahrendorf says: 'If, however, every society is in this sense [the sense explained above—steps (i)-(iii)] a moral community, it follows that there must always be at least that inequality of rank which results from the necessity of sanctioning behaviour according to whether it does or does not conform to established norms' (p. 100). And a little later: '. . . the hard core of social inequality can always be found in the fact that men are subject, according to their attitude to the expectations of their society, to sanctions which guarantee the obligatory character of these expectations' (p. 100).

These 'explanations' leave it, it seems to me, extremely vague just where the causal relation lies: is the inequality a result of the fact that wherever there are sanctions there is inevitably a stratum of punishers and rewarders as opposed to a stratum of punished and rewarded? Or, alternatively, does it result from the fact that wherever there are norms there are inevitably those who cannot, or would not, conform?

If the former interpretation is correct, then what is it that groups the punishers and the punished together into two fixed lasting strata? Is it not the case that each norm may be associated with its own, *ad hoc*, punishers and punished? Thus, to continue Dahrendorf's own examples, the career woman who is 'punished' by her female neighbours for not taking part in their gossip, which is the norm among them, may nevertheless belong to a group of 'punishers' owing to her being among the most eloquent in defending the ideology of the state—where to defend this ideology whenever it is attacked is another norm in her community.

If, on the other hand, the latter interpretation is the correct one, as is perhaps suggested by Dahrendorf's examples, one may go on and question the status of the 'fact' mentioned in it: is it *empirically* true that there are deviators to any given norm? Or is it perhaps a hypothesis concerning human nature? Can there really be no norms to which there is virtually general conformity, or that the cases of deviance from them are too marginal and insignificant to account for the establishment of social stratification? And, again, even granted this 'fact', one is still left with the same difficulty which related to the first interpretation: each norm may have its own groups of conformers and deviators, but just what is it that unites the conformers and deviators of all (most?) norms into the 'lasting structures of social positions' which Dahrendorf sets out to explain?

All these questions and queries point to the problematic and unsatisfactory aspects of the derivation Dahrendorf professes to have achieved. Independently of the ways in which these difficulties could perhaps be settled, however, there remains the fundamental question regarding Dahrendorf's entire programme. Of it he says explicitly: '. . . the derivation [of social stratification] suggested here has the advantage of leading back to presuppositions (the existence of norms and the necessity of sanctions) which at least in the context of sociological theory may be regarded as axiomatic, and which do not therefore require further analysis for the time being' (p. 104). It is precisely this 'advantage' which I wish to challenge. I do not know whether it is indeed a matter of common agreement among sociologists to accept 'the existence of norms and the necessity of sanctions' as axiomatic. It seems to me, however, that to presuppose that is to presuppose a lot; a whole theory in fact. And if one does not supply any theory which accounts for the origin of these norms, their nature, the conditions under which they are formed and changed etc., one must be relying on some intuition which is supposed to lend the whole idea of the existence of norms an air of obviousness, plausibility, and familiarity.

This, however, must seriously be questioned. In what sense is social inequality 'explained' if the explanation ultimately draws on an intuitive acceptance of the existence of norms and the necessity of sanctions? Is the latter set of assumptions really that much more 'familiar' to us than the notion of social inequality as to justify taking norms and sanctions as the *explanans* and social inequality as the *explanandum*?

To be sure, it is not a sound methodological principle to require that the *explanans* be always more 'familiar' (in some specified sense) to us than the *explanandum*. We accept, for instance, explanations for the familiar physical world in terms of such remote, and sometimes abstract, concepts as electrons, genes, etc. In such cases, however, the *explanans* is a whole *theory*, which is taken to be better than all the alternative theories purporting to explain the same *explanandum* on the basis of various considerations and experiments. In cases like the present one, on the other hand, there being no theory and other things being equal, it *is* correct, I feel, to lay down the principle that an explanation should draw on concepts and principles more firmly established to explain the more questionable ones. In this respect I contend that it makes little sense to base one's account of inequality on the notions of norms and sanctions the way Dahrendorf does; the more so as the crucial step in his 'derivation' was found to be highly questionable.

My own aim in what follows is, in fact, in broad outline very much the opposite of Dahrendorf's programme: I shall start with the notion of inequality as introduced above, which I take to be as simple, familiar, and little loaded a notion as any, and attempt to construct upon it a conceptual scaffolding capable of accommodating, among other notions, that of norms. Let it be emphasized in this connection, finally, that the notion of a *status quo* of inequality differs from the notion of social inequality (or social stratification) as used by the social theorists in that it does not necessarily presuppose the entire social scene: the parties sharing it may range from individuals, through families, groups, firms, etc., to social classes and to states. Nor is it intended, for that matter, to imply a sociological context exclusively: it may relate to economic or military contexts too.

In sum: having decided to take a certain notion of inequality as the starting-point for the discussion, the legitimacy of the question concerning the origin of social inequality in general has been acknowledged. Of the various answers given it, Dahrendorf's drew our attention since in a sense the programme underlying it is just the opposite of the programme I set out to achieve here: he explains social inequality in terms of norms and sanctions. On examining his analysis, however, an important link in his purported derivation, as well as the methodology of his entire programme, was found to be seriously wanting. Furthermore, attention was also paid to the fact that my concept of a *status quo* of inequality is different from the concept of social inequality dealt with by Dahrendorf (as well as by other theorists), in its involving virtually no presuppositions and thereby in its being of a more general nature.

2. *The Disfavourably Placed Party*

I introduce now the first hypothesis concerning the *status quo* of inequality: the disfavourably placed party will attempt to improve his position. The conditions which must be met if this hypothesis is to hold are the following:

(1) The disfavourably placed party is *aware* of his being disfavourably placed in comparison with the other party to the situation. That is, he is assumed to possess correct knowledge of, or adequate information about, his own position in the situation.

(2) Realizing his inferior position, the disfavourably placed party is *interested* in a change in the situation such that his position in it will improve: he is assumed to be self-interestedly motivated.

The spelling out of this condition, obvious as it may seem, is important in that it precludes possible alternative attitudes on behalf of the underdog: an attitude of apathy, or a fatalistic belief that a change can ultimately work only for the worse and that it is therefore best to cling to whatever he has in the situation as it is, or of accepting his inferior position as part of the 'natural order of things' he can do nothing about.

(3) Not only is he taken to be interested in improving his position, he is also assumed to be willing to *act* on his interests and actively to attempt to further them.

The conjunction of the conditions 1–3, with various possible modifications, is often taken to be tantamount to an assumption of *rationality*. However, I wish at the moment to do no more than just draw attention to this point: what I shall have to say presently will be at some variance with received views of rational behaviour, so that this topic will soon be returned to. The hypothesis of attempting to improve an inferior position is straightforward enough as long as the 'party' under discussion is made up of a single individual. But how does it fare when the 'party' is in fact a large group? Are the conditions 1–3 still meaningful in this case? Or do we need to change our terminology?

Talk of group (or class) awareness, or 'consciousness', of group (or class) interests of various kinds, and of groups (or classes) acting on behalf of their common interests to further their common goal is, to be sure, abundant in sociological, economic, and political writings. This, though, does not testify to the lack of problems connected with the use of such concepts and expressions. The main problem is, of course, how to arrive at—and to account for—the aggregate awareness, interests, and actions of individuals. Closely related to this problem is the question of outlook and methodology: a collectivist approach to the group concepts is bound, for instance, to regard any answer given to the problem of aggregation by an adherent of the individualistic approach as committing the fallacy of composition, whereas the latter will surely accuse any answer given by the former of metaphysical reification.

However, independently of what solution is adopted for the problem of aggregation, I shall assume that in any specific context some such solution can be, and in fact is, adopted. Consequently, I shall assume that in any specific context some content and meaning is given to the group concepts in question, and that therefore we may go on talking of the disfavourably placed party's awareness, interests, and actions regardless of whether the 'party' denotes individuals or groups. (I shall in what follows use the pronoun 'he' for 'party'. This is for convenience only; it should be taken to prejudge the issue neither of the size of this party, nor of its sex.)

There is another interesting problem concerning the issue in hand which merits mentioning. It is dealt with as part of Olson's main thesis as developed in his book *The Logic of Collective Action* (1965). Olson argues there that from the assumption that individuals, in a group, act out of self-interest to further their individual objectives, it does *not* follow, as is usually taken for granted, that groups of individuals will act to achieve their common or group interests. Indeed, he even goes much further and states that 'unless the number of individuals in a group is quite small, or unless there is coercion or some other special device to make individuals act in their common interest, *rational, self-interested individuals will not act to achieve their common or group interests*' (p. 2, italics in original).

The main relevance of Olson's thesis is, to be sure, to the discussion of PD norms. It suggests, in fact, viewing PD norms as the 'special device' needed to make individual members of a group ignore their distributively rational choices which inevitably lead to a bad result for all. This device will thus make them act in their group interest (which happens to coincide with their individual interests, given that they just have to settle for second best, as the best results for each are necessarily different and incompatible states of affairs). As to the present context, it suggests making the case that if the parties in a *status quo* of inequality consist of large groups, the prevalence of certain PD norms among the members of the disfavourably placed party might be necessary in order to guarantee their acting in their common interest.

In any event, Olson's thesis points out a potential source of difficulty connected with our hypothesis that the underdog will attempt to improve his position: when large groups are involved, then, according to Olson, the fact that the members of a party are aware of their inferior position and the fact that they realize that it is in their interest to change the situation so that their position in it is improved do *not* jointly suffice, in general, to make them in fact *act* on this interest. That is, in the case of large groups, it is claimed that condition 3 is quite independent of conditions 1 and 2; even when the latter pair are met, 'special devices' might nevertheless be needed to ensure that condition 3 is met too.

3. *Improvement of Absolute Position*

The hypothesis that the disfavourably placed party will attempt to improve his position can be given two distinct interpretations: it may refer to *absolute* improvement of position, or to *relative* improvement of position. Given that one can rank-order alternative states of affairs according to one's preferences over them, and provided that this ordering is done with regard to one's *own* position in each of these states regardless of the positions in them of the others, then an absolute improvement of one's position will be a transition from the *status quo* to another state which ranks higher on one's preference ordering than does the *status quo*. Put otherwise, given that one can assign one's own position in each of the alternative states of affairs a certain pay-off on some ordinal scale, and that these pay-offs are determined independently of the pay-offs of any of the other parties to these states, then one will be said to have improved one's absolute position if one made a transition from the *status quo* to a state with a higher pay-off for oneself.

An improvement of one's relative position, on the other hand, will be such as does take into account the positions of, or the pay-offs to, the other parties to the situation. It will be discussed in the next section.

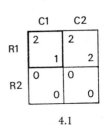

4.1

To take a simple example, suppose the situation is as depicted in the two-person two-choice matrix (4.1).

Suppose now that for some ('historical') reasons the prevailing *status quo* is the state represented by the thickened top-left cell, R1–C1. The *status quo* is, then, one of inequality, with Row-Chooser as the favoured party (with a pay-off of 2 as against 1 to Column-Chooser). Now if Row-Chooser were to remain at R1 while Column-Chooser switched to C2, then Column-Chooser, the disfavourably placed party, will have improved his absolute position—his pay-off being raised from 1 to 2. Row-Chooser's absolute position would in this case remain unchanged. (If Row-Chooser were to move from the *status quo* by switching to R2, he would thereby worsen his own as well as Column-Chooser's absolute positions.)

This type of situation, where it is possible for the underdog in a *status quo* of inequality to improve his absolute position with the other party's absolute position remaining intact (or, indeed, improving also),[1] appears to be quite straightforward and unproblematic. There is a sense, in fact, in which one may feel that such a change *should* take place: that the *status quo* is 'unjustified', or unstable, or sub-optimal, as compared with the state represented by the cell R1–C2. Indeed, the state resulting from Column-Chooser's improving his absolute position is, in this case, Pareto-optimal, since it satisfies the condition of leaving everyone (in this case just Row-Chooser) at least as well off as he was before, and making at least one person (in this case Column-Chooser) better off.

[1] As in this example:

	C1	C2
R1	2 · 1	3 · 2
R2	0 · 0	0 · 0

However, it is possible for the disfavourably placed party to improve his absolute position in a way which does *not* coincide with Pareto-optimality, but which is, rather, at the expense of the favourably placed party. Consider, for instance, the case represented by the matrix 4.2, where, again, the *status quo* of inequality is represented by the thickened R1–C1. Here, if Column-Chooser moves to C2 he improves his absolute position (with pay-off 2 instead of 1) while Row-Chooser's absolute position is worsened (with 0 instead of 2). Row-Chooser will, of course, be interested in preventing Column-Chooser's 'violation' of the *status quo*: he may,

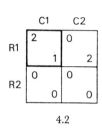

4.2

for example, seek a way of successfully and persuasively committing himself to a conditional choice of R2 in case Column-Chooser moves from his *status quo* position C1 to C2, so that Column-Chooser will be effectively deterred from this move— which would result, in this case, in the state represented by R2–C2 with a zero pay-off for both.

However, if one does not allow such 'strategic moves' (see Schelling, 1960, esp. pp. 121–31 and also p. 164 below) as a conditional commitment, then matrix 4.2 reflects Column-Chooser's genuine strategic advantage over Row-Chooser: Column-Chooser will be able to improve his absolute position at the expense of Row-Chooser who can do nothing about it, thereby creating a new *status quo* of inequality (namely, R1–C2) which favours the former underdog.

It is of some interest to recall in this context what is commonly accepted as one of the essential propositions of the liberal economist: 'In the liberal's ideal representation of the economic world', states Raymond Aron (1965, p. 136), 'each man, working in his own interest, works in the interest of the group.' Translating it into our terminology, the idea is that if each 'player' acts so as to improve his own absolute position, the absolute position of 'society' is thereby improved as well. This idea, when simplified so as to apply to a world of two persons only, can be put into a matrix form, or rather into a succession of matrices, somewhat like 4.3.

In each matrix, the state represented by the cell R1–C1 is the *status quo* at a certain period of time; by moving to R2 (C2)

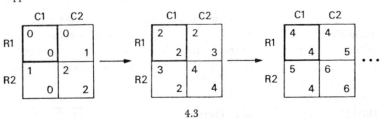

4.3

Row-Chooser (Column-Chooser) improves his own absolute position, and if *both* act so as to improve their own absolute positions, the resulting state is the one represented by R2–C2— which is 'society's' best. Now this R2–C2 becomes the new *status quo*—as represented by R1–C1 in the next matrix—which will again be abandoned by the two parties seeking to 'work in their own interest', and so it goes on. (See also above, Chapter III, p. 103.) (Incidentally, let it be pointed out that even before Adam Smith's celebrated 'invisible hand' argument, Montesquieu discusses cases—in *Spirit of the Laws*, i. 25—where 'each individual advances the public good, while he only thinks of promoting his own interests'.)

Marx's world-view, on the other hand, is 'a sort of inversion' of the liberals': for him, 'each man, acting rationally in his own interest, contributes to the destruction of the interest common to all' (Aron). A quite adequate representation of *this* view is the matrix representation of the Prisoners' Dilemma, where each party's improvement of his own absolute position is at the direct expense of the other's, and if both attempt it simultaneously they cause a social disaster.

The fact that by unilaterally 'violating' the *status quo* one (not necessarily the *dis*favourably placed one) can improve one's absolute position means that the *status quo* lacks stability: that it is not in equilibrium. An important qualification should, however, be made right away: the *status quo* is, in this case, not in a *game-theoretical* equilibrium; the latter concept being characterized as a state such that 'it does not behove either player to change his choice if the other does not' (Luce and Raiffa, 1957, p. 62). But this game-theoretical equilibrium is an equilibrium only in a rather limited sense. If one allows the other party to change *his* choice too, then a situation is conceivable in which it *is* possible for an underdog in a *status quo* of inequality to

improve his absolute position and yet the
strategic structure is such that it renders
the *status quo* stable none the less.

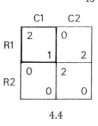

4.4

Consider the situation represented by the
matrix 4.4.

The disfavourably placed party in the *status
quo* of inequality represented by R1–C1, viz.
Column-Chooser, can improve his absolute
position by moving to C2; the *status quo* is thus not in a game-
theoretical equilibrium. But Column-Chooser's switch to C2
can be 'punished' by Row-Chooser's switch to R2, the resulting
state being R2–C2 which, from the point of view of Row-
Chooser, is just as good as was the original *status quo* (with an
equal pay-off of 2), but which leaves Column-Chooser worse
off than he was in the original *status quo* (with a pay-off of 0
instead of 1). Row-Chooser's available 'retaliatory' move to R2
serves, then, to bring Column-Chooser back to the *status quo*, or
possibly to prevent Column-Chooser from trying to improve his
own absolute position by abandoning the *status quo* in the first
place. Thus, due to the strategic structure of the entire situation,
the *status quo* may be said to possess stability, even though it is
not a game-theoretical equilibrium.

Indeed, a similar conception of stability seems to underlie
George Homans's concept of 'practical equilibrium' (1950,
p. 282; 1961, pp. 113–14). His idea is that established patterns
of conformity, or regularities, are not automatically self-
sustaining, nor is it the case that no one involved in them has
any incentive to deviate from them. Rather, they persist because
departure is met by resistance. And resistance, in turn, 'consists
in the way the elements of the systems are interrelated: a change
in one element results in a change in others that counteract it
and bring it back to its original state. A system in which this
occurs is said to be in equilibrium.'[2] Homans qualifies his concept of equilibrium by adding to it the adjective 'practical' in
order—in his words—'to avoid the almost mystical arguments
that have encrusted the latter word [i.e. equilibrium] in social
science' (1961, p. 113). This seems to be amply justified within
the framework of Parsonian theories and jargon. In the present

---

[2] Walter Buckley, *Sociology and Modern Systems Theory*. Englewood Cliffs, N.J.:
Prentice-Hall, 1967, p. 32.

study, however, which does not relate to this framework, the stress on 'practical' seems irrelevant. Instead, what is important to emphasize in our study is that the equilibrium in question is attained in virtue of the strategic structure of the situation. Therefore, when this broader concept of equilibrium will be returned to below, it will be referred to as 'strategic equilibrium'.

The desire to improve one's absolute position is a legitimate one within game-theory; indeed it is implied by its basic assumptions concerning the rationality of the players. Generally speaking, they amount to the postulate of the self-interestedness of the participants in a game situation, or, alternatively, to the postulate of the participant's acting (choosing) so as to maximize something (e.g. value, utility, expected utility).

For the sake of greater clarity with regard to the concept of improvement of one's *relative* position, to be introduced in the next section, it is of importance to emphasize once more the following point. Although game theory is concerned with interdependent decisions in situations of personal interactions, it does not allow one's utility function (i.e. preference rank-ordering over the possible states of affairs) to be influenced by this interaction. Each participant is envisaged as rank-ordering the states *in isolation* from the interaction situation, or in a sense even *prior* to it. He is supposed to enter the interaction situation already equipped with this ordering. And then, once in it, he is supposed to act (choose) so as to achieve the highest possible state in his ordering regardless of the positions and preference patterns of the other participants—which he is nevertheless supposed to be fully informed about. Thus it is only an improvement of one's absolute position, as discussed in this section, which is allowed for by the framework of game theory.

4. *Improvement of Relative Position*

4.1 *Presentation*

The disfavourably placed party in a *status quo* of inequality will be considered to have improved his relative position if he has made a move towards narrowing the gap between his own and the other party's positions.

As an important special case this includes a move towards a state of equality between them.

A simple and useful taxonomy of the cases in point is provided according to whether the improvement in one's relative position is at the same time an improvement in one's absolute position as well, whether it leaves one's absolute position unchanged, or whether it in fact worsens it. In each of these cases a further distinction can be drawn between the achievement of gap-narrowing and the achievement of equality. That is, six cases —grouped into three groups—are distinguished altogether.

Group one. The first two cases will be exemplified by situations represented by the two matrices 4.5 and 4.6,

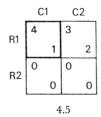   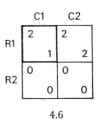

4.5   4.6

where, as usual, the *status quo* is the thickened R1–C1 cell, Column-Chooser is the underdog, and his abandonment of the *status quo* by moving to C2 achieves gap-narrowing in matrix 4.5 and equality in matrix 4.6. (Let it be mentioned that matrix 4.6 is identical with matrix 4.1—p. 142 above—which served to exemplify an improvement of absolute position coinciding with Pareto's principle.)

In both these cases Column-Chooser improves his absolute position as well as his relative one.

Group two. The cases where the absolute position of the dis-favourably placed party remains unchanged while his relative position improves are exemplified by the matrices 4.7 and 4.8,

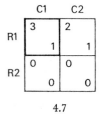   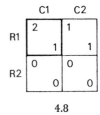

4.7   4.8

the first one (4.7) depicting gap-narrowing and the second (4.8) equalizing.

Group three. The last two cases, where the underdog's absolute position in fact worsens with the improvement in his relative position are represented by matrices 4.9 and 4.10.

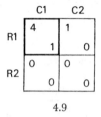
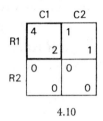

              4.9   4.10

(The pay-offs in the cells R2–C1 and R2–C2 in all six matrices have been kept fixed at zero so as to achieve as much similarity among the various cases as possible, thereby emphasizing the relevant differences among them. Also this neutralizes possible motives on behalf of Row-Chooser to abandon the *status quo*, which would complicate matters to no avail.)

The cases in the second and third groups are of interest to us, since in them the improvement in relative positions does not coincide with improvement in absolute positions and is therefore 'isolated' in them. I shall now comment on them in some detail, focusing on two main standpoints: Pareto-optimality in its relation to game theory, and the question of rationality.

4.2 *Relative Position Improvement in the Light of the Postulates of Game Theory and Pareto Optimality*

In the two cases belonging to the second group (exemplified by matrices 4.7 and 4.8) the *status quo* is a weak game-theoretical equilibrium: a game-theoretical equilibrium since no one *gains* by unilaterally deviating from it; and weak because one of the parties, i.e. Column-Chooser, does not in fact *lose* by unilaterally deviating from it. Game theory postulates that once in R1–C1, neither of the parties has any incentive to abandon it, and it therefore treats this state as stable (albeit in a weak sense). But if R1–C1 did not happen to be the prevailing *status quo*, game theory does not require Column-Chooser to choose C1 in preference to C2; rather, it assumes his *indifference* between these two alternatives (columns). So that given the situations as represented by the two matrices at hand, when no *status quo* is assumed, game theory will be unable to predict, or indeed to recommend, a 'solution'.[3]

Now if the four cells in each matrix of the second group are regarded not as representing four outcomes in a game situation, but instead as four possible states of affairs among which 'society' (in this case just Row-Chooser and Column-Chooser) is to choose the best, then Pareto's principle supplies the sufficient reason for picking out the state represented by R1–C1 as the social choice. R1–C1 should be the social choice since it is Pareto-optimal in the sense explained above (p. 142): while Column-Chooser is indifferent between it and R1–C2 (the candidacy of the cells R2–C1 and R2–C2 as the social choice being obviously ruled out right away), Row-Chooser strictly prefers R1–C1 to R1–C2. Hence the social choice, which is determined on the basis of the *individual* preference-rankings of the states, is the state represented by the upper-left cell R1–C1.

However, the concept of improvement of one's relative position as here developed provides a sufficient reason for the state represented by the upper-right cell R1–C2, rather than that represented by the upper-left R1–C1, being the final outcome of the interaction situation. While *before* the interaction situation Column-Chooser might have been indifferent between his two alternatives (i.e. columns), once *in* it he will have a good reason for preferring column 2 to column 1 (on the assumption that Row-Chooser would choose R1 in any case). This is so since in the state represented by R1–C2 his relative position, that is, his position as compared with that of Row-Chooser's, is better than what it is in R1–C1: the former state is more egalitarian than the latter. Similarly, if R1–C1 were the actual *status quo*, while game theory denies the existence of any incentive on the part of Column-Chooser to deviate from it unilaterally, the consideration of his relative position does supply Column-Chooser with a good reason for wishing to abandon the *status quo* in favour of the less discriminatory state represented by R1–C2.

---

[3] This is true when only pure strategies are allowed. In mixed strategies, Row-Chooser would stick to R1 (which is a dominant choice), and Column-Chooser would use a $(\frac{1}{2}, \frac{1}{2})$ probability distribution over C1 and C2.

The 'good reason' Column-Chooser has for preferring C2 to C1 is thus obviously at variance both with the postulates of game theory and with Pareto's principle. These postulates pertaining to rational behaviour, the question naturally arises: What sort of consideration is the improvement of one's relative position? Is it in fact irrational?

4.3 Envy and Rationality

The important part of the answer lies in the observations that the practice of assessing one's own relative position in alternative states of affairs exists and is, furthermore, prevailing and commonplace; that the precept of 'Keep up with the Joneses' is widely adhered to; that men are often moved by envy. The possibility of one's own value system ('utility function') being influenced by—and dependent upon—those of the other participants in the interaction situation is ruled out by theories of rational behaviour because of, among other things, the apparently insurmountable methodological problems connected with the comparability of value systems. Moreover, these theories derive much of their potency (as well as much of their weakness) from the fact that they recognize a single, clearly defined, motive for human choice and action: that of ruthless self-interest in the sense of striving to improve absolute positions. But once the notion of 'self-interest' is widened so as to include considerations of relative positions as well, grounds are provided on which a large variety of actions hitherto 'impermissible' can be explained and justified. Consequently the force of these theories, and particularly their predictive power, is seriously compromised.

However, I am not here concerned with explicating the concept of rationality, or with providing a theory of rational choice and behaviour. Nor is it in my interest to confine the discussion to the 'perfectly rational men' as conceived by such theories.[4] Rather, I am ultimately aiming at the explanation of norms in terms of some basic interaction situations and the various strategies connected with them. And for this purpose one has to allow the persons dealt with to be more 'human': one has to accommo-

---

[4] Notwithstanding their usefulness as an analytical tool, these 'rational men' are often referred to by critics of the theories of which they are the heroes as 'perversely simple', 'ascetic almost to the point of lunacy', 'free from normal human complexes and complexities', and the like. (See Frankel, 1969, p. 402.)

date the real-life drive to improve relative positions in addition to the undisputed drive to improve absolute positions. Furthermore, although the introduction of this motive admittedly exceeds the bounds of the rationality assumptions of the various theories of rational behaviour (e.g. classical and welfare economics, theory of decision making, theory of games), it does not *ipso facto* condemn our agents to *irrationality*. It might be helpful to picture 'irrationality' as lying at one end of a large continuum, at the other end of which lies the narrowly defined 'perfect rationality' of the rational behaviour theories, with a considerable yet ill-demarcated area of non-rationality (or, better, of 'non-perfect-rationality') in between.[5] It is somewhere in this interval, then, that our agents, along with most flesh-and-blood agents, are supposed to be located; the battle-cry of irrationality thus loses much of its poignancy.

In his paper 'Justice as Fairness' John Rawls is concerned with a community of wholly rational men, whom he describes as follows (1962 (1958), p. 137):

They know their own interests more or less accurately; they are capable of tracing out the likely consequences of adopting one practice rather than another; they are capable of adhering to a course of action once they have decided upon it; they can resist present temptations and the enticements of immediate gain; *and the bare knowledge or perception of the difference between their condition and that of others is not, within certain limits and in itself, a source of great dissatisfaction* (my italics).

It is only the last requirement, as Rawls himself points out, which presents an addition to the usual requirements from 'rational men': Rawls regards rational men as 'free, to some degree, from the fault of envy'; he does not allow them to be motivated in choice and action by considerations of their relative positions in alternative states of affairs. That Rawls is somewhat unhappy with this requirement which, it seems, would bar most real men from the province of rationality, is evidenced by his use of quite a number of escape clauses and

---

[5] Schelling even points out (1960, p. 16) the multidimensionality of the concepts of rationality and irrationality, so that the continuum of which they are the two polar ends cannot in fact be a one-dimensional scale: 'Rationality is a collection of attributes, and departures from complete rationality may be in many different directions.'

relative terms; e.g. 'within certain limits', 'in some degree', 'is not . . . a source of *great* dissatisfaction', and a few more qualifications in the unquoted explanatory sentences in that context.[6]

It is indeed precisely on this point that Charles Frankel, in his 'Justice and Rationality' (1969), attacks him: '. . . why is envy "irrational"? . . . It is a genuine human emotion, and its satisfaction, if a man feels it, is as much a part of his self-interest as the satisfaction of any other interest. And from this point of view, if Peter is envious of Paul and we cut Paul down to Peter's size, thus making Peter feel better, we contribute to Peter's advantage' (pp. 409–10). And somewhat later: 'Envy, though not all men feel it, is not an esoteric human emotion. It is a fairly powerful and widespread one. . . . The government of men depends on dealing with envy, not ignoring it. To exclude envy from our abstract rational calculus may be a methodological convenience, but it is also a moral prejudice and an unrealistic one' (p. 410).

We have to be clear about the issue at stake. The question is not one of truth and falsity: whether men are or are not moved by envy. Rather, the question is one of usefulness and adequacy of an explication. Rawls's programme is one of explicating the concept of justice in terms of a non-moral (yet normative) concept of fairness, based on a 'thought-experiment' pertaining to a community of rational men. For this conceptual exercise, as well as for independent reasons, Rawls frees his rational men, at least to some degree, from the 'fault of envy'.

In his criticism, and quite apart from his doubts concerning the soundness of Rawls's entire programme, Frankel argues that whatever the degree of success the explication achieves, it is bound to be devoid of real interest since it suppresses and

---

[6] In *Theory of Justice* (1971, esp. pp. 530–41) Rawls admits that envy does exist and that it must in some way be reckoned with. Indeed, he devotes two sections to the analysis of envy, in which he draws some important distinctions, such as between general and particular envy, between envy and resentment, and between benign envy, emulative envy, and envy proper. He even comes up with the conclusion that there are circumstances in which envious feelings are not irrational. He says: 'When envy is a reaction to the loss of self-respect in circumstances where it would be unreasonable to expect someone to feel differently, I shall say that it is excusable' (p. 534). His chief concern, however, is not so much with excusable envy as such, but with the question whether his 'well-ordered society' might generate it to such an extent that it would be rendered unworkable and incompatible with human good.

ignores a 'genuine human emotion' which, he maintains, is essential in any discussion of justice. In explicating the concept of rationality in his 'The Aim of Inductive Logic' (1962), Carnap faced a similar problem with regard to prejudice: to postulate in advance that rational men can have no prejudices is, it seems, too much of an abstraction from real men and too high a price for a neat *explicatum*; and yet the idea that rational men may be guided by prejudice is counter-intuitive, to say the least. Carnap resolved this dilemma in the following way: a rational man may, he maintains, have prejudices. He will be considered irrational, however, if he refuses to change them in face of counter-evidence.

In a similar fashion we may now state that, for our purposes, rational men need not be free from envy. What will count as irrational, though, is to act out of sheer envy so as to worsen one's own absolute position just to 'cut someone else down to one's own size'—when this is done as an end in itself and not with a view to some eventual betterment, or at least main-tenance, of one's absolute position. Anticipating the terminology we shall introduce later, envy will be considered acceptable in our framework only to the extent that it contributes to the making of a sound 'strategic move'. In order to grasp the idea, let us consider an example (which employs *threat* as a representa-tive strategic move).

Imagine two competing tycoons, say Ari and Stavros. Ari receives confidential information that the legendary and long-desired Mogul's diamond is up for sale at last. Needless to say he sets out to purchase it, and plans to present it to his wife at her birthday ball. But Stavros gets wind of this and, mad with envious rage, he threatens to embark upon a most damaging total price war between them if Ari proceeds to purchase the diamond. Now it is clear that the credibility of this threat which, if carried out, would be as costly to Stavros as it would be to Ari, depends greatly on the extent to which it is assumed that acting upon it would indeed gratify Stavros's envy. In such a case, then, we shall not say that since envy is 'ruled out' in advance, and since acting upon this threat is 'irrational', the threat is bound to lack sufficient credibility and is therefore void. On the contrary, Stavros's threat may very well be credible enough to achieve its aim of deterring Ari from purchasing the diamond.

In this sense, then, envy may be said to have contributed to the strategic move of a deterrent threat, and thus to help maintain Stavros's position intact (or even to improve it, through the 'victory').

Note, however, that if Stavros had *not* got wind of Ari's intention in time to prevent its being carried out by means of the deterrent threat, we would indeed consider it irrational if he were to start a price war damaging to both *after* the diamond had been purchased and with the pictures of its presentation in all the Sunday newspapers: this would be to act vengefully, out of sheer envy, worsening his own absolute position—as well as Ari's—as an end in itself and not as a part of some strategic scheme designed eventually to improve, or at least to maintain, his own absolute position.[7]

[As to the further question—What happens when the threat is made and fails to deter: is it then rational for Stavros to act on his threat and start the costly price war?—there is no clear-cut answer. It depends, for one thing, on the continuity of the relations between them; that is, on whether Stavros anticipates similar situations in the future. To the extent that he does, it

---

[7] Put in a matrix form, the situation might look somewhat like the one illustrated here (where A1 and A2 denote Ari's options of maintaining the *status quo* and purchasing the diamond, respectively; S1 and S2 denoting Stavros's options of maintaining the *status quo* and starting a price war, respectively).

	S1	S2
A1	3 / 3	0 / 0
A2	5 / 3	0 [1] / 0

In the *status quo* they are equal; when Ari moves to purchase the diamond, Stavros's relative position worsens; a price war started by Stavros is equally damaging for both (with the possible qualification—indicated by the bracketed pay-off—that the possession of the diamond may give Ari an advantage (in prestige?) over Stavros even in the state of a war between them).

Now to Ari's intended move to A2 Stavros replies with the threat of moving to S2; to the extent that the threat is credible, Ari would forgo the diamond, Stavros would not start the price war, and the *status quo* would be maintained to Stavros's satisfaction.

However, if the state represented by A2–S1 is already the new, established *status quo*, that is, if Ari has purchased the diamond before Stavros could make the threat, Stavros would be irrational to switch to S2: there is nothing he stands to gain by it (the price paid for the equality in their relative position in A2–S2 being disproportionately high), and there is much for him to lose—assuming, that is, that Ari's 'retreat' to A1 is impossible, or does not make sense unless we change the story.

[In 1960, p. 48 Schelling presents a two-dimensional graph which illustrates the concept of the deterrent threat and which, when translated into a matrix form, is similar to the above matrix.]

may be rational for him to carry out his unsuccessful threat now, so as to establish the credibility of his future threats. For a more detailed discussion of this point I refer the reader to Schelling, 1960, pp. 39–40.]

To sum up: far from ruling envy out of our framework (with the qualifications noted above), we recognize that it may contribute to the intricate interplay which goes into the making of strategic moves. To Schelling's observations (supported by brilliant examples) that it is 'perfectly clear that it is not a universal advantage in situations of conflict to be inalienably and manifestly rational in decision and motivation', and that 'it may be perfectly rational to wish oneself not altogether rational, or—if that language is philosophically objectionable— to wish for the power to suspend certain rational capabilities in particular situations' (ibid., p. 18), we might add another: that a reputation for acting out of envy might in some situations be a genuine advantage in rendering one's threats credible and one's commitments irrevocable.

5. *Improvement of Relative Position at the Expense of Absolute Position*

We have to go back now and comment upon the cases belonging to Group Three (matrices 4.9 and 4.10, p. 148 above), where improving one's relative position is at the expense of one's absolute position. In both cases, the *status quo* of inequality— represented by the upper-left cell R1–C1—is a game-theoretical equilibrium in the strict sense: each party actually loses by unilaterally deviating from it.

Two points concerning these cases are clear and deserve to be emphasized. First, from the point of view of game theory it makes absolutely no sense for Column-Chooser to abandon the *status quo*. In other words, his deviation would be considered downright irrational. Second, there are situations ('scenarios') in which it is quite easy to envisage a Column-Chooser being driven—by envy, vengeance, indignation, or whatever—to abandon the *status quo* in favour of the 'equality in deprivation' achieved in the state represented by the upper-right cell R1–C2. 'The passion for equality' as Tocqueville puts it,[8] 'is ardent,

[8] Quoted in Aron, 1965, p. 226. See also Blau, 1967, ch. 6, e.g.: '. . . individuals who receive high rewards in groups where others do too are likely to be less satisfied with their attainment than individuals who are no better off, or perhaps even worse off, but who find themselves in groups where others receive fewer rewards' (p. 144).

insatiable, incessant, invincible; they call for equality in free-dom; and if they cannot obtain that, they still call for equality in slavery. They will endure poverty, servitude, barbarism, but they will not endure aristocracy.'

A dramatic paradigm for this act of dragging one's partner along with oneself 'into the gutter' just to achieve—or even to approach—a state of equality may be suggested by Samson's swan-song 'strategy' of 'Let me die with the Philistines' (Judges 16: 30). Samson preferred death, along with his captors, to the *status quo* of grinding corn in the prison house and making sport for his torturers.

A paper called 'Are Trivial Games the Most Interesting Psychologically?', by G. Marvell and D. R. Schmitt (1968), offers a rather interesting support for the hypothesis that people might sometimes be psychologically prompted to deviate from the obvious, rational, game-theoretical solution, although they thereby damage their absolute position. The authors report there on experiments with some simple, 'no-conflict' games, which—their mathematical solution being evident—are mathe-matically trivial. However, these games, the authors claim, might be most interesting psychologically, since in them the psychological element, namely motivation, can be studied in isolation, so to speak. Among the motivations they distinguish and discuss are what they call 'Maximizing Difference' and 'Inequity Pressure'. The first is exemplified by the game 4.11, where R1–C1 is the obvious, equilibrial, game-theoretical solution (R1 and C1 being the two players' dominant choices). The frequent experimental result of R2–C1 which the authors obtained can only be explained in terms of Row-Chooser's desire to increase the difference between his and Column-Chooser's gains—a desire apparently strong enough to cause him to sacrifice his absolute position somewhat (that is, to settle for a pay-off of 9 instead of 10) for its satisfaction.

	C1	C2
R1	10	3
	10	2
R2	9	2
	3	1

4.11

The second motivation is exemplified by the game 4.12, with the control game 4.13, where, again, R1–C1 is the obvious, equilibrial, game-theoretical solution. The experimental result that R1–C1 was in fact the actual outcome of the game repre-

	C1	C2
R1	9 / 3	2 / 2
R2	2 / 2	2 / 2

4.12

	C1	C2
R1	3 / 3	2 / 2
R2	2 / 2	2 / 2

4.13

sented by matrix 4.12 on fewer trials than it was in game 4.13 can only be explained either in terms of Row-Chooser's desire for a more 'just' outcome, even though it means a sacrifice on his behalf—in case R2–C1 was in fact the actual solution—or in terms of Column-Chooser's similar desire—in case R1–C2 was the actual solution.

Of the two points established in this section, viz. the game-theoretical irrationality of deviance from the *status quo* (in matrices 4.9 and 4.10) on the one hand, and the existence of motives for deviance on the other, it is the second which is of more concern to us. It is of course quite easy to reconcile these two points by labelling the deviance motivations 'irrational' and by admitting regretfully that irrationality exists, and on occasions, alas, prevails. However, this apparently innocent 'labelling' smacks of a persuasive definition, and in fact amounts to brushing aside *all* of the possible grounds for such deviance as irrational while overlooking the quite rational role it might play in the strategic structure of some conflict situations. We shall therefore lay down, along the lines developed in the discussion of envy above, that it would not be considered irrational for one to attempt to improve his relative position even at the price of worsening his absolute position as long as (i) the 'price' in terms of absolute position is sufficiently low in proportion to the prospective gain in relative position to be insignificant—as in matrix 4.12 above with regard to Column-Chooser; or (ii) it is employed in some 'strategic move' with a view to an eventual improvement, or at least maintenance, of one's absolute position—as in the Ari–Stavros case above and in situations to be discussed below.

6. *Interpersonal Comparisons*

One question cannot, it seems, be suppressed any longer: does all the foregoing discussion not presuppose interpersonal comparability of individual value-systems ('desirabilities', 'utilities')? Furthermore, do our matrices, and the concept of relative position improvement, not presuppose a common zero-point for the evaluation of the two parties' pay-offs?

The answer must be faced: interpersonal comparison of positions, on the basis of some common standard, is indeed at the root of much of the foregoing discussion. But we have to be clear about just what is involved here. Theories of rational choice, and economics in particular, are considered to have made their way once they have embarked upon purging themselves of the concept of cardinal utility—the cornerstone of classical utility theory—and of as many of its introspective elements as possible. Edgeworth's introduction of the notion of indifference curves (1881), Pareto's hypotheses in terms of *ordinal* utility (1906), and Samuelson's concept of 'revealed preference' (1938, 1948) are among the milestones of this advance. The rationale behind these efforts has been that the newer concepts and frameworks could do all that could be done by cardinal utility, with fewer —and considerably less disputable—assumptions. The idea, then, was to limit the number—as well as the strength—of the assumptions, and at the same time to increase their generality and to decrease to the minimum their psychological requirements and overtones.

Now as already emphasized above, I am not here aiming at a development of a theory of rational behaviour. The concepts and general approach of game theory serve as a helpful tool, suggest useful techniques, and help channel sources of insight; it is taken here as a diving-board, but by no means as a binding framework. So that the alleged advantage of present theories of rational behaviour, with game theory among them—namely that they side-step the tremendous theoretical and methodological problems connected with cardinal utility and the interpersonal comparisons of value-systems and yet are able to achieve all that they do achieve—is, for us, beside the point.

So far as the present study is concerned, the point is that people do as a matter of fact compare their own positions to that of others, and that their feelings as to their relative positions in a situation influence much of their attitudes, decisions, and actions. To start establishing this point would, it seems to me, be to document the obvious. It is of course true that one's assessment of one's relative position in a situation is, in turn, influenced by such things as one's biography, temperament, expectations; it is also true that people are often misinformed as to the actual positions of others, or, alternatively, that their assessment of it is a projection of their own; it is true that they sometimes make erroneous assessments, and that they might, out of various reasons, overstate or understate their own position in a situation as compared with that of the others. All this contributes, no doubt, to the enormous complexity one faces when attempting to provide a *theory* pertaining to these interpersonal comparisons and assessments of people's relative positions, or to provide some objective standard or criterion against which one could check these subjective and often incompatible assessments. But at the same time it is also true that by and large there is quite a high degree of correlation between people's actual positions and their mutual assessments thereof, and quite a high degree of implicit consensus as to the terms of these comparisons.

However, the following point cannot be over-emphasized: I am not here concerned with *accounting for* the phenomenon of people's relative position assessment; rather, I propose to *take it into account* in my attempt to single out and to characterize situations the structure of which is prone to be norm-generating. Furthermore, this structure need not be 'objective': what is of importance is the mere possibility that the disfavourably placed party in a *status quo* of inequality might form to himself a picture of the entire situation ('matrix') in such a way as would suggest to him that through a certain action—'strategic move'— of his he would have the advantage of the other party. Consequently, the 'objective' judgement that he in fact grossly overstated his deprivation in the *status quo* and was thus led to an 'unjustified' move is, to us, irrelevant.

7. *The Favourably Placed Party*

The main hypothesis concerning the favourably placed party in a *status quo* of inequality is that he is interested in the continuation of his privileged position and hence in the maintenance of the *status quo*. We shall assume that the situation is such that this party cannot, by a unilateral move, improve his absolute position any further, and also that he cannot improve his relative position in the sense of widening further the gap between himself and the other party. Now in order to maintain the *status quo* one might, in some cases, have to fortify it against potential sources of danger. This need arises when the *status quo* lacks sufficient stability: when it is not in equilibrium. It has already been pointed out earlier (p. 144) that the game-theoretical concept of equilibrium is a rather limited one: it pertains just to such states as do not provide any incentive for a *unilateral* deviance on behalf of either party. Such an equilibrium state is taken, within game theory, to be stable.

However, in the same context it was also noted that a state which is *not* a game-theoretical equilibrium can nevertheless be stable due to the strategic structure of the entire game (matrix 4.4, p. 145). By the same token, when all the alternative states —or moves—in a situation are considered, it is possible for a state to be a game-theoretical equilibrium and yet to be unstable and to stand in need of support. As examples one may take Marvell and Schmitt's games, depicted by matrices 4.11 and 4.12 (pp. 156, 157 above), where the motivations of maximizing difference and promoting equality might prompt one of the parties, or even both, to abandon a *status quo* which is regarded by game theory as a stable equilibrium. It is the existence of such motives, then, which is a potential source of danger and which might threaten the maintenance of a seemingly stable and (differentially) beneficial *status quo*.

A different type of example is provided by the situation represented by the matrix 4.14. The state represented by the upper-left cell R1–C1, if it happens to be the *status quo*, is stable by game-theoretical standards, since each party loses by a *unilateral* deviance from it. However, the fact that by *simultaneously* deviating from it they can both gain renders the *status quo* unstable according to the broader conception of stability adopted here. It is clear, incidentally, that if the two parties co-ordinate their actions and abandon the *status quo* together, the resulting state, represented by the bottom-right R2–C2, is a game-theoretical equilibrium which is unshakeably stable according to the present standards too. Note, though, that the fact that the new *status quo* in the above case (viz. R2–C2) is equally optimal for both parties is *not* what

	C1	C2
R1	1 1	0 0
R2	0 0	2 2

4.14

accounts for its stability. For in matrix 4.15 the state represented by the top-left R1–C1, which is neither equitable nor optimal for Column-Chooser (who would obviously have preferred the state R2–C2), is nevertheless a game-theoretical equilibrium which is at the same time stable by our standards as well: it is on no account susceptible to threats. Row-Chooser enjoys it, while Column-Chooser is intimidated from abandoning it by the fear of getting −30.[9]

	C1	C2
R1	10 6	4 −30
R2	5 4	8 8

4.15

To sum up: game-theoretical equilibrium is neither a necessary nor a sufficient condition for the stability we are after. To check the stability of a certain state, *all* the alternative states of affairs in the situation have to be compared to it, and not—as is done in game theory—only a subset thereof. A state will be considered stable only if the pay-off structure is such that the web of all possible moves, and strategic moves, tends to protect it. In general, this will be the case when one of the following two conditions is met. (i) No party has an incentive to deviate from it—either alone or in co-ordination with others—to improve either his absolute or his relative position. Or (ii) when there does exist a motivation for deviance on behalf of some party, the structure of the situation is such that it makes the risk of a considerable loss too great (as in matrix 4.15), or that it might be too costly for that party in terms of an effective pending punishment (as in matrix 4.4). In other words still, it is the desirability to each party of *each* of the alternative states of affairs, as well as the price paid for acting so as to attain it, which have to be considered and mutually compared when the stability of a certain *status quo* is in question. It would be appropriate, I think, to refer to this type of stability as *strategic stability*, since, as shown, it depends on the strategic structure of the entire situation.

[9] This matrix is used by Luce and Raiffa (1957, p. 110) to exemplify what they call 'psychological dominance': the equilibrium point R1–C1 is said to dominate psychologically the second equilibrium point R2–C2—preferred by Column-Chooser—since Column-Chooser will not dare choose C2 for fear of ending up with −30.
  This discussion, interestingly, belongs to a section which laments the 'pitiful incompleteness' of the game-theoretical analysis connected with the solution concept, which is partly due to the fact that 'the structure developed in these sections does not adequately reflect many of the psychological factors of the non-cooperative games'.

Let it be noted, though, that whereas the stability associated with the game-theoretical equilibrium is well-defined, the bounds of the concept of strategic stability are somewhat blurred. There may be many boundary cases where there will be no clear-cut answer to the question of the strategic stability of a certain given *status quo*. This is so because strategic stability depends, among other things, upon psychological factors and upon such relativistic notions as 'too high a price', 'too great a risk', etc.; and where these are involved, no precision can be expected. The classification of the boundary cases, and the stipulation of various conditions under which they will be taken to be strategically stable (unstable) is, it seems to me, quite an interesting area for further study. But it should be realized that it is of no pertinence to the present study. What is of significance for us at the moment is just that there are *clear cases* of states which, notwithstanding their being in a game-theoretical equilibrium, are strategically unstable.

8. *The Paradigmatic Situation*

8.1 *Characterization*

In the light of the points established in the last section it is possible to distinguish the following four cases:

(i)   A *status quo* which is in a game-theoretical equilibrium and which is strategically stable as well.

(ii) A *status quo* which is neither in a game-theoretical equilibrium nor is it strategically stable.

(iii) A *status quo* which is not in a game-theoretical equilibrium and yet is strategically stable.

(iv) A *status quo* which is in a game-theoretical equilibrium and yet is strategically unstable.

We shall here be interested in states which are unstable and which, at least in the view of *one* party to the situation, stand in need of some device which would render them stable. The second of the four cases will, however, be dismissed as uninteresting, since a state which is neither in a game-theoretical nor in a strategic equilibrium cannot be expected to endure at all: at least one party to this *status quo* will find it advantageous, as well as non-punishing, to abandon it right away. On the other hand, states which belong to the fourth of the above cases do possess the 'superficial', game-theoretical stability in that it pays no party to deviate from them unilaterally. These states are potentially threatened, and hence not completely and safely stable, only in a less immediate sense. It is precisely this feature of a *status quo*, namely its appearing stable on the surface and yet its being fundamentally in danger, which serves the purpose of the analysis to be offered presently of the 'fortifying function' of norms.

Our attention will be focused, then, on states belonging to the fourth of the above cases. To this we must add the basic requirement with which we started: that the state be a *status quo* of inequality. Thus the complete characterization of the case to be analysed is given by saying that it is *a status quo of inequality which is in a game-theoretical equilibrium and which is strategically unstable*.

As a paradigm for this case let us use the situation depicted by matrix 4.16 (hence— 'the paradigm matrix'). The state represented by the thickened R1–C1 is the *status quo*; it is a *status quo* of inequality which discriminates in favour of Row-Chooser. Neither party can improve his absolute position by a unilateral deviance from the *status quo*—which is to say that the *status quo* is in a game-theoretical

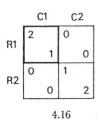

4.16

equilibrium. But, by moving to C2 Column-Chooser can improve his relative position—at the expense of his absolute position—for this move brings about a state of equality (represented by the top-right R1–C2), albeit that it is 'equality in misery'. This, apparently, amounts to saying that the *status quo* is not in a strategic equilibrium.

However, we have concluded earlier (p. 153), while discussing the notion of relative position improvement, that we shall not accept as rational, or as a 'legitimate' motivation, acting so as to worsen one's own absolute position just to cut someone else down to one's own size, when this is done as an end in itself and not as part of a strategic move intended eventually to improve, or at least to maintain, one's original absolute position. To appreciate this point, and its significance to the case in hand, let us digress for a moment and examine the matrix 4.17 situation. This situation is identical with the situation depicted by the paradigm matrix (4.16) above, but for the state represented by

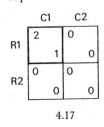

4.17

the bottom-right cell R2–C2. Here, indeed, for Column-Chooser to abandon the *status quo* in favour of the state represented by the top-right R1–C2 would be taken to be irrational. This is not to deny, though, that one *might* be motivated, in certain situations, to do just this —out of sheer envy, revenge, indignation, or what have you. In fact Samson's 'Let me die with the Philistines', referred to above (p. 156), is a case in point: Samson chose to lose all, i.e. to die, but in such a way that he would kill his captors along with himself, so that 'I may be at once avenged of the Philistines for my two eyes' (Judges 16: 28).[10]

To say that this type of 'Samson's strategy' is irrational and unacceptable in our framework is to say that we would *not* consider the *status quo* in such cases (i.e. cases like the one depicted by matrix 4.17) as strategically unstable and as standing in need of fortification: deviance from it cannot be employed as a part of a strategic move aimed at some ultimate benefit in absolute terms. This means that on the whole these situations would belong to the *first* of the four cases listed above—their *status quo* being both in a game-theoretical and in a strategic equilibrium —and are thus of no concern to our present analysis. So let us return to the 'paradigm matrix' (4.16) which, it is claimed, exemplifies situations belonging to the fourth case in which we are interested. As the only difference between this matrix and 'Samson's matrix' is in the bottom-right cell R2–C2, this cell must account for the relevant distinctions between the two corresponding situations.

8.2 *The Disfavourably Placed Party's Strategic Move*

The term 'strategic move' has been employed a number of times already. Up to now it was hoped that it was suggestive

[10] If matrix 4.17 is not suggestive enough as a representation of the '*status quo* of inequality' in which Samson is a blind and humiliated grinder in the prison house of his enemies, the *status quo* can be changed into, say, (10, 1). Incidentally, one might argue that Samson's miserable existence was in fact worse than death, and that by dying he was actually redeemed, that is—that he improved his absolute position rather than worsened it (in other words, the argument claims that the *status quo* should have been represented by, say, (5, −5))—or at least that *Samson* might have felt so. However, this sort of dispute must, by the nature of things, be left open.

enough to be self-explanatory. But as it is going to play a crucial role in what follows, the time has come to introduce it properly. A strategic move, first of all, is a move. It is distinguished, though, from an ordinary move, which is a mere adoption of a certain course of action (i.e. in the matrix-language, a mere decision on a certain row or column), in several respects. Following Schelling (1960, p. 160), it will be characterized as follows. One's aim in using a strategic move is to bring about a state ('outcome', 'solution') which is optimal for one's self. Given that the situation is an interaction situation (between two, for simplicity), one cannot bring about this state alone; one needs the co-operation of the other. But, unless this particular state happens to be optimal for the other party as well, there is no reason to suppose the other will in fact co-operate. So what one needs is some method of inducing the other party to choose in one's favour. This inducement will be achieved once one succeeds in affecting the other party's expectations concerning one's own behaviour. And one will be able to influence the other's expectations through visibly and persuasively constraining one's own behaviour.

Now the constraints one can put on one's own behaviour comprise mainly an irrevocable commitment to one particular and unconditional course of action (i.e. in the matrix-language, a commitment to stick to a particular row or column under any circumstances), or a commitment to a particular conditional response to the other party's possible choices (e.g. in the matrix-language, a commitment to choose column 2 if the other chooses row 1 and to choose column 1 if the other chooses row 2). Essentially, this constraining of one's own options in order to influence the other party's choice by affecting his expectations is what strategic moves are all about. And according to what type of constraint is employed, whether it is conditional or not, what is the pay-off structure of the situation etc., such basic moves as threats and promises result.

The idea behind constraining one's own behaviour in the manner just explained is that thereby the original interaction situation is reduced to only a part (a segment) thereof (e.g. in the matrix-language, by committing one's self to an unconditional choice of column 2, an originally four-state situation is reduced to only a two-state situation, viz. the two states in the second column only). And the best choice for the other party in this partial interaction situation should—if the strategic move was well planned—bring about the state which was the optimal one for one's self in the original interaction situation. In this way, by using a strategic move, one achieves one's aim of inducing the other party to choose in one's favour. As the present section deals with a specific strategic move in a specific set-up, I shall consider myself exempt from giving a detailed general example at this point: what follows will in fact illustrate the above.

Let us turn back now to our paradigm matrix (4.16) and observe that its Column-Chooser, who is the underdog in the *status quo*, would clearly prefer an alternative state in the situation, viz. the one represented by the bottom-right cell R2–C2, to become the *status quo*. But it is just as clear that he cannot by himself bring it about. It needs the deviation of *both* parties from the *status quo* to arrive at this state, and there is every reason to expect Row-Chooser not to co-operate. Furthermore, the mere existence of this alternative state of affairs, in which the parties' positions are reversed and Column-Chooser is the one favoured by the inequality, may well suffice to make Column-Chooser all the more exasperated at the *status quo* which discriminates against him. Whereas in a situation like the one represented by 'Samson's matrix' (4.17, p. 164) it is quite likely that Column-Chooser might come to accept the *status quo* as part of 'the natural order of things' and might be content with what he's got, the situation here is different: the alternative state represented by the bottom-right R2–C2 is a constant reminder to Column-Chooser that things can be different, that the tide may turn, indeed that he himself might help turn the tide.

Now there is one thing Column-Chooser *can* do: he can try to convince Row-Chooser that he is committed, in a binding and irrevocable way, to abandon the *status quo* and to deviate to C2. In reply to this move of Column-Chooser's, and depending on how resolute he appears, it is reasonable to assume that Row-Chooser would hasten to salvage what he can, i.e. would hasten to abandon the *status quo* too—the state represented by the bottom-right R2–C2 being preferable for him to the 'equality in misery' state represented by the upper-right R1–C2 to which Column-Chooser is dragging him. But this, of course, is just what Column-Chooser intended to achieve in the first place: through his determination to use the threat of dragging Row-Chooser along with himself 'into the gutter' he might succeed in coercing him to renounce his position of superiority and in forcing his accommodation.

This procedure, whereby one *status quo* may be replaced by another to the advantage of the former underdog, is by no means a mechanical one; that is, one which, once triggered off, proceeds 'automatically' in its predetermined course. Like all strategic moves, its success depends to a large extent on the credibility of a threat conveyed, on the appearance of determination on either side, on a contest of personalities—quite apart from the actual and objective 'power structure' of the situation. It is possible, for example, that Row-Chooser may *not* be convinced of Column-Chooser's being so indignant at the *status quo* that he actually prefers anything, including an 'equality in misery' to it; he might come to the conclusion that Column-Chooser abandons the *status quo* (or threatens to) just so as to force his own accommodation. And if so, he might decide to commit himself visibly and irrevocably to remaining at his *status quo* choice of R1 come what may—in the hope that, through attrition, he would force Column-Chooser's capitulation and return to the *status quo ante*. It follows that although Column-Chooser may use the state of 'equality in misery', represented by R1–C2, as nothing but a pressure device, that is, as nothing but a stage in his strategic move intended ultimately to attain the desirable state represented by R2–C2, the move will not work unless he is really so indignant at the *status quo* of inequality as genuinely to prefer 'letting himself die with the Philistines' to it.[11] Or at least he has to *appear* to Row-Chooser to be as indignant and determined as that.

In short, it may be rational for Column-Chooser to employ the strategic move of threatening to abandon the *status quo* with the hope of thereby bringing about a new and advantageous

[11] Again, if the matrix is not suggestive enough for Column-Chooser's indignation, change the pay-offs in the *status quo* into, say, (10, 1): here, where the inequality is 'enormous', by moving to C2 Column-Chooser loses very little in absolute terms (from 1 to 0), improves his relative position in so far as he achieves equality, and can perhaps rejoice at Row-Chooser's 'fall'. In addition to that, of course, Column-Chooser stands a chance of gaining all if the other capitulates.

(for him) *status quo*; but he has to be—or at least to appear to be—*irrational* in his preferring the 'equality in misery' state to the *status quo* for this strategic move to come off. The upshot is the following: there are states of inequality which appear on the surface to be stable but which are, in a somewhat subtle and complicated way, strategically unstable. They may be in equilibrium, but it is a rather flimsy one; far from being self-perpetuating, they are susceptible to threats. Now the assumption that the party discriminated in favour of is interested in the preservation of such a *status quo* leads reasonably to the assumption that he will seek to fortify it against its potential undermining. It is at this point that norms, meant to counter the *status quo*-upsetting strategic moves, enter the picture.

9. *Fortifying Methods*

9.1 *The Possible Methods*

We want to consider now the devices the favoured party might use to achieve the fortification—and thus to promote the stability—of the *status quo*. There are several possible ways. The most obvious, perhaps, is to do it by force: to deter the disfavourably placed party from even contemplating deviance through exploitation of potential force, and actually to apply force to punish any actual attempt at deviance. That is, to coerce the other party into remaining at the *status quo* through the use—or the potential use—of manifest and brute force.

The drawbacks of this method, however, seem to be just as obvious.[12] In outline, the first and foremost disadvantage of having to rely on naked force is its personalizing and antagonizing aspect. The parties, that hitherto could have stood in no particular relation to each other, are necessarily brought into contact by it: relations of domination and subjection are thereby established, and along with them are sown seeds of further friction, tension, and conflict. Coercion by force is bound to make an enemy of the other party, with all the cost and the strain that this implies. In short, to rely on manifest physical force to preserve the *status quo* might well be too crude, costly, and inconvenient; it might backfire in that it might antagonize the underdog into being all the more determined

[12] For a discussion relevant to the present one see, for instance, Thibaut and Kelley, 1959, esp. pp. 130–4.

to upset the *status quo* at the very first sign of weakness on the part of the dominator. It thus calls for keeping guard constantly by regular policing and monitoring, and for being prepared to put oneself to the test at any moment. All this is indeed aptly captured by the saying, attributed to Napoleon, that 'You can do anything with bayonets, except sit on them.' Some further elaborations on this topic, i.e. of force as a possible device of fortifying the *status quo*, will be offered soon.

Another 'device' for preserving the *status quo* without resorting to force might be for the favoured party to share some of the benefits of his favoured position with the other party. That is, voluntarily to narrow the gap between them, or, if you will, to 'bribe the other party off'—to buy peace and stability by occasional gratuities at any sign of approaching trouble. This may be fine as far as it goes, but it has its obvious drawbacks too. The crucial one is, of course, that unless the favoured party is prepared ultimately to renounce his superior position altogether and to create complete equality between himself and his partner, the whole manœuvre is pointless. Concessions might buy peace for a while, and then for another while. But as long as the favoured party is determined to maintain his position of superiority, there must be a point at which no more concessions will be readily granted and at which, therefore, either the favoured party will find himself resorting to open force, or else the disfavoured party might employ his strategic move and uproot the other from his position of superiority. Furthermore, too many concessions made in the past might convince the underdog that provided he displays sufficient resolve to abandon the *status quo* and not to return to it, the other party will be quick to capitulate and to abandon it too.

There are a few other, somewhat more 'sophisticated', ways to promote the stability of the *status quo* the favoured party might consider. For instance, he might try to conceal and blur his favoured position as much as possible so that it will not be too striking on the surface at least. (Unless he belongs to those who find no relish in their being in a superior position as long as the underprivileged do not know precisely to what extent they *are* underprivileged.) Or he might attempt, by all possible means, to dissociate himself from the other party in such a way that the latter will not even include him in his 'group of reference' to the members of which he compares his position. But this might be difficult to achieve. Or again, it might be possible for him to emphasize to the other party, through propaganda, education, or what not, how very much better for him the present *status quo* is, compared with some other state in the past. The past state might, for that matter, be real or fictional; the point is to try to make the disfavoured party compare his present position exclusively to some past state which was worse for him, and to divert his attention from possible future states which might be better for him.

Now it is the central thesis of this chapter that there is another significant device to render the *status quo* stable: to fortify it by norms. The idea is that once it is in some sense normatively required that the *status quo* endure, the nature of the possible calculations and considerations of deviance fundamentally changes: it is no longer evaluated only in terms of being 'costly' or 'risky', but as being *'wrong'* or *'subversive'*. Once there is some value attached to the *status quo*, deviance is no longer reacted to predominantly by explicit and institutionalized *punishments*, which are the instrument and manifestation of naked force; instead, to follow S. F. Nadel's distinction,[13] it is countered with the finer, subtler, and less institutionalized forms of *penalties*. The latter comprise the various social sanctions ranging from disapproval and distrust to maybe internment and mental hospitalization.

9.2 *Force v. Norms*

It must be noted that, formally speaking, the methods of norms and force as possible fortifiers of the *status quo* in question are functionally equivalent (compare Ch. II Sec. 8 above): provided the norms are effective, they both amount to making deviance from the *status quo* more costly through the imposition of sanctions. Or, to employ once again the matrix-representation language, they both amount to reducing the pay-off to Column-Chooser in the top-right cell R1–R2 in our paradigm matrix (4.16, p. 163). The difference between

[13] S. F. Nadel, 'Social Control and Self-Regulation', in *Social Forces*, 31 (1953), pp. 265–73. The counterpart of his punishment–penalty distinction, incidentally, is that between *rewards* and *premiums*.

the two methods, then, apparently does not lie on the formal level of discussion. (However, see below.) It rather lies in the nature of the sanctions to be imposed, and also, perhaps more importantly, in the strings touched by the type of deterrence associated with these sanctions. While the threat of punishment (in the sense of the above distinction) might deter through appealing to what is often referred to as one's *'tastes'*, that is, one's self-interest in a more or less economic sense, the threat of penalties on the other hand is apt to deter through touching upon one's *values*, moral or otherwise. (See, e.g., Arrow, 1963, p. 18.) To be sure, the punishment–penalty distinction is by no means a clear-cut one. It would indeed be nearer the mark to say that there is some sort of scale at the one end of which are clear cases of punishment by sheer force and at the other end cases of penalties by social disapproval associated with normative gaffes. But the fact that the distinction isn't clear-cut serves to bring out the point that, although significantly different in nature, employment, and connotations, the formal function of force and norms—through their practical expression in punishment and penalties—is, in this context, one and the same.

There is, however, one fundamental difference between these two methods, which pertains to the formal level as well as to the non-formal aspects of the issue. When the favoured party protects the *status quo* by force, the application of force is of necessity *discriminatory*: it is applied by the favoured party against the disfavoured party whenever the latter attempts to deviate. This means, in terms of the paradigm matrix, that the only change in the matrix will be a reduction in the pay-off for Column-Chooser at the top-right cell $R1–C2$ representing Column-Chooser's unilateral deviance from the *status quo*. On the other hand, when the *status quo* is fortified by norms, the sanctions backing them must by their nature be imposed *impersonally*, on whoever attempts to deviate from it.

It is true, of course, that in practice it will most certainly be only the underdog who will be sanctioned, since only he is liable to deviate. But the point is that, *as a matter of principle*, norms, unlike force which is directed by the favoured party against the disfavoured party as such, are *impersonally* directed at him who violates the *status quo*, whoever that may be. In this precisely lies the great advantage of norms over force, from the point of view of the favoured party. There is a price, though, that this party has to pay for this advantage; we shall return to this point below (Section 13.2). In terms of the matrix, then, fortifying the *status quo* with norms amounts in fact to a reduction *both* in Column-Chooser's pay-off in the upper-right cell R1–C2 representing Column-Chooser's unilateral deviance, *and* in Row-Chooser's pay-off in the bottom-left cell R2–C1 representing Row-Chooser's unilateral deviance.[14]

Going back to our initial point, and considering that only the underdog might have an incentive to violate the *status quo*, the two methods of force and norms as possible stabilizers of the *status quo* are similar in that they both make it more costly for him to do so; they differ, however, in the nature of this cost and in that in the case of norms there is an aura of impersonality and impartiality whereas force is personal and discriminatory.

There is one more difference that is worth mentioning. It was just pointed out that the direct and personal use of force to safeguard the maintenance of the *status quo* is costly in that, among other things, it requires constant policing, monitoring, and surveillance. The point I wish to make now is that not only is the method of force more costly than that of fortifying the *status quo* by norms; it might also be less effective. This will be so provided the norms are widely adhered to in the relevant social unit; and, moreover, provided that they are adhered to by virtue of their being *internalized* by its members. Once norms are internalized, one abides by them not out of fear of the pending sanctions associated with them, but out of some inner conviction. And when this is so, one is likely to conform to the norms even in one's thoughts, intentions, and in what one does

---

[14] In the case of force the paradigm matrix changes, then, into something like matrix 4.16(a), and in the case of norms into something like matrix 4.16(b).

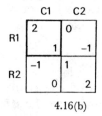

4.16(a)   4.16(b)

in private. When adherence to the *status quo* is induced by force, on the other hand, what can be punished is only one's overt and observed behaviour.

In this respect, then, norms can reach areas, so to speak, which cannot be reached by force. And so in this respect effective norms are more effective than effective force in so far as fortifying the *status quo* is concerned.

10. *Norms of Partiality*

Norms which help perpetuate a *status quo* of inequality in situations of the paradigm type will be called *norms of partiality*. Such norms serve to promote the interests of the party favoured by the inequality. At this point the question of examples naturally arises: what specific norms are, or can be considered, norms of partiality? Faced with this question, though, I confess to an uneasy feeling, even embarrassment. But this is not due to there being no examples. Rather, it has to do with the degree of abstraction one should expect from an answer to this question. For, as a matter of fact, my attempt so far has been to provide what might be termed a 'theory of norm-contexts' which is supposed to connect typical contexts with norms: that is, to characterize and to investigate the formal structure of contexts in which one might expect norms to be generated.

It is clear that the more specified the context, the more likely one is to be able to associate it with a specific norm. However, an increasing specification of the contexts inevitably leads to a loss in the capacity to generalize over contexts—and this, after all, is what I am after. Consequently, what can be expected to exemplify norms of partiality, in the sense here accorded to this term, will in fact have to be a type, or a cluster, of norms which, in various specific contexts, will be variously formulated and embodied. The best such example is, I think, the cluster of norms associated with private property, an important sub-class of these being those connected with the inheritance institution. The concept of trespass, the notions of the sanctity of individual property and of the rights of inheritors, and the norms associated with them, are all meant, essentially, to preserve, protect, and perpetuate the position of the 'haves' —and their descendants—in states which are inherently states of inequality.

Again, the question of how these norms are actually formulated, or in what they are actually embodied—in legal codes, customs, etc.—can be answered only within specific historical and social contexts. These are questions which are clearly of an empirical nature, and at them my armchair speculations must come to a halt. (For example, states which stand for a more equitable distribution of wealth have reformed the inheritance institution—mainly, but not exclusively, through taxation—so as to prevent the perpetuation of significant differences in rank and wealth indefinitely.) But generally speaking, and that is the main point, my contention is that the character of some of the possible defence mechanisms of the institutions of private property and of inheritance is that of norms of partiality.

Let me add that the Marxists' claim is in fact a much stronger one: It is that the very institution of the state, and all the social systems and institutions that support it, inevitably represent norms of partiality. In particular, it might be said that according to them a state's legal code is a cluster of partiality norms: they regard it as being oriented towards the protection of the positions and the property of the strong.[15]

There exists an interesting and provocative interpretation of Locke's political theory which bears on the issue in hand. It is C. B. Macpherson's (1954), and, according to it, it is possible to show that the transition from the state of nature to civil society was conceived by Locke to have been brought about to protect a state of inequality in possessions.[16] 'The great and chief end therefore, of Men's uniting into Commonwealths, and putting themselves under Government, is the Preservation of their Property' (*Second Treatise of Civil Government*, no. 124). In this sense Locke's civil society might be said to embody norms of partiality aimed at the protection of private property, the unequal acquisition and accumulation of which has already in the state of nature caused disparity among people (no. 50).

[15] See, e.g., Paul M. Sweezy, *The Theory of Capitalist Development* (1942), Oxford University Press (3rd edn.), 1949, ch. 13; John Plamenatz, *Man and Society*, Vol. 2, Longmans, 1963, pp. 351–72.

[16] Macpherson points out the crucial ambiguity in Locke's use of the key term 'property': it is used simultaneously in a wide sense, meaning 'lives, liberties, and estates', and in a narrower sense meaning only possessions, i.e. goods or land (ibid., p. 222).

Talking about the existence of such an interpretation of Locke, two senses of interpretation have to be distinguished:

(i) A 'philological' interpretation; that is, an interpretation which results from a close and rigorous analysis of a given text, and the ultimate end of which is to unfold the precise original intention of the author.

(ii) An interpretation in the sense of a 'rational reconstruction'. According to this conception, although the given text does put constraints on any possible interpretation, the interpretation has to do no more than be *compatible* with the text in at least one of its possible readings. The aim of such an interpretation is not necessarily to unearth the author's original intention, but to expose some fruitful intuition underlying the text. Moreover, this intuition may or may not be the author's, and it may or may not be his consciously.

Now even if Macpherson's interpretation of Locke is not up to the standards of a textual interpretation in sense (i) (as indeed is claimed, e.g., by Alan Ryan),[17] it presents, I think, an impressive example of interpretations in sense (ii). And as my present needs are mainly illustrative, they can be met quite adequately, it seems to me, by an interpretation of the rational reconstruction variety. So each occurrence of 'Locke' in what follows might, for the sake of scholarly pedantry, be replaced by 'Macpherson's Locke'. The basic claim, once again, is the following: in Locke's political theory the transition from the state of nature to civil society took place—at least according to one interpretation of the text—for the sake of the protection and preservation of private property. In Macpherson's words, Locke's theory is one which sought 'to protect and promote the property institutions' (p. 229), 'to provide a moral basis for a class state' (p. 224), to 'consolidate the position of the men of property' (p. 229). By implication, the constitution as well as the specific norms of civil society are, according to this conception, bound to be oriented towards the preservation of the state of inequality in possessions established already in the

[17] Alan Ryan, 'Locke and the Dictatorship of the Bourgeoisie'. This paper follows Macpherson's in the above-cited volume (pp. 231-54).

state of nature. Thus, what might be termed Locke's 'fundamental norm', as well as the specific ones constituting it, are conceived—in the light of Macpherson's interpretation—as norms of partiality *par excellence*.

Locke's political theory is commonly compared to and contrasted with that of Hobbes. The significant difference between them is usually located in their opposing views of human nature and consequently in their opposing conceptions of the pre-contractual state of nature. In the light of the above, though, I wish to propose another way of confronting the political theories of Hobbes and Locke.

It will be remembered that in Chapter II Hobbes's original situation of mankind was presented as a Prisoners' Dilemma-type situation. To overcome this type of dilemma, it was suggested, what are needed are norms which would protect the unstable-yet-mutually-beneficial state (of peace, in the Hobbesian case) and prevent its deterioration into the stable-yet-mutually-unbeneficial state (of war, in the Hobbesian case). These norms were referred to as PD norms. Thus, Hobbes's social contract, which made the transition from the state of nature into the civil state (or the commonwealth) possible, could, it was suggested, be conceived of as a 'fundamental norm' of the PD type, as it leads to the installation of a sovereign the specific edicts of whom would be oriented towards preventing the deterioration into a state of war of all against all.

With Locke, on the other hand, the view is here offered that, the state of nature already being—according to him—a state of inequality, the transition from it into the civil state is achieved through a 'fundamental norm' of the partiality type: that is, the establishment of authority the specific edicts of which would be oriented towards the preservation of the inequality in property.

11. *Functional Explanation*

In the course of the discussion in this Chapter a situational problem has been delineated in considerable detail. It is claimed that a *status quo* of inequality which is in a game-theoretical but not in a strategic equilibrium is potentially threatened; and that it is in the interest of the party favoured by the inequality to eliminate—or at least to reduce to the minimum—this potential threat. Employing Parsonian jargon, this defines a structural-functional problem. What is wanted, therefore, is an appropriate set of 'mechanisms' that would safeguard the stability of the *status quo*; thus, to continue with the same terminology, a structural-functional imperative (or need) is cited. It is then being argued that a sufficiently shrewd attachment of a normative value to the preservation of the *status quo*, and the specific norms derived therefrom, might serve this imperative and thus help resolve the structural-functional problem.

When viewed in this light the entire discussion in this chapter seems to fall, roughly, under what Parsons refers to as 'dynamic structural-functional analysis': it consists of the specification of a situation which gives rise to a certain type of need, and it then points to a mechanism through which it can be served, while attempting to draw in, on the way, the relevant psychological and motivational factors. On the other hand, an account of norms which presents them as serving the interest of a superior, perhaps dominating, party in the perpetuation of his position of superiority or dominance quite clearly belongs to the realm of the so-called conflict school. That is, to the explanations of social phenomena in terms of conflicting factional interests, coercion, and exploitation, propagated by what is usually known as the conflict (or coercion) school of sociology. But, of course, the conflict theory of society (as represented, say, by C. Wright-Mills) stands in the most extreme opposition to the functionalist theory of society (as represented by Talcott Parsons).[18] How is it possible then that the account given here of norms apparently follows the general pattern of *both* theories? Put otherwise, the question to be considered is: How is it possible that the clearly conflictistic account of norms of partiality given here can also be viewed as a functional explanation?

Traditional functionalism is characterized as those analyses

---

[18] It might be of interest to note that Ralf Dahrendorf maintained for a while the position that these two theories in fact complement each other rather than contradict and exclude each other (e.g., 1959, pp. 163, 170). Later, however, he changed his mind and turned a full-fledged conflictist (e.g., in 'In Praise of Thrasymachus', in his volume, *Essays in the Theory of Sociology*, London [Routledge & Kegan Paul], 1968. Interestingly, in this paper he proposes to regard Socrates and Thrasymachus as the first 'integrationist' and 'conflictist', respectively).

that use in an essential way concepts such as adaptation, integration, consensus, equilibrium, functional prerequisites, and some others, and that explain social patterns by their effects rather than by a one-way causal relation in terms of the conditions preceding them.[19] In addition to these basic components of a functional explanation as conceived traditionally, Robert Merton adds a few further requirements which he thinks a functional explanation must fulfil ((1949) 1957, p. 25). Among these he requires that 'standardized [i.e., patterned and repetitive] social activities or cultural items [be] functional for the *entire* social or cultural system', and also that 'these items [be] consequently *indispensable*'. Vague as all the central terms in the above characterization might be, it does, it seems to me, convey some impression as to what traditional functionalism is all about.

Criticism of it is, of course, abundant; it ranges anywhere from pointing out the vagueness, even vacuity, of the basic concepts employed by functionalists to such ideological accusations as that functionalism is a position which leads to a conservative outlook. But to examine the criticisms would carry us too far afield, especially as it would require going much deeper into functionalism itself—as an approach and as a theory—than is necessary for making the present point.

The point is that the account given here of norms cannot be regarded as functional, since it lacks, or violates, at least two of the main features of functionalism as presented above. First, the need the norms of partiality come to satisfy is not a need of the entire society; it is a need of but one faction thereof, and the existence of these norms is, to a certain degree, to the detriment of the other. Secondly, the requirement that the 'cultural item' to be functionally explained contribute to the 'integration' of society is not met in our case. Whatever might be the explication of this key notion of 'integration', it undoubtedly stands in opposition to conflict. And so the norms which serve to perpetuate a state of affairs in which one party has the advantage of the other, dominates, or possibly even exploits the other, can more truly be said to work toward social conflict than toward social integration and harmony. (Although, admittedly, when

[19] See 'Varieties of Functional Analysis' by F. M. Cancian, in the *International Encyclopedia of the Social Sciences*, D. L. Sills (ed.), 1968.

compared to force norms will help 'play the conflict down', impersonalize, even conceal it—whereas force would have aggravated the conflict and brought it into the open.)

True enough, when sufficiently pressed and stretched, the central concepts of functionalism might be made to accommodate our norms of partiality within the framework of functional explanation: they seem capable of almost endless conceptual acrobatics. But then these concepts, together with the whole functional doctrine, might just as well be regarded as completely void. The main point, once again, is that when functionalism is taken at its face value, the account given here of norms of partiality cannot be regarded as a functional explanation since it violates the two requirements just considered (viz. they satisfy a need of but one faction of society, and they cannot be said to contribute to social integration).

There are, on the other hand, a few elements which are central to functionalism and which are present in the account given here of norms of partiality. The most prominent of these are the crucial and pivotal role played by the notion of equilibrium, and the fact that the norms under study were not explained in terms of a one-way causal relation, but rather in terms of their effect and function. In fact the account offered here of norms of partiality falls under what is sometimes called *formal functionalism*,[20] that is, the formal scheme of explanation which is again concerned with explaining social patterns in terms of their effects, but which is not restricted only to those patterns whose effects are both beneficial and necessary to the existence of the entire society. This is the functionalism modelled on the biological homeostatic and self-regulating systems, and which is called 'formal' since unlike traditional functionalism it is not committed to any theoretical orientation, nor does it include any substantive hypothesis about empirical matters.

There is another point on which the present account can be viewed as in the functional trend or, more appropriately, as conforming with the main features of what is sometimes called the early functionalism of Malinowski.[21] This early functionalism

---

[20] See: (1) the *International Encyclopedia of the Social Sciences* (op. cit., p. 241 n.); (2) Carl G. Hempel, 'The Logic of Functional Analysis', in Brodbeck (ed.), 1968; (3) Ernest Nagel, *The Structure of Science*, London: Routledge & Kegan Paul, 1961, pp. 520–35.

[21] See Maurice Mandelbaum, 'Functionalism in Social Anthropology', in:

was opposed to the historical ('evolutional', 'diachronic') explanations prevailing until then (i.e. until 1922) in social anthropology. (Let it be remarked, parenthetically, that functionalism in sociology is a considerably later movement than functionalism in social anthropology: the former is usually regarded as having been originated in the year 1949, with the contributions of Parsons and Merton, and the latter—in the year 1922—with the contributions of Malinowski and Radcliffe-Brown.) It favoured instead a structural ('synchronic') orientation, putting a premium on the functional *interdependence* of social institutions, and claiming that 'an understanding of any trait is to be derived from understanding its functioning within its own particular context, rather than from tracing down its migrations' (Mandelbaum, ibid., p. 308). Thus, when functionalism is understood in opposition to a historical approach rather than in opposition to a conflict (or coercion) theory of society, it is quite clear that the present account of norms *is* a functional one in its main features.

12. *Latent Functions and Latent Interests*

12.1 *Latent Functions and the Conspiracy Fallacy*

One of Robert Merton's important contributions to functional analysis was his introduction of the notion of *latent functions*, in contradistinction from *manifest* functions ((1949) 1957). The distinction between them is that manifest functions of a social institution are those which are both intended and recognized, and latent functions are those which are neither intended nor recognized.[22] When we say that the function of norms of partiality is to stabilize and fortify a certain state of affairs, and that this serves the interest of one of the two factions in the society involved, it is meant to be understood as a latent function; i.e. as a function not consciously sought, and not even consciously recognized by those whose interests are furthered by it. Indeed, it might be the case that to a large

S. Morgenbesser, P. Suppes, M. White (eds.), *Philosophy, Science, and Method*, New York: St. Martin's Press, 1969, pp. 306–32 (esp. pp. 307–14).

[22] Carl G. Hempel remarks that this definition of Merton's allows for functions which are neither manifest nor latent; e.g., those which are recognized but not intended. He suggests therefore to base the distinction on the element of intention only. (See his 'The Logic of Functional Analysis', in Brodbeck (ed.), 1968, p. 189 n.)

extent there is a conviction, ideological or otherwise, on the part of the beneficiary party, that the prevailing norms regarding, say, the regulation of office, private property, and the like, are beneficial to the *entire* society. Moreover, the effectiveness of these norms would quite likely have been hampered had they been consciously conceived as explicit restrictions imposed by the beneficiary on the deprived. Had their function been manifest—that is, consciously perceived and sought—an unmasking of these norms would sooner or later be bound to occur, and they would be seen for what they are: a cynical ideological cover for mere force, coercion, and exploitation.

This point is of considerable importance since the extensive use of the terminology of game theory made in the exposition of this chapter is inherently problematic. We spoke of rational individuals (or groups thereof) who, fully knowing the situation they're in, use whatever means they have to pursue their own interests. And then, when it is said that certain norms are—or provide—a 'solution' to a certain situational problem, the impression might be created that somebody actually sat down, analysed the situation, came up with what—for him—was a desirable solution to the problem presented by it, and set out to put it into practice. Now this precisely commits what, following Popper, we shall call the 'conspiracy fallacy'. Popper discusses and criticizes a view which, he maintains, is widespread and influential, and which he calls the conspiracy theory of society ((1945) 1966, pp. 94–5). According to this view whatever 'bad' happens in society (such as war, poverty, unemployment) must be the result of direct and sinister design by some powerful individuals who profit from it. This view gives rise to a conception—mistaken, to be sure—of what an explanation in the social sciences is: an explanation of a social phenomenon, according to it, 'consists in the discovery of the men or groups who are interested in the occurrence of this phenomenon . . . and who have planned and conspired to bring it about' (ibid., p. 94).[23]

Thus, when the social phenomenon to be explained is the existence of certain norms of partiality, our account of them

---

[23] As Robert Nozick points out (1974, p. 19), conspiracy theories (or 'hidden-hand explanations') are, in an obvious sense, diametrically opposed to invisible-hand explanations (see p. 11, above).

can readily be regarded as committing the conspiracy fallacy—
as it apparently boils down to no more than pointing out the
'someone' who, in a particular set-up, is interested in the
existence of these norms and who is in a position to enforce
them. This, however, is false, and, furthermore, is far from
being the case empirically. It is the technique of the discussion
which is misleading by using quasi-conspiratorial modes of
speech borrowed from game theory. It presents a latent function *as if* it were a manifest one. But this was done only for
convenience of presentation, as a didactical concession, and
should by no means be taken as an empirical statement.

12.2 *Latent Interests and Dahrendorf's Model*

In parallel to the distinction, within the functional (integra-
tional) school, between manifest and latent functions, there is
an analogous distinction within the rival school of conflict
(coercion). The distinction here is the Marxian one, between
subjective and objective interests; the latter being the non-
psychological 'true' ones which are conditioned by social
position. (Marx in fact equates 'common situation' with
'common interest'.)[24] Ralf Dahrendorf, however, has proposed
to change this terminology, presumably not least because of
the cynical overtones attached to the notion of 'objective interest' ever since the Stalinist era. He proposes (1959, pp. 173–
9) to talk instead of manifest and latent interests,[25] thus
making the analogy between this distinction and the functionalist one discussed above all the more apparent. One's
manifest interests, then, are those which have psychological
reality, and which account for one's conscious goals. One's
latent interests, on the other hand, are independent of one's
conscious orientations; they are predetermined by the social
role one plays.

Relating my account of norms of partiality to the framework
of the conflict doctrine, I may now say the following: when it is
said that these norms function as stabilizers and fortifiers of
a certain discriminatory *status quo*, and that this promotes the

[24] In *Das Elend der Philosophie*. New edn., Berlin, 1947, p. 187.
[25] Incidentally, when introducing these terms Dahrendorf refers the reader back
not only to Merton's distinction, but to Freud's categories of 'manifest' and 'latent
dream contents' (p. 178 n.).

interests of the party favoured by this *status quo*, it should be clear that the interests referred to may be this party's (merely) *latent* interests. Let it be emphasized once again that one should not be misled by the quasi-conspiratorial modes of speech, adopted for clarity of exposition, which present interests which may in fact be latent as if they were manifest. In this connection it should also be clear that all that was said earlier (p. 180) regarding the effectiveness of the norms in question as depending upon their satisfying a latent—as opposed to a manifest—function will hold good when translated into the conflict-school framework; that is, into the terminology of interests.

To recapitulate: in the last two sections I have cautioned against the conspiracy fallacy, and explained how the present account of norms of partiality should, despite the quasi-conspiratorial modes of speech it employs, be understood within the frameworks of the two major trends in the social sciences. Of those two major trends it seems that it is to the school of conflict that the account attempted here of norms of partiality more appropriately belongs; this is even suggested by their name. These norms are, after all, claimed to be partial to one of the parties involved in an at least latent conflict of interests; they help stabilize and maintain a *status quo* which, for this party, conveys benefits denied to the other. In this sense the present account falls into line with the basic thesis of the conflict theory of society, that norms, and social institutions in general, are but means of domination and exploitation.

It seems appropriate, therefore, to confront the present account of norms of partiality with a counterpart segment of a theory which subscribes to the conflict school. As Ralf Dahrendorf appears to me to be perhaps the most sophisticated of present-day conflict theorists, I shall try first to present his 'model of conflict group formation' (as expounded in the fifth chapter of his *Class and Class Conflict*)—very briefly and schematically—and then to highlight the points of convergence with, and divergence from, my presentation.

(i) Frame of reference. The unit of social organization with which Dahrendorf deals is what he calls 'imperatively co-ordinated associations'—or 'associations' for short—(the expression is in fact a translation of Max Weber's *Herrschaftsverband*) such as the state, a church, an enterprise, a trade union. (This category is supposed to be the conflictistic counterpart to the integrationistic 'social system'.)

(ii) Dahrendorf's most basic hypothesis, from which all the rest is supposed to follow analytically, is that authority relations are a universal element of human societies. This means that in all societies there are always relations of super- and sub-ordination; that there is always a division involving domination and subjection.

(iii) Authority being a dichotomous 'zero-sum' concept, the distribution of authority in any given association is ultimately the 'cause' of the formation of exactly two conflict groups—those who have authority and the 'outs'.

(iv) The next step is now provided by the proposition that 'differentially equipped authority positions in associations involve, for their incumbents, conflicting interests' (p. 174); that is, those in domination and those in subjection have, in virtue of their being in domination or in subjection, conflicting interests. This conflict of interests is thus socially structured, i.e. determined by social positions (rather than by personalities).

(v) Having explained, at this point, the sense in which these conflicting interests should be understood as 'objective', or latent, Dahrendorf goes on to specify their substance: '. . . they are interested in the maintenance or modification of a *status quo*. . . . of the two aggregates of authority positions to be distinguished in every association, one—that of domination— is characterized by an interest in the maintenance of a social structure that for them conveys authority, whereas the other— that of subjection—involves an interest in changing a social condition that deprives its incumbents of authority' (p. 176).

(vi) Finally, Dahrendorf turns to the Weberian notion of legitimacy, and in this connection states that 'In every association, the interests of the ruling groups are the *values* that constitute the *ideology of the legitimacy* of its rule, whereas the interests of the subjected group constitute a *threat* to this ideology and the social relations it covers' (p. 176, my italics).

I shall now relate this admittedly sketchy fragment of

Dahrendorf's theory to the present study. The points of convergence are, it seems to me, quite clear. Very generally, both Dahrendorf and myself have in mind a bipolar structure consisting of two parties (iii), one of which is interested in the maintenance of the prevailing *status quo* which confers upon him some sort of benefits, while the other is basically interested in changing this *status quo*, which for him entails some sort of deprivation (v). Furthermore, in both Dahrendorf's view and mine the interests of the deprived party constitute a certain threat to the existing 'social order', while the interests of the beneficiary party are in one way or another connected with the realm of values—with ideology or with norms (vi).

The points of divergence, however, are of more interest to us, since they might help clarify several aspects of the present study. In the first place, the frame of reference is different. While Dahrendorf's model pertains to any and every (imperatively co-ordinated) association, mine is restricted to those the main features of which permit them to be represented by a matrix similar to the paradigm one (p. 163 above). The significance of this restriction is mainly in that I base my analysis not only on the given *status quo* of inequality (or of 'differentially equipped authority positions'), as does Dahrendorf, but on the desirability patterns of the *alternatives* to it in terms of unilateral and mutual deviations from it.

In the second place, the starting-point is different. In order to grasp the difference, a wider theoretical viewpoint is needed. There are two families of theories pertaining to social stratification (that is, to the division into social classes). One of them attempts to account for social stratification in terms of a single basic dimension for comparison. Marx's sole comparison dimension, for instance, was that of private property; Dahrendorf's is that of authority.[26] Dahrendorf's emphasis on authority resulted, in fact, from his realizing the difficulty which the Marxian approach faces when trying to handle the difference, in modern industrial society, between proprietorship and management (i.e. to handle the fact that in the case of large firms the owner of the firm is today often not identical with its director).

[26] Gamson points out (1968, p. 7) that in fact Dahrendorf's position is a *generalization* of Marx's: that property relations are a special case of authority relations.

According to the opposing approach, on the other hand, social stratification can be accounted for only when a variety of comparison dimensions are considered. (The theories of Weber and his followers belong here.) Examples of such diverse dimensions might be wealth, blood, political power, education, etc.—the idea being that none of them is considered more fundamental than the others, none of them is considered derivative from the others. Indeed, the variety of dimensions for comparison might in principle, according to this conception, determine a variety of divisions into classes. My approach differs from these two in that it is non-committal as to the number—and content—of the dimensions of comparison. It concentrates exclusively on the *structure* of the inequality and is indifferent to the criteria according to which it is appraised. Hence my approach, while being compatible with the two, is identical with neither.

The third point now follows. By postulating the universality of authority relations Dahrendorf in his analysis in fact presupposes the existence of norms and sanctions. Dahrendorf describes authority as 'legitimate power' (p. 166) and explains it as the social control—in terms of norms and sanctions—the rulers are expected to exercise over the ruled, this expectation being due to their social position rather than to the character of their contingent incumbents. A little later (p. 168), while stressing again the 'omnipresence' of authority, he says that 'authority relations exist wherever there are people whose actions are subject to legitimate and sanctioned prescriptions'— which amounts, for him, to saying that authority relations exist always and everywhere.

However vague and wanting these formulations might be found to be, they quite clearly tie in with Dahrendorf's 'derivation of social stratification' expounded in his article 'On the Origin of Social Inequality'. As we have seen earlier (p. 137) he considers it an advantage of his 'derivation' that the presupposition it leads back to is the existence of social norms backed by sanctions—a presuppostion he feels to be self-evident. The analysis offered here is quite clearly in sharp opposition to that of Dahrendorf. Far from presupposing the existence of norms, my analysis of the *status quo* of inequality constitutes an attempt to point out a certain need occurring in a quite specific set-up, and then to propose that it might be satisfied by a certain type of norms. In this sense my programme has been to explain the existence of these norms in terms of the function they fulfil in situations of a certain type; the situations being specified, in turn, in terms of the desirability patterns of the prevailing *status quo* and its various deviance-alternatives.

13. *Norms of Partiality and Coercion*

The function of norms, generally speaking, is to put restraints on possible courses of conduct, to restrict the number of alternatives open for action. When a certain course of conduct is normatively denounced (is considered 'wrong'), it becomes a less eligible course of conduct than it might otherwise have been: although through lying, for example, one might quite conveniently get away with some misdeed, its being recognized and acknowledged as normatively (morally) prohibited normally makes it a less attractive way out, or even precludes its having been considered an alternative in the first place. In this sense, then, norms might be said to be *coercive*, to the extent that they function as constraints on actions; that is, to the extent that they prevent one from doing an action one might have done had there been no norm denouncing it, or at least to the extent that they render a certain course of action less eligible than it might otherwise have been.

Let us elaborate this point a little further. There are three important elements in coercion: threat, deterrence, and assurance. Any coercion attempt consists, in the first place, of a threat:[27] if you do A, certain consequences harmful to you will ensue. This threat is aimed at deterring you from doing A; in this sense you are being coerced into not doing A. Any coercive threat, furthermore, requires corresponding assurance that if you refrain from doing A, in compliance with the threat, the harmful consequences will *not* be brought about. As Schelling points out (1966, p. 74), 'the object of a threat is to give somebody a choice'. He then goes on to explain that ' "One more step and I shoot" can be a deterrent threat only if accompanied by the implicit assurance, "And if you stop I won't".'

---

[27] A threat in this case is meant to cover cases of *warning* too. For the distinction between threat and warning see (1) Schelling, 1960, p. 123 n.; (2) Nozick, 1969, p. 441.

In the case of norms all three elements of coercion are present. When according to a certain norm doing A is prohibited, one is deterred from doing A by the threat of the imposition of some sanction (some penalty). The corresponding reward for refraining from A in compliance with the norm, though, often goes beyond the mere assurance that the sanction would not be imposed: it often consists of a positive premium such as approval by society, or corroboration of one's reputation for credibility, integrity, reliability, etc.

Having stated the general point that norms can be viewed as a tool of coercion, we shall turn now to consider the three following topics: (1) the question of who is the coercer, in relation to the impersonality of norms; (2) the notion of self-coercion, in relation to the impartiality of norms; (3) the question: Is coercion a 'zero-sum' concept?

13.1 The Coercer and the Impersonality of Norms

The notion of coercion is usually taken to presuppose a *coercer* (see Nozick, 1969, p. 144; Hayek, 1960, p. 133): a person P who coerces another person Q into doing (refraining from doing)[28] an action A, through threatening him with a sanction S. The question, therefore, is whether there is a coercer P in the case where Q is made to refrain from A by a norm prohibiting actions of the type of A. To answer this question we must emphasize once again the point alluded to earlier (p. 171) concerning norms of partiality *vis-à-vis* force. Norms, and the sanctions backing them, are—or at least usually appear to be—impersonal. Unlike the clear cases of coercion, where it is a case of 'P coerces Q into non-A', or 'P threatens Q with a sanction S if Q does A', with norms it is a case of 'don't do A', or 'if A then S' (or, more precisely, 'if A then S ought to be'). With norms the sanctions are imposed on behalf of society—be it through an institutionalized instrument thereof (e.g. the law) or not, but not on behalf of one identifiable person or faction of society in whose *self-interest* it

---

[28] In contrast with Nozick, who does not distinguish between coercion into doing A and coercion into refraining from A, Schelling shows that there is considerable asymmetry between these cases: he even gives them different names—'compellence' and 'deterrence', respectively (1966, pp. 69–78). Since norms more usually involve a deterrent (rather than a compellent) threat, we shall speak of coercion into non-action rather than into action.

is to impose them. It is precisely in this impersonality of norms, however, that lies their foremost advantage for those in whose power and skill it is to manipulate them for the pursuit of their own interests.

This, then, is what the favoured party in our *status quo* of inequality is supposed to be interested ('latently') in the partiality norms for: to safeguard the preservation of the *status quo* which favours him. The dominated, disfavourably placed party is thus being coerced into non-deviance from (and hence maintenance of) the *status quo* which discriminates against him, by a set of ostensibly impersonal norms denouncing and prohibiting any deviance-attempt rather than by naked power applied explicitly by those in the favoured position. Furthermore, norms are rather easily accepted as part of the 'natural order of things'. To be sure, one might be quite resentful of this natural order, or of one's lot therein, and regard it as discriminating against one. But usually there is very little one is going to do about it unless—and until—the object of one's resentment is personified: only few will start a revolution against an elusive oppressive 'system'; many more might revolt against an identifiable oppressive ruler.

To sum up: with regard to norms of partiality it is claimed that they might be conceived of as a sophisticated tool of coercion, used by the favoured party in a *status quo* of inequality to promote its interest in the maintenance of this *status quo*. It will be considered sophisticated to the extent that the air of impersonality remains intact and successfully disguises what really underlies the partiality norms, viz. an exercise of power.

13.2 *The Impartiality of Norms and Self-coercion*

The price that has to be paid for the advantage of the seeming impersonality of norms of partiality is that their incidence has to be impartial and universal. These norms have to apply to the privileged as well as to the deprived, or else they lose much of their effectiveness as a disguise for the real exercise of power underlying them. In theory, though, if one could issue norms by which one need not abide oneself, it would seem to be an ideal means of domination and coercion. It would be to enjoy the best of two worlds: not to suffer the costs associated with the exercise of direct and personal power, and yet not to be bound and restrained by one's own legislation. Historically, this sort of situation existed whenever the ruler was conceived by the people as God and hence his decrees were not supposed to apply to himself—as in the case of the Pharaohs in ancient Egypt.

But of course in these situations norms and force are used as complementing each other, not as substitutes for each other. Also, more importantly, in these cases the basic relation of rulers versus ruled is abundantly clear, whereas in the situations here under study the dominance relation is not at all apparent, indeed it is concealed and disguised. Our analysis assumes a favourably versus disfavourably placed party; not rulers and subjects.

In this connection, of a ruler abiding by his own norms, it might be interesting to recall the story of King Saul and his son Jonathan, as told in the first book of Samuel, Chapter XIV. Saul issues a decree that 'Cursed be the man that eateth any food until evening, that I may be avenged of mine enemies.' Jonathan, however, did not hear the oath his father charged the people with, '. . . wherefore he put forth the end of the rod that was in his hand, and dipped it in an honeycomb, and put his hand to his mouth.' Later on that day, when Saul seeks counsel of God and is not answered, he understands that something went wrong, and he summons the chiefs of the people to 'see wherein this sin hath been this day. For, as the Lord Liveth . . . though it be in Jonathan my son, he shall surely die.' And then, when through a process of drawing lots Jonathan is caught and admits what he has done, Saul says: 'God do so and more also, for thou shalt surely die, Jonathan.' (Jonathan was rescued, though, by the people who would not let their war hero be killed by the king.)

(Let it be added that this willingness on the part of Saul to abide by his own decree even when he himself may suffer (see also vv. 40–42) is particularly interesting in the context of the book of Samuel, one of the main objects of which is to caution the people of Israel against their desire for a king (instead of the Judges they have had before): it claims (Chapter VIII) that a king would have no scruples about exploiting the people for his own interests.)

Of course, in order to preserve his law-abiding image, a ruler might abuse his authority by issuing *ad hoc* edicts that would legitimize whatever he might intend to do. A nice example is afforded by the following:

Some of the most flagrantly obvious special laws involved Trujillo's family or marital relations. In 1935 Trujillo sought a divorce from his second wife, Bienvenida Ricardo, whom he married six years earlier and by whom he was childless, in order to marry his mistress, María Martínez, who had already borne him a child. He therefore had Congress pass a law declaring that a couple could be divorced after five years of childless marriage if one of the partners so desired. Trujillo was divorced from Bienvenida and married to María within a matter of days.

(Howard J. Wiarda, *Dictatorship and Development—The Methods of Control in Trujillo's Dominican Republic.* Gainesville, Florida: University of Florida Press, 1968; pp. 67–8.)

A record of sorts was achieved by Indira Gandhi, Prime Minister of India, when she drafted (3 Aug. 1975) retroactive legislation changing the election laws, under which she was convicted of improper campaign practices taking place about four years earlier, in such a way as would retrospectively legalize her past deeds and remove the basis from under the Supreme Court's actions against her. (See the *New York Times*, 4 Aug. 1975.)

But let us return now to the initial point of this section, i.e. that for norms of partiality to be effective they have to be impartially and universally applied.

In terms of the coercion conception this amounts to saying that to the extent that norms of partiality can be regarded as an indirect tool of coercion in the hands of the favoured party, this party must be considered to be engaged in some sort of self-coercion. When put in this light, the universal and impartial incidence of norms of partiality means, for the favoured party, some sacrifice of his freedom of action, a voluntary renouncement of certain options and, in general, an imposition of self-restraints. (In terms of the matrices, the above statement 'translates into' the statement that unilateral deviance from the *status quo* is costly not only to the disfavourably placed party but to the favoured one too. That is, there is a reduction in pay-offs for the unilateral deviator whoever he is. This was exemplified above, p. 172 n.)

The question now naturally arises, whether this notion of self-coercion makes any sense, and whether it can be regarded as a reasonable price to be paid for the advantages—to the favoured party—associated with norms, rather than force, as fortifiers of the *status quo*. Having in earlier sections listed and discussed in considerable detail the advantages of norms of partiality over force—in so far as they can be regarded as functionally equivalent and provided that the norms are indeed effective—it seems to me that they quite clearly outweigh the disadvantage of their being self-binding. This will be seen to be all the more so once it is borne in mind that the self-restraints the favoured party is assumed to be imposing upon himself through norms of partiality concern only the contingency that he himself deviates from the *status quo*; but of course the whole point is that, excepting radically changed and unpredictable circumstances, he will *not* deviate. (Remember that one of the assumptions concerning the favoured party was that, in the situations under consideration, he cannot improve his position, either absolute or relative. Of course once this assumption no longer holds, the favoured party might come to want to abandon the *status quo* in favour of a better state for him, and then he might find the norms binding him to the maintenance of the *status quo* a real disadvantage and a hindrance.)

Hence the answer to the question of the price is, I submit, decidedly in the affirmative: the cost of binding oneself through the norms of partiality must be considered reasonable by the favoured party when weighed against their gains; the necessary qualifications, however, being that these norms be effective as a substitute for force, and that the circumstances that dictate the interest of the favoured party in the maintenance of the *status quo* not change. As to the notion of self-coercion itself, as employed in this context, I see nothing particularly paradoxical about it. Indeed, it may sometimes be a strategic advantage to have one's hands tied in certain ways. As Schelling points out, '. . . the power to constrain an adversary may depend on the power to bind oneself; . . . to burn bridges behind one may suffice to undo an opponent' (1960, p. 22).

In our case, in fact, the effect of deterrence the norms of partiality are supposed to have (see p. 187 above) may be all the more enhanced once it is clear to all that the norms apply to all and that the sanctions associated with them would be imposed on whoever deviates from the *status quo*, regardless of who he is or to which 'camp' he belongs. In the same vein, the fact that Saul was ready to abide by his own decree even though it happened to turn against his own son was likely to increase significantly—if not drastically—the effectiveness of his other decrees. The absence of any precedents in which someone privileged was spared the sanction, the absence of any loopholes which might facilitate a discriminatory application of the norms, contribute to their deterrence value, so that in general it is quite conceivable that the favoured party realizes that he might come to benefit from the increased deterrence potential of the norms of partiality, achieved by virtue of their universal and impartial incidence. Consequently it is quite reasonable to expect him to engage willingly in this sort of self-coercion—despite the fact that under unusual and rare circumstances he might himself be the victim of these norms. It might finally be recalled in this connection that in the case of PD norms too it was shown that it might be a strategical advantage to reduce some of one's own pay-offs (associated with some of the relevant action-alternatives) so as to get rid of embarrassingly attractive options, and thus pave the way toward a mutually desired and beneficial solution.

13.3 *Is Coercion a 'Zero-Sum' Concept?*

For Parsons, power is 'a facility for the performance of function in and on behalf of society as a system' (1957, p. 139). To this integrationist orientation of his, he opposes—and criticizes —the approach of the 'conflict oriented' thinkers (such as Max Weber, H. D. Lasswell, and C. Wright Mills). He calls their conception of power 'zero-sum', and explains that for them '. . . power . . . is interpreted exclusively as a facility for getting what one group, the holders of power, wants by preventing another group, the "outs", from getting what it wants' (ibid.); or again, elsewhere, that for them 'power is the capacity of one unit in a system to gain its ends *over the opposition of other units*' (1960, p. 182). In other words, according to Parsons the conflict conception of power is tantamount to that of coercion, and it can be characterized as 'zero-sum' in so far as one group of persons is envisaged as possessing power to the extent that the other is deprived of it.[29] Parsons, needless to say, vehemently rejects this view.

In his evaluation of the two opposing views of Parsons and Mills, Ralf Dahrendorf does not question the validity of characterizing coercion as a 'zero-sum' concept. He actually elaborates this conception, and qualifies it in an interesting respect (1959, p. 170 n.). He points out that in principle, or 'mathematically', the 'zero-sum' conception of power (or of *authority*, as he prefers to call it) is compatible with both groups having no authority at all 'in the sense of a complete absence of authority'. However, the fact that for him 'the presence of authority, and its unequal distribution, are universal features of social structure' requires that the possibility of there being situations of zero power (authority) be considered excluded. The idea that power, or authority, always sums up to zero should, he maintains, be interpreted to mean that the power of one group is always greater than zero, so to speak, and that of the other group is correspondingly smaller than zero (i.e. they hold 'negative power').

In Dahrendorf's own view, though, neither of the two approaches—that of Parsons and that of Mills—should be regarded as the only valid or applicable one: '. . . on the highest level of abstraction it is illegitimate to emphasize either of these to the exclusion of the other' (ibid.). According to him, 'They constitute complementary, rather than alternative, aspects of the structure of total society as well as of every unit of this structure' (ibid., p. 163).[30]

To sum up thus far: those who deal with the coercion theory of society, whether accepting it or rejecting it, tend to conceive of the concept of coercive power as a 'zero-sum' one. That is, they take it to presuppose that the interests of the two parties involved are diametrically opposed, and understand it to imply that the extent to which one group has power is precisely

[29] Gamson (1968, pp. 108–9) offers two interpretations to this zero-sum (or indeed constant-sum) conception of power: the first is in terms of *influence*, the second in terms of *resources*. He takes the second to be more pertinent and meaningful.

[30] It has been noted earlier (p. 177 n. 18, above) that Dahrendorf later changed his mind on this matter and came to prefer the 'ugly', coercion approach over the integration approach.

the extent to which the other group is denied it. Furthermore, the implication is that the group which has power uses it coercively against the other group to promote its own factional interests.

Now when it is said that norms of partiality may be regarded as, in a sense, a tool of coercion, is it meant to be understood as falling in line with this widespread conception of coercion? Indeed, *can* it be taken in this way? It will be remembered, in the first place, that the paradigm matrix (p. 163), which represents the paradigmatic situation potentially generating norms of partiality, was *not* a zero-sum matrix (that is, it is not the case that the cells are oppositely ordered by the parties, or that the numbers in each cell add to zero). The interests of the parties in the situation depicted by it, although in conflict to a certain degree, are far from being strictly opposed. Indeed the situation allows, or even calls for, a considerable degree of co-operation: the joint interest of the parties is to avoid being stuck at the states represented by the top-right cell, R1–C2, and by the bottom-left cell, R2–C1, in which both gain nothing. Also, once the underdog has succeeded in visibly committing himself to deviate from the *status quo*, the other party, as we already know, is very likely to deviate too, however grudgingly. And in doing so he in fact 'co-operates' with the underdog to achieve a state (represented by the bottom-right cell R2–C2) which, although worse for him than the original *status quo*, is still better than the state (R1–C2) resulting from the underdog's unilateral deviance. The situation thus combines varying degrees of conflict and co-operation.

Moreover, the *status quo*, albeit discriminatory, is not 'bad' to one party to the extent that it is 'good' to the other. It is, to be sure, a *status quo* of (relative) inequality, but not a state in which one party gets absolutely all the benefits and the other party is correspondingly absolutely deprived of everything. So is it really possible to maintain that via the norms which function so as to sustain and perpetuate the *status quo*, the disfavourably placed party is *coerced* by the favoured party into non-deviance?

My answer is in the affirmative: there is a latent exercise of power here which does amount to coercion. And the argument which supports this answer is that it is wrong to regard coercion as a 'zero-sum' concept in the sense just explained. To establish this, it should be pointed out that if the interests of the parties are absolutely opposed, then the situation is one of sheer contest of power and will between them. The attempt of each to win is, in such cases, tantamount to the attempt of each to hurt and frustrate the other. In cases of coercion, on the other hand, what is required is some *bargain* between the parties. It is not in general true that the coercing party is chiefly interested in that the other be downcast. Rather, he needs the other's co-operation—even if it be forced—in order to achieve his own aims. This involves being able to offer the other party something for doing what he wants, or at any rate being able to arrange for him to be worse off if he does not comply. And this in turn implies that the situation of the parties is not zero-sum.

Precisely this happens in the situation at hand. The favoured party is not taken to be particularly interested in keeping the other low, as an end in itself; it is not the case that he thrives on the other's deprivation. What he *is* interested in, though, is solely the maintenance of a *status quo* which discriminates in his favour, and he needs the other to 'help' him in that. By making deviance from the *status quo* more costly, by means of the threatened sanctions associated with the norms of partiality, a sort of 'coercive bargain' is struck. The bargain aspect of it consists, among other things, in that the favoured party's deviance is just as punishable as the other party's; the coercion aspect of it consists in the fact that, after all, the disfavoured party is made to comply with someone else's will and interests which oppose—even though only to a certain degree—his own. He is denied the possibility of using the one strategic move which might improve his position—or at least this possibility is made that much more costly; and hence he is being coerced into remaining in his discriminated-against position.

To conclude: the bias of integration theorists toward emphasizing only the co-operative aspects of norms is a result (at least in part) of their mistaken conception of coercion as a 'zero-sum' concept. They realized that most of the social situations they were dealing with were not zero-sum structured (that is, did not involve a *strict* conflict of interests). And, being convinced that coercion relations pertain exclusively to situations the main features of which are of the zero-sum type, they tended to account for norms only in terms of their contribution to social integration.

Trying, very schematically, to make these theorists' implicit bias explicit, we shall get something like the following argument:

1. Social norms exist in situations which are not zero-sum structured.
2. Coercion is a zero-sum concept (i.e. it applies only to zero-sum structured situations).

Therefore

3. Social norms cannot be explained in terms of coercion. (And hence the element to be emphasized in any account of norms is integration.)

What I have attempted to show in this section, then, was to reject proposition 2 as false—and thus to expose this 'integrationist argument' as unsound.

By way of summing up it might be said that both the integration and the conflict schools have overstated their cases, the former concentrating on the harmonizing aspect of social norms, the latter on their coercive aspect. In the light of the last two chapters, dealing with norms of co-ordination and of partiality respectively, both these schools are seen to present only part of the picture. Each of them corresponds to just one of the several social contexts—three of which have been delineated and analysed in this study—which are prone to generate norms.

BIBLIOGRAPHY

ARON, Raimond, *Main Currents in Sociological Thought* (i) (English trans.). Penguin Books, 1965.

ARROW, Kenneth J., *Social Choice and Individual Values* (Second Edition). New York: John Wiley & Sons, 1963.

BARRY, Brian, *Political Argument*. London: Routledge & Kegan Paul, 1965.

BLAU, Peter M., *Exchange and Power in Social Life*. New York: John Wiley & Sons, 1967.

BRODBECK, May (ed.), *Readings in the Philosophy of the Social Sciences*. New York: Macmillan, 1968.

BUCHANAN, James, and Gordon Tullock, 'Economic Analogues to the Generalization Argument.' *Ethics*, Vol. 74 (1964).

CARNAP, Rudolf, *Meaning and Necessity*. Chicago: University of Chicago Press, 1956 (1947). [Also in it: 'Empiricism, Semantics and Ontology', pp. 205–22.]

—— *Logical Foundations of Probability*. London: Routledge & Kegan Paul, 1962 (1950).

—— 'The Aim of Inductive Logic' in: E. Nagel, P. Suppes, and A. Tarski (eds.), *Logic, Methodology and Philosophy of Science; Proc. of the 1960 International Congress*. Stanford, 1962.

CAWS, Peter, *The Philosophy of Science*. Princeton, New Jersey: D. Van Nostrand Company, 1965.

DAHRENDORF, Ralf, *Class and Class Conflict in Industrial Society*. London: Routledge & Kegan Paul, 1959.

—— 'On the Origin of Social Inequality' in: Peter Laslett and W. G. Runciman (eds.), *Philosophy, Politics and Society* (Second Series). Oxford: Basil Blackwell, 1962.

DORMAN, Neil A., 'The Refutation of the Generalization Argument.' *Ethics*, Vol. 74 (1964), pp. 150–4.

FRANKEL, Charles, 'Justice and Rationality' in: S. Morgenbesser, P. Suppes, and M. White (eds.), *Philosophy, Science and Method: Essays in Honour of Ernest Nagel*. New York: St. Martin's Press, 1969 (pp. 409–14).

GAMSON, William A., *Power and Discontent*. Homewood, Illinois: The Dorsey Press, 1968.

GAUTHIER, David P., 'Morality and Advantage.' *Philosophical Review*, Vol. 76 (1967), pp. 460–75.

—— *The Logic of Leviathan*. Oxford: Oxford University Press, 1969.

GOFFMAN, Erving, *Where The Action Is*. London: Allan Lane, The Penguin Press, 1969.

HARSANYI, John C., 'Individualistic and Functionalistic Explanations in Light of Game Theory: The Example of Social Status' in: I. Lakatos and A. Musgrave (eds.), *Problems in the Philosophy of Science*. Amsterdam: North Holland, 1968 (pp. 305–22). (See also: L. P. Foldes's comment and Harsanyi's reply there, pp. 322–48.)

HART, H. L. A., *The Concept of Law*. Oxford: Oxford University Press, 1961.

HAYEK, Friedrich A., *The Constitution of Liberty*. Chicago: Gateway Edition (1960), 1972.

HOBBES, Thomas, *Leviathan* (edited by Michael Oakeshott). Oxford, 1948.

HOMANS, George C., *The Human Group*. New York: Harcourt, Brace & World, 1950.

—— *Social Behaviour: Its Elementary Forms*. New York: Harcourt, Brace & World, 1961.

KEYNES, J. M., *The End of Laissez-Faire*. London: L. &. V. Wolf, 1926.

LEWIS, David K., *Convention*. Cambridge, Mass.: Harvard University Press, 1969.

LOCKE, John, *The Second Treatise of Civil Government and a Letter Concerning Toleration* (ed. J. W. Gough). Oxford: Basil Blackwell, 1948.

LUCE, R. Duncan, and Howard Raiffa, *Games and Decisions*. New York: John Wiley & Sons, 1957.

LYONS, David, *Forms and Limits of Utilitarianism*. Oxford: Oxford University Press, 1965.

MACPHERSON, C. B., 'The Social Bearing of Locke's Political Theory' (1954) in: C. B. Martin and D. M. Armstrong (eds.), *Locke and Berkeley*. London: Macmillan (Modern Studies in Philosophy) (pp. 199–230).

MANDELBAUM, Maurice, 'Societal Facts.' *British Journal of Sociology*, Vol. 6 (1955).

MARVELL, G., and D. R. Schmitt, 'Are Trivial Games the Most Interesting Psychologically?' *Behavioural Science*, Vol. 13 (1968), pp. 125–8.

MERTON, Robert K., 'Manifest and Latent Function' in his *Social Theory and Social Structure* (1949) (revised and enlarged edition). New York: The Free Press, 1957.

MILL, J. S., *Principles of Political Economy*. London: Longmans, Green, 1926.

MINTZ, A. 'Non-Adaptive Group Behavior.' *Journal of Abnormal Psychology*, Vol. 46 (1951), pp. 150–9.

MORGENBESSER, Sidney, 'Psychologism and Methodological Individualism' in: S. Morgenbesser (ed.), *Philosophy of Science Today*. New York: Basic Books, 1967 (pp. 160–74).

NOZICK, Robert, 'Coercion' in: S. Morgenbesser, P. Suppes, and M. White (eds.), *Philosophy, Science and Method: Essays in Honour of Ernest Nagel*. New York: St. Martin's Press, 1969 (pp. 440–72).

—— *Anarchy, State, and Utopia*. New York: Basic Books, 1974.

OLSON, Mancur, Jr., *The Logic of Collective Action*. Cambridge, Mass.: Harvard University Press, 1965.

OSKAMP, S., and D. Perlman, 'Factors Affecting Cooperation in a Prisoners' Dilemma Game.' *Journal of Conflict Resolution*, 1965, pp. 359–74.

—— 'Effects of Friendship and Dislike on Cooperation in the Mixed-Motive Game.' *Journal of Conflict Resolution*, 1966, pp. 221–6.

PARSONS, Talcott, 'The Distribution of Power in American Society.' *World Politics*, Vol. x, No. 1 (Oct. 1957).

—— *Structure and Process in Modern Society*. New York: Free Press of Glencoe, 1960.

PILISUK, M., S. Kiritz, and S. Clampitt, 'Undoing Deadlocks of Distrust: Hip Berkeley Students and the R.O.T.C.' *Journal of Conflict Resolution*, 1971.

POPPER, K. R., *The Open Society and Its Enemies* (Vol. ii). London: Routledge & Kegan Paul, 1966 (1945).

—— *The Poverty of Historicism*. London: Routledge & Kegan Paul, 1961 (1957).

RAPOPORT, Anatol, *Two-Person Game Theory*. Ann Arbor, 1966.

RAWLS, John, 'Justice as Fairness' in: Peter Laslett and W. G. Runciman (eds.), *Philosophy, Politics and Society* (Second Series). Oxford: Basil Blackwell, 1962.

—— *A Theory of Justice*. Cambridge, Mass.: Harvard University Press, 1971.

RAZ, Joseph, *The Concept of a Legal System*. Oxford: Oxford University Press, 1970.

ROSS, Alf, *Directives and Norms*. London: Routledge & Kegan Paul, 1968.

ROUSSEAU, Jean Jacques, *On the Origin of Inequality* (trans. G. D. H. Cole). Great Books of the Western World, Encyclopedia Britannica. London, 1952.

SCHELLING, Thomas C., *The Strategy of Conflict*. Oxford: Oxford University Press, 1960.

—— 'Strategy, Tactics and Non-Zero Sum Theory' in: *Theory of Games; Techniques and Applications*. The Proceedings of a conference under the aegis of the NATO Scientific Affairs Committee, Toulon, 1964.

—— *Arms and Influence*. Yale University Press, 1966.

—— 'Some Thoughts on the Relevance of Game Theory to the Analysis of Ethical Systems' (1968) in: I. R. Buchler and H. G. Nutini (eds.), *Game Theory in the Behavioral Sciences*. University of Pittsburgh Press, 1969.

SEN, Amartya, 'Choice, Ordering and Morality' in: Stephan Körner (ed.), *Practical Reason*. New Haven: Yale University Press, 1974 (pp. 54–67).

SHWAYDER, David S., *The Stratification of Behaviour*. London: Routledge & Kegan Paul, 1965.

SINGER, Marcus, *Generalization in Ethics*. New York: Alfred Knopf, 1960.

SMART, J. J. C., 'Extreme and Restricted Utilitarianism' (1956) in: Philippa Foot (ed.), *Theories of Ethics*. Oxford: Oxford University Press, 1967 (pp. 171–83).

SMITH, Adam, *The Wealth of Nations* (1776). London: Routledge & Kegan Paul, 1913.

STOUT, A. K., 'But Suppose Everyone Did the Same.' *The Australasian Journal of Philosophy*, Vol. 32, No. 1 (May 1954), pp. 11–29.

STRANG, Colin, 'What if Everyone Did That?' (1960) in: J. J. Thomson and G. Dworkin (eds.), *Ethics*. New York: Harper & Row, 1968 (pp. 151–62).

SUPPES, P., and R. C. Richardson, *Markov Learning Models of Multiperson Interactions*. Stanford: Stanford University Press, 1960.

THIBAUT, John W., and Harold H. Kelley, *The Social Psychology of Groups*. New York: John Wiley & Sons, 1959.

ULLMANN-MARGALIT, E., 'The Generalization Argument: Where does the Obligation Lie?' *The Journal of Philosophy*, Vol. 73, No. 15 (2 Sept. 1976), pp. 511–22.

URMSON, J. O., 'Saints and Heroes' (1958). Reprinted in: Joel Feinberg (ed.), *Moral Concepts*. Oxford: Oxford University Press, 1969 (pp. 60–73).

WALLACE, D., and P. Rothaus, 'Communication, Group Loyalty and Trust in the PD Game.' *Journal of Conflict Resolution*, 1969.

VON WRIGHT, Georg Henrik, *Norm and Action*. London: Routledge & Kegan Paul, 1963.

INDEX

agreement, 21, 44, 68, 70, 84, 87, 90–100
  cartelization agreement, 45, 128
  enforceable, 21, 22, 35
  explicit, 10, 20, 111, 113, 116–17, 124
  implicit, 75–6, 100, 124
  mutual contracts, Hobbes, 65–7;
    Spencer, 74–5
  presupposes norms, 75–6
altruism, 48
  altruists' dilemma, 48 n.
anonymity, 25, 47, 85–6, 97
Aron, Raymond, 143, 144, 155 n.
Arrow, Kenneth J., 107, 171

Barry, Brian, 62, 102 n.
Blau, Peter M., 105, 155 n.
Bohm, P., 127 n.
Braithwaite, R. B., 6
Brodbeck, May, 14 n.
Buchanan, James M., 60, 61, 62
Buckley, Walter, 145 n.

Cancian, F. M., 178 n.
Carnap, Rudolf, 1, 2, 4, 6 n., 153
cartel (monopoly, oligopoly), 42–5,
  IV.5.5 (127–9)
Caws, Peter, 2
Chinoy, Ely, 96
Chomsky, Noam, 2
Clampitt, Stuart, 48
coercion, 53, 66, 134, 167, 168, 181,
  IV.13 (187–97)
  coercion (conflict) school of sociology,
    177, 180, 182–3
  self-coercion, IV.13.2 (189–93)
  as 'zero-sum' concept, IV.13.3
    (193–7)
  see also exploitation; integration
    school of sociology
collective goal, 131
  see also co-operation
conformity, 12–13, 71, 84–5, 98–100
  adherence, 68–73
  conformism, III.2.3 (93–6)
  conformity and (or v.) compliance,
    38–9, 77, 89
  general conformity (compliance),
    118–20

'connotations' of games, 14–15, 84,
  111
control, social, 44–5, 105, 186
conventions, 16 n., 74–6, 92, 96 ff., 107,
  112–13
covenant (Hobbes), 65, 67–73
custom, law, legal regulations, 7,
  92–3, 105, 126, 174
habit, 34, 38, 100
co-operation, 38 n., 77, 122–4, 165,
  195–6
  'antagonistic', 120
  co-operative action, 41
  co-operative goal, 129–33
  and coordination, III.6 (129–33)
  and division of labour, 49
  and friendship, 45–8

Dahrendorf, Ralf, 135–8, 177 n.,
  IV.12.2 (182–7), 194
Darwin, Charles, 11
Davis, Kingsley, 96
decrees, 76, 90–2, 97 ff., 113
deterrence, 39, 66, 168, 177, 187,
  192–3
  v. compensative device, 37
  deterrent threat, 154 (see strategic
    moves)
  discipline as a deterrent device, 35
division of labour, 38 n., II.8.1 (48–9),
  74
dominant action (choice, strategy), 19,
  20 (dominance principle), 30–2, 36,
  41, 44, 48 n., 51–3, 57, 67, 72, 114–15,
  122, 124 (see also equilibrium; solution; strategies)
Dorman, Neil A., 59, 62
Durkheim, Emil, 14 n., 74, 76, 135

Edgeworth, F. Y., 158
effectiveness, efficacy (of norms), 39–40,
  43, 49, 120, 181, 183, 189
  source of effectiveness, 76, 89, 97,
    III.3.2 (98–101), 105–6
envy, IV.4.3 (150–5), 157, 164
equilibrium, 19, 30–6, 39–40, 52, 60,
  71 (quasi-equilibrium), 80–2 (co-
  ordination equilibrium), 84–5, 87,